Shipbuilders of the
Venetian Arsenal

The Johns Hopkins University Studies

in Historical and Political Science

109th Series (1991)

The Johns Hopkins University Press

Baltimore and London

ROBERT C. DAVIS

Workers and Workplace in the Preindustrial City

Shipbuilders of the Venetian Arsenal

© 1991 The Johns Hopkins University Press

Printed in the United States of America

Johns Hopkins Paperbacks edition, 2007

9 8 7 6 5 4 3 2 1

The Johns Hopkins University Press
2715 N. Charles Street
Baltimore, MD 21218-4363
www.press.jhu.edu

The Library of Congress has cataloged the hardcover edition of this book as follows:

Davis, Robert C. (Robert Charles), 1948 —
 Shipbuilders of the Venetian arsenal : workers and
workplace in the preindustrial city / Robert C. Davis.
        p.   cm. — (The Johns Hopkins University studies
in historical and political science ; 109th ser., 1)
   Includes bibliographical references and index.
   ISBN 0-8018-4095-3 (alk. paper)
   1.   Shipbuilding industry — Italy — Venice — Employees —
History.   I. Title.   II. Series.
HD8039.S512I83   1991
331.7′623821′094531—dc20   90-43807

ISBN 10: 0-8018-8625-2 (pbk. : alk. paper)
ISBN 13: 978-0-8018-8625-6

A catalog record for this book is available from the British Library.

Contents

Illustrations and Tables

Acknowledgments

L ike most works of research, this book represents something of a team effort, for a good many scholars, organizations, and friends gave their time and assistance so that it could be realized.

I would first like to thank the directors of the Italian Fulbright-Hays Program, the Gladys Krieble Delmas Foundation, and the Charles Singleton Program, all of whose very generous financial support made it possible for me to enjoy nearly two years of unbroken research time in Venice.

In addition, I would like to thank those of the very supportive circle of scholars and friends living or working in Venice who helped to introduce me to the city, its archives, and its ways. Particular thanks are due to Cristina Perissinotto, for months of thoughtful assistance, as well as to Anna Bellavitis, Humphrey Butters, Jill Carrington, Salvatore Ciriacono, Paula Clarke, Jon Glixon, Reinhold Mueller, Donald Queller, Alessandra Sambo, and Helena Szepe. Thanks also to Franco Angiolini, Mirella Grandi, Vittorio Sciuti Russi, and Stuart Woolf for introducing me to the larger world of Italian scholarship.

Those here in America who have helped are almost too numerous to list. I would particularly like to thank Richard Rapp, however, for generously sending me his entire microfilm collection of the seventeenth-century *anagrafi dei piovani* and for generally starting me on my way. My appreciation and special thanks also go to Robert Forster, Guido Ruggiero, Anne Schutte, and Domenico Sella, all of whom carefully read and corrected parts of this manuscript; as well as to Ann Geddes, Richard Kagan, Susan Nicassio, and Arie Zmora, who also took the time to read and comment on early versions of this work.

My gratitude especially belongs to Richard Goldthwaite, who assisted and directed me from my first days at Johns Hopkins until the final version of this work nearly six years later. Of his patience, critical facilities, commitment, and sense of purpose, I cannot speak highly enough; no aspect of this study does not reflect in some way his constant and constructive advice.

Finally, I would like to thank my parents for all their support and enthusiasm; and I especially thank my wife, Cindy, who had to listen to every chapter as it was being written, and whose comments were as helpful as her graphics and artwork were essential to the finished work.

Introduction:
Workers in the
Factory of Marvels

This is a study of the shipbuilders who worked in the Venetian Arsenal and of the social community that they formed, together with their wives, families, and neighbors. As artisans, these men belonged to a multitude of craft guilds, for then as now many different skills were necessary in the art of shipbuilding. They were all united, however, by their common connection with Venice's complex of public shipyards and armories known as the Arsenal, so much so that they eventually took its name for their own, and became known as the *arsenalotti,* "the sons of the Arsenal." Such a strong identification between craftsmen and workplace represented much more than just a linguistic curiosity, for the Arsenal created these workers and gave shape to their community even while they themselves provided the productive force of the Arsenal. This study is thus focused both on the shipyards of the state and on the neighborhoods of the shipbuilders, for both made up the social world of the arsenalotti. But it is also necessary to look well beyond the confines of the shipbuilding district of the city into yet a wider circle, for the arsenalotti played out their role on the larger stage of Venice, if not that of the entire Venetian empire. Their reputation and fame were gained in a greater urban and imperial context as much as in the Arsenal itself, and it was their variety of functions in Venetian society at large that transformed the arsenalotti from common shipbuilders and manual workers into an institution in the *Republica Serenissima*.

Like *arsenalotti*, the term *arsenale* was itself of good Venetian coinage, probably dating in some form back as far as the seventh century. For Venetians of the seventeenth century, living in a thousand-year-old Republic that still seemed good for another millennium, the public Arsenal had unquestionably become an institution worthy of an empire. Looking at their state shipyards, contemporaries saw the foundation not only of the Republic's once-legendary commercial strength (now perhaps showing some warnings signs of decline), but also of Christian Europe's best defense against the Moslem east (see fig. I.1).

In his guide to Venice, which he aimed at both curious Italians and visiting foreigners alike, Francesco Sansovino had offered his own version of how the Venetian Arsenal got its name, one which evoked the institution's civic and religious primacy:

> The base and the foundation of the greatness of this Republic, rather the honor of all Italy and to say it better and with more honesty, of all Christendom, is the house of the Arsenal, which derives from *Arx*

Figure I.1. Exterior view of the Arsenal gates

Senatus, that is, the fortress, the bastion, the defensive line, and the supporting wall of the Senate and of our faith against the arms of the Infidel.[1]

Considering the Arsenal the outstanding military establishment not only of their own city but of the entire western world, Venetians naturally spoke of it with a certain pride, as much when discussing it within their own state bureaucracy as they did to outsiders or tourists. In 1676, the Marine Secretary Zuane Bernardo prefaced his biannual report to the ducal Collegio with the words: "The name and concept of the Arsenal grows always more famous, even among the farthest nations; it is rightly recognized as the Factory of Marvels [*L'Officina delle Meraviglie*], the treasury of arms, and the most vigorous weapon in the defense of precious Liberty."[2]

Foreign dignitaries and Grand Tourists came to Venice during these years with the particular intention of visiting the Arsenal; filling their journals with superlatives, they leave some idea how this Factory of Marvels appeared to contemporaries. Peter Mundy, travelling in company with the British ambassador to Constantinople in 1620, judged the Arsenal to be "the most worthy [of] notice of all that is in Venice"; Richard Lassels asserted that it was "the greatest piece of Oeconomy in Europe." The early seventeenth-century English wanderer Thomas Coryat visited the Arsenal and passed along the story that the Marquis of Guasto, Charles V's commanding general in Italy, had once enthusiastically called it "the eighth miracle of the world"; Coryat went on to call the shipyards "the richest and best furnished storehouse for all manner of munition, both by Sea and Land, not only of all Christendome, but also of all the world, in so much that all the strangers whatsoever are moved with great admiration when they contemplate the situation, the greatnesse, the strength, the incredible store of provision thereof."[3]

Clearly, it was the immensity of the Arsenal and its great wealth of war materiel that so astonished foreign visitors. The entire complex covered around sixty acres at this time and was surrounded by roughly two and a half miles of walls and moats: a contemporary English guidebook termed it "as big as the city Canterbury."[4] Once within, tourists were shown a dazzling display of military hardware, and many of them dutifully recorded the remarkable statistics provided by their obliging guides. John Evelyn, who visited the Arsenal's storehouses in 1645, reported that he saw "a court full of cannon, bullets, chains, grapples, grenadoes, &c, and over that arms for 800,000 men . . . together with weapons of offence and defence for sixty-two ships." Philip Skippon noted in his diary that he had seen "arms in two rooms for three thousand horse . . . arms for ten thousand horse in another room; and in another, arms for fifty gallies . . . a very great mortar-piece . . . and a room call'd by some *The Garden of Oranges,* which is full of bullets."[5]

Besides showing off the Arsenal's treasure troves of weaponry and its many curious engines of war, Venetian guides were particularly eager to lecture Grand Tourists on the shipyards' legendary efficiency. Few visitors failed to comment on the orderly arrangement of both finished goods and primary materials, from the neat pyramids of cannon balls kept in the *Giardin di Ferro* to the heaps of timber that Skippon noticed seasoning under water.[6] Particularly impressive, however, were the prodigies of shipbuilding said to be carried out within the Arsenal. Mundy reported that "they are able in few dayes to build, rigg, furnish, arme and sett forth a good fleete of gallies"; Sir John Reresby wrote that, "once, upon an emergency, it is said, they prepared and rigged forth thirty galleys in ten days' time." Diarists would inevitably also feel compelled to pass along a story which over the years had taken on almost mythical proportions: how an entire galley had been built and launched in 1574 for the entertainment of the French King Henry III, just in the time it took him to eat his dinner.[7]

Yet seventeenth-century diarists and visitors to the Arsenal devoted at best only a few lines to the legions of craftsmen that made this fabled efficiency possible; what little they wrote of Venetian shipbuilders emphasized their immense numbers and an almost military organizational discipline. Lassels noted that 1,500 to 2,000 of these "Artificers" came to work in the Arsenal every day; their wages, said to total 250,000 ducats annually, "would pay two armyes."[8] John Evelyn wrote that these were craftsmen who were always busy about their tasks, models of disciplined and industrious behavior; he observed with approval that they would even "march out in military order . . . every evening."[9]

The seventeenth century was a time when visitors to the Venetian Arsenal could still find much there to admire. Even if the shipyards were increasingly taking on the air of a monument to the Republic's past imperial glories, they were nevertheless still an enormous manufacturing complex: quite capable of the kind of sustained ship production needed during the latter part of the century, for the Republic's protracted and painful rearguard wars in Crete and the Morea. This study of the Arsenal and its shipbuilders has been set in the seventeenth century (specifically in the years 1621 to 1670) in part just for this reason: for while previous works on the institution are both numerous and rich, only fairly recently have scholars begun to abandon the traditional assumption that all that is worth telling about the Arsenal and Venetian shipbuilding finished with the glories of Lepanto.[10]

The seventeenth century still remains largely uncharted territory in Venetian scholarship, both for the Arsenal and its workers and for the Republic as a whole. Yet the 1600s have been lately emerging at the center of a wide-ranging debate on the process and nature of economic and social decline, not only in Venice, but in Italy and the entire Mediterranean world. Work with new sources has allowed historians to re-evaluate in particular the tenacity of Venetian commercial enterprise in the face of challenges from the Atlantic maritime states; the economic decadence that was once commonly accepted to have overtaken the Republic as early as 1500 has by now been pushed ahead to 1630 or even later.[11] Central to any debate on Venice's economic health must be her shipbuilding industry, the provider of the Republic's commercial muscle and the supporter of perhaps 10 percent of the city's working population. Although the present study is primarily a work of social history, I hope it will also provide a better understanding of how the Arsenal as an institution contributed to the larger Venetian economy over the course of the century. New documentary materials in fact make it possible to show that the decades of stagnation in naval construction following the disastrous 1590s were eventually turned around, with a strong resurgence of shipbuilding activity in both public and private shipyards by the 1650s that provides good evidence that the Republic's shipbuilding sector could still be vital.[12]

Any research on this period could well be said to perform a service in opening up a rather neglected historical landscape, but the 1600s also have virtues of their own that make them especially attractive for a social historian with an interest in the Venetian Arsenal. Archival materials abound that are not especially numerous from the Republic's previous centuries (nor indeed sometimes from that which followed): four different censuses detailed the arsenalotti community between 1624 and 1661; these are backed by an unbroken series of parish resisters of births, marriages, and deaths, which only came into being toward the end of the sixteenth century. Although the primary administrative records of the *Senato Mar* and the *terminazioni* of the Patroni of the Arsenal run continuously from the 1400s until the fall of the Republic, certain series of reports and studies are peculiar to the seventeenth century. Particulartly rich are sixteen such reports from the Secretaries of the Marine (*savii agli ordini*) to the Collegio and three others from the Inquisitors of the Arsenal.[13]

Most important for this work, however, has been the series of petitions (*suppliche*) presented to the Pien Collegio by the arsenalotti themselves. Surviving in particularly large numbers from the seventeenth century, such petitions have allowed this study of Venetian shipbuilders to escape an overdependence on administrative and governmental sources and become more truly a social history. During just the half century between 1621 and 1670 shipbuilders presented the Collegio with nearly a thousand petitions, and many of these artisans loaded their formal requests for position or preferment with a wealth of personal details and observations of their own (see Appendix 1). As such, these petitions have permitted an unusual glimpse into an almost mythical institution, presenting the Arsenal of Venice, that Factory of Marvels with all its complexities and prodigies of manufacturing, from the point of view of those who actually did the work.

Therefore the first two chapters of this study will focus on the Arsenal workplace—ground which may well have been covered before, but here more from the perspective of the shipbuilders themselves than in the context of the administration and organization of the shipyards. The rich seventeenth-century sources have made it plain that these years were by no means stagnant ones in Venetian state shipbuilding, even if both the physical Arsenal and its workforce may have ceased to grow by 1600, for the shipbuilders themselves continued to evolve socially. The petitions of the period make it clear that it was particularly during the first half of the century that the arsenalotti "matured" as a workforce: becoming disciplined to the demands of integrated wage labor placed upon them by the Arsenal, while at the same time becoming more thoroughly self-conscious of themselves as a worker group with traditions, privileges, and status in the larger society.

The seventeenth-century Arsenal workforce should also be considered for the particular significance which it had in the larger history of European labor, as a reminder of the variety of modes of workplace organization that flourished in the premodern manufacturing world. The long-standing debate over the rural putting-out system's "protoindustrial" role in bridging from the independent craftsman to the factory system has tended to obscure the place in the industrializing process of large, state-run manufactures like the Venetian Arsenal.[14] Although before the Industrial Revolution such naval dockyards were indeed often the only sizeable industrial centers in most European states, most of the study directed to these institutions until now has been limited to the context of military production and state finance; the shipyards have received far less attention for the role they played in the organization and shaping of large forces of workmen.[15]

Seemingly defined by bureaucratic and military structures and operating largely independently of the workings of profit and the marketplace, such large, state-run shipyards have generally not appeared especially central to the key social and economic determinates of the industrializing process.[16] Nevertheless, the massive, concentrated workforces of large manufactures like the Arsenal presented for the first time kinds of management and labor problems that would be much more typical of the industrial factory than of the putting-out system: the disciplines of wages and time, the need for coordinated work gangs, and the formation of specialized and uniform "company towns" on the fringes of the workplace. The task of the present study has been to chart the peculiarly Venetian solution to the potentially destabilizing situation of running a large-scale manufacturing operation within a premodern, urban society. The "making" of the arsenalotti out of independent Venetian shipbuilders provides an especially useful illustration of how such a traditional society of orders, within the limits of its strengths and weaknesses, could tackle such "modern" problems in the age before industrial capitalism.

The arsenalotti never became a worker class. Rather than experience a sense of alienation from their workplace, they ran it themselves; far from being marginalized, they became thoroughly integrated into the ruling order of the Republic, to the extent of gaining a stake in the well-being of its patrician regime. This study has operated on the assumption that these shipbuilders derived their distinctive character as much from their civil role as from their workplace, and that they thus cannot be approached in isolation from the larger context of Venetian society. Fortunately, this society is already one of the better-known of early modern Europe, thanks to generations of scholarly spadework; more important, however, is that historians are increasingly starting to interest themselves in the world beyond that of just Venice's glittering patriciate, broadening the Republic's historiography to begin the elaboration of the complex web of relationships in which even the most ordinary craftsmen moved during the days of the Republic. For arsenalotti and artisans generally, Venice is emerging as an urban world that was rich with family and guild obligations, patronage linkages to higher social orders, minute and paternalist government regulation, and religious and civic celebrations.[17]

This study, then, proposes to follow the arsenalotti outside of their workplace in the state docks. First to their particular community surrounding the Arsenal, where they lived in an isolation and a state of self-sufficiency that made the district virtually an urban village, resolutely turned away from the cosmopolitan, mercantile world bustling all around it. Here will be found a prototype company town, completely given over to the shipbuilding trades and overwhelmingly dependent on the Arsenal in its midst; yet the district was also, and perhaps somewhat surprisingly, a highly feminine community, where women dominated in terms of numbers and played a key economic and social role.[18] Finally, the remaining two chapters of this work will move beyond these community boundaries, to the arsenalotti's larger social world, where shipbuilders distinguished themselves both as the Republic's worker militia and often as the bullies of the town as well. Indeed, the two roles were inextricably linked, for the arsenalotti never shied away from demanding from other artisans the respect to which they considered their public offices and special state work entitled them.

As a work that attempts to combine (or at least to straddle) both institutional and social history, this study has necessarily had to draw on a broad range of methodologies. Particularly useful have been the descriptive techniques and categories of cultural anthropology, which I have borrowed freely, if not always with complete discretion, for what they could tell me about status, dominance, violence, honor, and shame, whether focusing on the work in the shipyard docks or on shipbuilders' public lives in the streets and *campi* of seventeenth-century Venice. Enjoying from the outset of this research such a generous collection of worker petitions on which to draw, I have always attempted to portray this social world as the arsenalotti themselves saw and experienced it; if I have been able to do so convincingly, it is largely because of other scholars who have already shown the possibilities in cultural anthropology

for bringing back to life the often obscure popular perceptions and
mentalities of early modern Italy.[19]

With this study, then, I aim to further the already lively activities underway in Venetian social history and to make a small contribution toward beginning what might be termed an historical ethnography of the city's unique worker population. In the end, I hope to produce a portrait of the Arsenal masters that is both less mythical and more human than Venetian historiography has traditionally allotted to them, as the heroic but anonymous workers in the Factory of Marvels. If, in the process, these shipbuilders turn out to have had feet of clay, at least they may end up as more truly a part of their own contemporary social and cultural world, both as seventeenth-century Venetians and as workers of early-modern urban Europe.

1

Formation and
Nature of the
Arsenal Workforce

The world of the arsenalotti was anchored in the Arsenal where these artisans worked: the Venetian state shipyards gave purpose, hierarchical structure, and economic vitality to the community of workers that surrounded them. The production demands of the Arsenal not only brought together large numbers of artisans but also ultimately determined what kind and caliber of workers they would be. Yet the creation of this workforce was often a halting affair; at times it even appeared as if the Arsenal itself might grind to a stop for lack of suitable workers. Much of the difficulty lay not so much in getting the masters to enroll with the shipyards as in disciplining them to the demands of the workplace once they were inside. Indeed, in this respect the Arsenal had to confront many labor problems that resemble those the first English factory owners would face over a century later, for to maximize production in the shipyards, workers' habits of individual independence often had to give way before the rigidity of group discipline. The solutions found to these problems by the Republic were not those that eventually prevailed in the British Midlands. Instead, as in so many other matters, the Venetian approach to workforce formation would be uniquely its own: a fundamentally preindustrial response based on a society of castes rather than of classes, one that indeed turned out to be particularly suited to the social world of the Republic.

The Ordinary Workforce

Not all master craftsmen who came to work in the Arsenal were shipbuilders, and not even all those who were could be considered true arsenalotti. In fact, the Arsenal had three separate manufactories operating within its more than sixty acres: besides departments devoted to the building, outfitting, and repairing of ships, there were also two largely separate divisions charged with the production of ropes or cables and with the manufacture of arms and gunpowder. Both of these (comparatively) minor sections of the Arsenal maintained their own supply depots for raw materials and finished products and had their own particular administrative organization; the master ropemakers (*filacanevi*) and cannon casters (*fondatori*) who worked in them kept distinct relations with those whose business was shipbuilding.[1] Furthermore, many workers in the shipyards proper served more as auxiliaries than actually as shipbuilders: several hundred porters (*facchini* or *bastasi*) to provide the necessary muscle for this preindustrial workplace and a disparate collection of wallers (*mureri*), blacksmiths (*favri*), and sawyers (*segadori*) all crowded the Arsenal every day.[2] Whether master craftsmen or not, most of these workers kept a casual relationship with the Arsenal and were not usually considered genuine arsenalotti by contemporaries.

Arsenalotti were rather the masters of the shipyards' three so-called major guilds: the shipwrights, the caulkers, and the oarmakers who carried out the actual shipbuilding in the Arsenal. They also formed the great majority of those who worked there: together with their apprentices, masters of these three guilds would have accounted for at least 75 percent of the total workforce in the state shipyards. Known as the *maestranze ordinarie*, or regular workforce of the Arsenal, these masters had by the early 1500s won for themselves the particular privilege that distinguished them as arsenalotti: once enrolled in the *libro delle maestranze*, or workforce pay roster, they could find paying work in the Arsenal whenever they should choose to do so. Even if they were too old, sick, or incompetent to do anything useful, the state guaranteed them their daily pay, or *ordinario*, as long as they managed to show up at the shipyards in the morning.[3]

The guildsmen with this special connection to the Arsenal were those concerned with the major aspects of shipbuilding. The shipwrights *(marangoni)* produced the keel, frame, and ribbing of a ship, the "live work." Those known as *calafati* were responsible both for attaching the hull and cabins (the "dead work") and for the actual caulking of the exposed seams.[4] Finally, oarmakers *(remeri)* produced the thousands of oars used to propel the galleys and galleasses in which the Arsenal specialized.

In addition to these three major guilds, several smaller groups of artisans carried out subsidiary crafts as members of the Arsenal's ordinary workforce, but in lesser guilds affiliated with one of the major corporations. Chief among these were the mastmakers *(alboranti)* and the pulleymakers *(tagieri),* both attached to the guild of the shipwrights.[5] Also important, however, were a few wood carvers *(intagliadori)* responsible for decoration, some cask makers *(botteri),* and the guncarriage makers *(carreri).* Although counted and paid as part of the ordinary workforce, the *carreri* also fell under the direction of the armaments division of the Arsenal.[6]

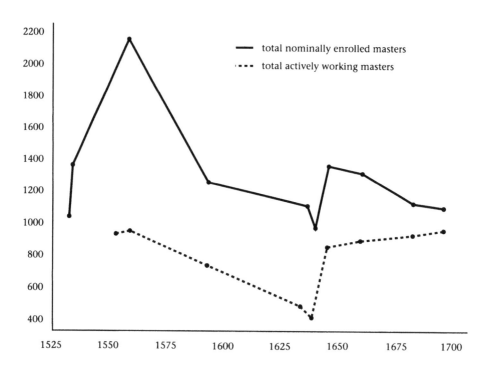

Graph 1.1. Enrollment of major guildsmen in the Arsenal, 1503–1696
Note: Derived from sources listed in Table 1.1

Table 1.1 Major Guildsmen in the Arsenal, 1503–1696

	Shipwrights		Caulkers		Oarmakers	
	Masters	Apprentices	Masters	Apprentices	Masters	Apprentices
1503[a]	*361*					
1531	*221*					
1536	(581)		(415)		(40)	
1538	(693)		(652)		(36)	
1553	*600*		(556) *250*	(350)	*60*	
1554	(1016)				(146)	
1559	(1024) *600*		(1013) *300*		(146) *60*	
1560	(1200)		(1000)			
1563	(1001)					
1565	(993)					
1591	(431) *200*		(786) *450*		(161) *100*	
1598[b]	(488)				(131)	
1605			(815)			
1606[c]			(828) *396*			
1609[d]			(825)			
1620			*440*			
1622			(627) *331*			
1623			(600) *320*			
1624			(594) *256*			
1629[e]	(700) *430*	(250)	(620) *290*	(200)		(30)
1630[f]	*217*	*165*	*277*	*121*	*56*	*20*
1633[g]			[373 shipwrights and caulkers]			
1636[h]	(564) *218*		(447) *147*		(120) *40*	
1639[i]	(446)		(456)		(90)	
1641[j]	(539)	(439)	(550) *312*	(316)	(150 incl. apprentices)	
1645[k]	(691) *400*		(564) *369*	(286) *260*	(142) *70*	
1660[l]	(616) *420*		(591) *380*		(115) *70*	
1660[m]					*40*	
1666[n]			(500)	(130)		
1679[o]	(541) *394*	(107) *75*				
1682[p]	(532) *420*	(179) *120*	(555) *440*	(188) *130*	(90) *65*	(43) *25*
1696[q]	(579) *424*	(174) *140*	(661) *500*	(290) *220*	(82) *64*	22

Note: Figures in parentheses = total number enrolled; figures in italics = number actively working.
[a]Figures for 1503–91: Lane, *Navires et Constructeurs,* 231.
[b]Figures for 1598 and 1605: Romano, "Economic Aspects of the Construction of Warships," 71.
[c]Figures for caulkers in 1606, 1622, 1623, 1624, and 1641: from ASV:SM, filza 324, 9 Nov. 1641.
[d]Figures for 1609 for caulkers: ASV:SM, filza 235, 16 Apr 1622.
[e]ASV:SM, reg. 87, 24 Nov 1629.
[f]ASV:SM, filza 274, 7 Dec 1630.
[g]ASV:Collegio V (Segreta), bu. 57, Relazione of Alvise Molin; figures only for total of shipwrights and caulkers working.
[h]ASV:SM, filza 304, 14 Apr 1636.
[i]ASV:Collegio V (Segreta), bu 57, Relazione of Priamo Lezze.
[j]ASV:Collegio V (Segreta), bu. 57, Relazione of Polo Contarini; figure for shipwrights includes 27 mastmakers.
[k]ASV:Collegio V (Segreta), bu. 57, Relazione of Andrea Marcello; figures for shipwrights include 33 pulleymakers enrolled and 19 pulleymakers working.
[l]ASV:Collegio V (Segreta), bu. 57, Relazione of Piero Mocenigo.
[m]ASV:SM, filza 510, 2 June 1660.
[n]ASV:CRD suppliche, filza 67, 28 Sept 1666.
[o]ASV:Collegio V (Segreta), bu. 57, Relazione of Zuane Bernardo.
[p]ASV:Collegio V (Segreta), bu. 57, Relazione of Vettor Grimani.
[q]ASV:Collegio V (Segreta), bu. 57, Relazione of Francesco Cornero.

Tallies of masters enrolled in the three major shipbuilding guilds in the Arsenal, although by no means complete, are at least sufficient to give some indication of the overall size and long-term variations of the state's shipbuilding workforce during the sixteenth and seventeenth centuries (see table 1.1).

Although enrollment did not always vary at the same pace for each guild, the general trends in workforce fluctuation are still fairly clear during these two centuries: after a strong initial buildup in the mid-1500s, shipyard enrollment then experienced an equally strong and rapid decline, with low points reached around 1590 and 1630. Thereafter, a new period of modest growth began which eventually produced a workforce that, while only about half the size of the 1560s, at least remained fairly stable until the end of the seventeenth century (see graph 1.1).

This view of Arsenal enrollment in the long term produces a different picture from most previous studies of Venetian shipbuilding, which have focused attention on the sixteenth century, when the Republic's ship production boomed and the Arsenal workforce reached its maximum size. The traditional consensus has long connected the sharp drop in workforce size after the Battle of Lepanto with the end of centuries of growth, a decline that once begun became inescapable, as state shipbuilding joined the general broad economic and political decline of the Republic.[7] Such a conclusion becomes less tenable when consideration is given to the growth and stability of the Arsenal workforce after the 1630s. When the entire two centuries of growth and decline are placed in perspective, it is indeed the rapid increase of the Arsenal workforce in the mid-1500s, more than later declines, that appears to have been the exceptional occurrence: a sudden and unusual expansion brought on by the threats of Turkish war that for little more than a generation doubled the number of enrolled arsenalotti. When, after Lepanto and Venice's separate peace, the immediate Turkish naval threat receded, the Arsenal's enormous workforce was hastily cut back to a level appropriate to the Republic's limited available resources. What is most striking about Arsenal enrollment levels of the later seventeenth century is not so much that they were reduced from the 1560s, but that they were stable: an indication that the state was indeed determined to keep a shipbuilding workforce, but one that would be held steady at what might be considered a "pre-emergency" size of before the 1540s.

Much of the exceptional boom in workforce enrollment in the Arsenal in the 1540s and 1550s can be linked to recruitment policies undertaken by the state in previous decades. Worried about a grow- ing Turkish threat from the east, the Senate decided to double the Republic's regular fleet of warships, to 100 light galleys (*galie sotili*) and 12 great galleys (*galie grosse*).[8] To bring about the rapid increase in shipbuilders which such policies demanded, the Senate decided to alter the state's traditional relationship with Venetian shipbuild- ers. Previously, the number of artisans actually enrolled with the Arsenal had been kept fairly limited: only a few dozen shipwrights out of a regular workforce of several hundred or so were inscribed with the right to work in the state shipyards whenever they pleased. The state was evidently reluctant to extend the privilege of enroll- ment beyond this small circle: caulkers and oarmakers working in the Arsenal had not enjoyed such rights, and indeed there appears to have been no need to offer such an expensive concession to work- ers, since a sufficient number was usually at hand to guarantee nec- essary production levels.[9] When emergencies had demanded a quan- tity of shipping in a hurry, it was customary to enlarge the Arsenal workforce simply by declaring a draft (*leva*) and pressing into tem- porary service the required number of local shipbuilders and related craftsmen.

This working situation changed by the early sixteenth century, however. The production demands of the hundred-galley program were so great that pre-empting independent workers no longer was an adequate means of meeting what amounted to permanent emer- gency conditions. To persuade shipbuilders to make themselves available for state service voluntarily, the Senate decided to liberal- ize Arsenal enrollment policies. Henceforth, all shipbuilders who came to the Arsenal in this period would also be allowed to enroll themselves on the work rosters of the shipyards as members of the ordinary workforce. Indeed, craftsmen would not only gain the as- surance of paid work in the Arsenal whenever they chose for the rest of their lives, but they might also expect to pass the right on to their sons. Oarmakers were granted the privilege in 1532 and the caulkers a decade later, although only on a half-time basis.

Since at this time the Arsenal was paying experienced shipbuild- ers at or near the going rates in the private sector, the result of the offer, as might be expected, was a rush for inscription. Craftsmen from all over the Republic were willing to enroll with the Arsenal, knowing that enrollment gave them access to the public payroll when they needed it without forbidding employment in the city's private shipyards (*squeri*) should it be easier or pay better. Having soon realized that their decision had amounted to open-ended subsidizing of the city's shipbuilding community, senators began to doubt the wisdom of the system, the more so as independent shipbuilders who were accustomed to work on their own evidently had some trouble adjusting to the discipline demanded within the state shipyards. Several significant riots of these arsenalotti broke out during the latter sixteenth century over questions of pay and working hours; on one occasion the Collegio itself was occupied by angry shipbuilders.[10] Barely a generation after their adoption, the Senate thus decided to retreat from its enrollment policies, without abolishing them altogether: outside shipbuilders found it increasingly difficult to enroll, and the number of apprentices each master could take was cut back.[11] Only occasionally (as in the years just before Lepanto) were such restrictions relaxed, as the Senate let attrition reduce Arsenal enrollment from its expensive peaks of the 1560s down to the pre-emergency levels of the 1520s and 1530s.[12]

The very success of Lepanto was to prove a major factor in the subsequent decline and restructuring of the Arsenal workforce. Venice's share of the booty after the victory included so many Turkish galleys that normal shipbuilding was virtually suspended while dozens of prizes were repaired and refitted. Ship's carpenters, who had previously been the backbone of the Arsenal workforce, were no longer nearly as useful as were the caulkers, whose skills were necessary for refitting both the Turkish prizes and Venice's own battered galleys. New ship production in the Arsenal after 1576 ground almost to a complete halt: no galleys at all were built in the shipyards for more than a decade.[13] Although shipwrights still had their right to come to the state shipyards, the government gave them no encouragement to do so; few were allowed to enroll their sons as apprentices, a restriction that deprived masters of both the extra income and the assistance they normally expected from a helper. For many shipwrights the situation by the 1590s had become intolerable, the more so because a depression in the private shipbuilding sector deprived them of outside work as well; in the end, they staged something of a mass desertion from the Arsenal, and over 500 masters left the trade altogether, going over to house carpentry or other crafts. When the Arsenal's need for repairs and refitting eventually declined as well, the state began to apply the same restriction to caulkers: by 1605 these craftsmen were also no longer signing on new apprentices.[14] Like shipwrights, caulkers unable to find work in the city's private shipyards were forced either to learn new trades or to leave Venice altogether and try their luck with foreign princes.

In its determination to reduce expenditures, the Senate came close to wiping out the city's entire shipbuilding sector, and with it a reserve of skill and experience that represented one of the Republic's most important human resources. Without a flow of new apprentices, the workforce became steadily more aged and moribund, until the Arsenal *Patroni* noted in 1617 that masters were dying off at an alarming rate: nearly 600 in just one decade, not counting "a considerable quantity that have died outside [the city] and [those] that were enslaved by the Turks."[15] Caulkers, who had until recently greatly outnumbered shipwrights in the Arsenal, were suddenly in short supply, and the Patroni began to send worried messages to the Senate about how frames finished by the carpenters were waiting years for their planking and caulking.[16] Indeed, so few competent masters were available for work that it began to seem as if Venice might have to abandon both public and private ship construction altogether and start buying its vessels from outside manufacturers such as the Dutch.[17]

Some attempts were made during these years to reorganize what available workforce there was more effectively. Caulkers, who previously had been inscribed on the Arsenal rosters to work only every other week, were given the option to come in continuously, as long as they were willing to master both the caulking and planking branches of their craft.[18] Since the Senate did not move at the same time to loosen restrictions on apprentices and pay, the response of these workers was poor, and their numbers continued to decline alarmingly.[19] In the end, the Senate had to face the expense and open the Arsenal workforce once again to new apprentices. Beginning in 1614, a succession of large blocks of boys were enrolled, usually at the rate of 100 or 200 caulkers or shipwrights at a time.[20] By degrees the Arsenal workforce was rebuilt, and at the end of the 1620s total enrollment of shipwrights and caulkers surpassed even that of the 1590s.

The practice of enrolling large groups of new apprentices every two or three years had its problems, however. Many arsenalotti who had been away from the Arsenal during the short inscription periods missed their chance to enroll their sons—they flooded the Patroni with complaints of unfairness; the Senate repeatedly had to approve he funding for an extraordinary enrollment to satisfy those whose

boys who had been left out.[21] More important, the practice of enrolling apprentices in large blocks simply began afresh the earlier
problem of instability in the ordinary workforce, starting up a new
cycle of rapid increase after the previous poorly controlled decline.

Partly as an attempt to eliminate such fluctuations in workforce
size, the Senate decided in 1629 to institute a new way of enrolling
apprentices, "to prevent a further decline in the workforce of the
Arsenal." The chief secretary (*scrivan grande*) of the Arsenal was
ordered to institute a new register, or *alfabeto:* here would be inscribed the names of the legitimate sons of each serving master at
the moment of their baptism. When these boys reached ten years of
age, they could be apprenticed to their fathers (or grandfathers, if
necessary) in a continuous flow, instead of in large blocks, as had
previously been the case.[22] The concept was simple, but it nevertheless affected the arsenalotti as profoundly as had the opening of the
official workforce roster and the guarantee of permanent employment had done back in the 1530s.

Coming at a time when many guilds in Venice were loosening
their entrance requirements and multiple guild membership was becoming commonplace, the arsenalotti baptismal register marked the
countervailing trend in an industrial sector that had once been
known for its openness to outside talent.[23] Venetian shipbuilders
had long considered themselves a breed apart, but the Senate's edict
virtually defined them as a separate caste of artisans, one of the most
exclusive of the city. Noting its similarity with the more celebrated
official list of sons of the Venetian nobility, some historians have not
surprisingly termed this register a *"Libro d'oro,"* and indeed it appears to have had the effect of turning the shipbuilders quite literally
into an aristocracy among workers: thanks to their inscription as
boys on the new rosters, arsenalotti could look forward, as did the
Republic's patriciate, to being "little *rentiers* of the Venetian state
from [the moment of] their birth."[24]

Although the institution of the baptismal register in 1629 may
have further refined the arsenalotti's sense of themselves as a patriciate among Venetian workers, there could be no immediate confir-
mation of its impact on their enrollment. Unfortunately for the ex-
periment, less than a year after the register had been established,
plague struck the city. Its effects on the arsenalotti were devastating:
922 masters were reported to have died in less than a year; over 360
were lost among the caulkers alone.[25] Since virtually the entire cadre
of future apprentices had been wiped out at a stroke, the barely
instituted arsenalotti baptismal register appeared to the administra-

tors of the shipyards to be of scant use: as a result, it was neglected and finally abandoned for over a generation.[26]

In the meantime, to rebuild the workforce after the plague, the Patroni returned to earlier practices of rounding up craftsmen from all over Venice and its *dogado* and of inscribing large blocks of apprentices, regardless of whether or not they were near relatives of working masters.[27] Such big blocks of apprentices were enrolled that delays sometimes occurred before enough arsenalotti could be found to take them all; some masters had to inscribe two or three boys at a time.[28] Enrollment figures suggest that this rebuilding of the workforce was a success: in 1645 the total number of enrolled shipwrights and caulkers was only 5 percent less than it had been in 1629, just before the plague. Nevertheless, continually having to rely on its discretionary powers was evidently not to the liking of the Senate, for when the Patroni suggested in 1650 that the baptismal register be tried once again, the idea was quickly accepted. This time, however, the Senate chose to make the register a requirement as well as an honor for arsenalotti, changing the wording of its provision from the earlier version to stress that inscribed boys would have the obligation rather than the option of choosing a trade in one of the shipbuilding guilds.[29]

Finally established for good in 1650, the arsenalotti baptismal register did appear to provide a stable workforce for the state shipyards, although smaller guilds such as the oarmakers and the pulleymakers sometimes had trouble finding enough boys to replenish their ranks.[30] Between 1660 and 1696, the numbers of major guildsmen enrolled in the Arsenal varied by only 10–15 percent, with apprentices always in sufficient supply to replace masters who had died off. Whenever the quantity of entering apprentices threatened to exceed the needs of the Republic's shipbuilding program, moreover, the Patroni still had the freedom to restrict the number of inscribed sons each master might actually enroll. When in the 1670s it appeared that too many masters returning from the Cretan War were seeking to establish themselves and their families back in the state shipyards, the Senate was not slow at putting a brake on new inscriptions in the baptismal register: in 1676 it was decided to halt new apprenticeships completely for a while, although three years later inscriptions were allowed once again.[31]

Creation of a Stable Workforce

Thanks to the arsenalotti baptismal register, by the end of the 1600s the Republic could count on the stability of the Arsenal's workforce enrollment more than had been possible a century earlier. It was hardly enough simply to enroll a certain number of shipbuilders with the Arsenal, however; the state also had to be sure that a sufficient number of masters for regular production needs actually came to the yards on a daily basis, and that once there they did in fact do some work. Even as early as the fifteenth century, when the workforce numbered only a few hundred masters, there had been problems in getting shipbuilders to spend their whole day at the worksite; in the Arsenal of two hundred years later, where sometimes thousands of artisans and laborers were carrying out dozens of different tasks at the same time, insuring that masters regularly came to their workplace was one of the state's most difficult problems.[32]

Keeping a steady supply of hands at the worksite had been a problem in such trades as the construction industry since at least the Middle Ages, when a building boom similar to that experienced by the Arsenal had made organizing the work a difficult business. Private shipbuilding in Venice had been traditionally carried on in a manner similar to housebuilding, by a highly fluid workforce accustomed to move freely from yard to yard, or even abandoning the craft altogether for a time, to take up work fishing, rowing the gondola, or sailing cargo boats, should these trades pay better.[33] The state encountered additional difficulties in disciplining workers to the rhythms and demands of the Arsenal, however, since few Venetian shipbuilders adjusted easily to its integrated production schedules or the arbitrary powers of their bosses. Absenteeism was high, as masters for whom such discipline was distasteful found almost any activity more attractive than coming to the state shipyards and engaging in the highly regimented work that was expected of them.[34]

In considering the size of the workforce at the Arsenal, a careful distinction should therefore be made between the many masters who were nominally enrolled on the work rosters and the much smaller number who actually came to the shipyards on a regular basis. Since counts were sometimes made of enrolled arsenalotti, sometimes of masters coming to work, and sometimes of both at once, there has been considerable confusion in modern studies on the Arsenal as to the size of the actual workforce.[35] By accepting the Arsenal's enrollment figures as if they were the daily count of working artisans, some historians have portrayed a virtual army of craftsmen coming and going from the shipyards every day. In fact, the "4,000 to 5,000 men" supposedly working in the Arsenal in the sixteenth century to a great extent existed quite literally only on paper, since such figures represented simply the sum of all the shipbuilders of the *dogado* who had the right to work in the shipyards if they so chose.[36] Totals from 1559 indicate the extent to which enrollment figures taken alone can exaggerate the size of the active workforce in the Arsenal: although the names of 2,183 masters from the three major guilds appeared on the rosters, a head count made during a single week revealed that only 960, or less than 44 percent, actually came to work on a daily basis.[37]

Such a low rate of actively working masters indicates that, although sixteenth-century shipbuilders from Venice and its *dogado* were quite willing to enroll with the Arsenal for the benefits it promised, they actually went to work there only as a last resort. Whenever work was to be found in the city's private shipyards, they clearly preferred to take it: private employment probably provided a more relaxed working environment than did work in the Arsenal, and by the end of the sixteenth century it would certainly have paid better. Starved for workers after the plague of 1630–31, private shipyards offered far higher wages than the Arsenal, driving the ratio of actively working to enrolled masters in the state yards down as low as 36 percent. As long as they were making better pay on the outside, shipbuilders would have seen little enough reason to come to the Arsenal in their days off; with extra income they could instead buy themselves some free time and play the part of *solazieri*, idling about the taverns and *campi* of their district, looking for amusements. Many arsenalotti managed to find higher-paying work in the private sector for years at a time while in their prime, only showing up at the Arsenal in their old age, claiming what was effectively a state pension, since they were then too feeble to do actual shipbuilding any more.[38]

The Patroni and Marine Secretaries of the Collegio repeatedly warned that a large disparity between enrolled and active masters was costly to the state; the Arsenal, they wrote, was only serving to "nurse the young and care for the old": training apprentices and providing a safe haven for elderly masters unable to find private work any longer.[39] Sometimes, it is true, the state was perfectly willing to let shipbuilders find work elsewhere if it had no immediate use for them: in the years 1573 to 1600 and after 1669, masters still of vigorous working age were actually encouraged to leave the Arsenal temporarily, to relieve the government of the burden of their wages.[40] Nevertheless, during most of the seventeenth century the

Senate and Patroni pursued an opposite course, trying to persuade or force as many enrolled arsenalotti as possible to actively work at the state shipyards.

State policy on absenteeism among enrolled masters took a particularly coercive turn after the plague of 1630–31, when masters were in short supply and there were suddenly many more high-paying jobs available in the city. The Senate first resorted to its traditional methods of rounding up workers to meet the labor shortage in the Arsenal; although such actions soon aroused loud protests from both individual arsenalotti and their guilds, they were successful enough to convince the Senate to demand even a larger share of its workers' time.[41] Already by 1633, new legislation which cited "the present needs" required that all ship's carpenters, oar, mast and pulley makers come to work at least six months of every year. Those who failed to fulfill this "obligation" were threatened with a loss of 6 soldi per workday from their Arsenal wages. Should any master attempt to cheat the edict and inflate his total by signing in during the morning and not reporting back in the afternoon, the day would be deducted from his required six months and he would also lose the morning's pay.[42]

In passing this and similar edicts in the 1630s (some of which specified 150 workdays per year instead of six months), the Senate was finally requiring a minimum working commitment from its arsenalotti. No longer could a Venetian shipbuilder call himself a master of the Arsenal unless he actually did some work there: shipyard pensions would henceforth be reserved for those elderly craftsmen who had taken care of their obligations to the state when they were younger. Under the pressure of petitions from the Arsenal guilds, the 150-day rule was occasionally softened and some exemptions were granted to individuals, but the Senate refused to abandon it altogether. Indeed, in wartime, when the demand for workers was high, the Patroni could go still further and require that certain categories of masters report to work in the Arsenal at least two thirds of the workdays in every year.[43]

The state's principal weapon for seeing to it that shipbuilders performed their obligatory workdays was the Colleggietto. This board, which was composed of one secretary from each of the Collegio's three governing boards, a ducal councillor, a head (*capo*) of the Quarantia, and the Patroni and Provveditori of the Arsenal themselves, existed at least by 1504, when it had been charged with

setting the pay rates of shipwrights. By the 1530s its competence
had been extended to cover the wages of oarmakers as well; not long
after, the caulkers, whose working schedule required that they be
treated separately, were given a Colleggietto of their own.[44]

Initially, the Colleggietto was scheduled to meet every two years for general pay reviews. By the 1600s, however, as many as six or seven years might go by before the Collegio would get around to summoning the board, and even then sometimes only so that the doge and his secretaries could put a stop to the annoyance of so many petitions from the shipbuilding guilds and arsenalotti seeking raises.[45] It might also turn out to be impossible to call a Colleggietto on schedule because the previous one was still meeting, trying to finish its assigned business. Although the names of many workers had to be checked, the slow pace of the board was at times also caused by its own members, who were often called to other and sometimes conflicting duties, and so left the Colleggietto without the necessary quorum.[46] On the other hand, as one secretary himself admitted, the government itself was often reluctant to call for a Colleggietto, just for the increased cost a general pay review would mean for the state.[47]

The purpose of the Colleggietto, according to the Senate edicts that summoned it, was to "reward the good masters and punish the bad" ("premiar li buoni et punir [or 'castigar'] li cattivi"). It has been observed that the Colleggietto must in fact have done little enough punishing, since the nobles of the board had insufficient technical knowledge to judge any shipbuilder's merits fairly and therefore generally gave raises simply based on seniority.[48] Such an assessment of the Colleggietto's role overlooks the fact that the board could give masters raises only up to a certain fixed pay maximum. More immediately important, however, it also fails to take into account the power of the Colleggietto to expel arsenalotti from the shipyards altogether. At first, that task was carried out somewhat like a role call: arsenalotti who failed to show up (or at least to send someone in their place) when their Colleggietto met and called their names would be stricken *(cassato)* from the Arsenal roster.[49] Soon, arsenalotti were complaining that such an arrangement was unfair, since the sittings of the board were so erratic that there was no way of knowing when their names would be called. Perhaps for this reason the simple role call form of discipline was replaced (or at least supplemented) by the 1630s, at which time the Colleggietto automatically expelled only those masters who had failed to work their required 150 days (or six months) during the previous year; it was evidently the responsibility of the Arsenal timekeepers to supply the board with the information on how much each master had worked.[50]

Through its authority to expel them, the Colleggietto was undeniably effective in convincing the shipbuilders to take their public obligations seriously. Fifty-six arsenalotti petitioned the Collegio for readmission to the shipyards during the years 1621 to 1670 after having fallen victim to the board, and these were very likely only a minority of all those expelled. Several times, dozens of masters with poor attendance records were removed from the rosters in a single stroke, although on such occasions the simple need for workers forced the Senate to reverse the board and order that those expelled be readmitted with just a warning about absenteeism.[51] The Colleggietto could also sometimes prove too ready to listen to unsound advice in its zeal to impose discipline on workers. In 1648, the shipwright Nadalin di Biasio objected that when a recent Colleggietto had called his name, "it was responded by the workforce that I was dead," and so he was *cassato,* although in fact he was only at home sick. The shipwright Stefano di Grassi—also absent due to illness—went further and asserted that "someone wishing me ill appeared" *(ne comprarire alcun mio malevole)* and spread stories about him *sinistramente* to the Colleggietto, until the nobles on the board decided to strike off his name.[52]

The smooth running of the Arsenal required that arsenalotti put in a minimum amount of work at the shipyards and that they did so on a regular and predictable schedule. The Venetian calendar of festivals and holidays meant that the shipyards were normally functioning only around 265 days a year, and it was important to maximize the productive potential of what time was available.[53] Shipbuilding traditions could inhibit effective workforce mobilization, however, for in the Arsenal as in many preindustrial manufacturing centers the distinctions between work and recreation were not always clear.[54] The launching of a new galley called for celebrations, which included what even the Patroni themselves referred to as "the good and ancient customs" of distributing twenty liters of undiluted wine *(vino puro)* to each work crew of ten masters—after which work was no doubt over for the rest of the day.[55] Guild sodality also required that arsenalotti break off work to march in the funeral procession of a brother master. The enthusiasm of arsenalotti for these wakes was such that craftsmen of one major guild in the Arsenal often took part in processions honoring deceased masters of the other two, giving the Patroni the impression that the burial of a shipbuilder would result in the emptying of the entire Arsenal. Having realized that anywhere between 70 and 150 masters might well die yearly, the Patroni eventually ruled that masters might march only in processions honoring a fellow guildsman, an order that reduced but never eliminated the disruption that funerals could cause.[56]

The state had particular difficulty persuading arsenalotti to come to work in the shipyards on Mondays. "Saint Monday" was indeed honored by artisans in many trades all over preindustrial Europe: the beginning of the week was often a time to recover from the drinking bouts and festive activities which highlighted Sundays, and absenteeism and inattention to work were generally high. In cottage industries or light manufacturing, craftsmen could make up the drop in production caused in missing Mondays by working longer and harder hours at the end of the week. In the Venetian Arsenal, however, the process of ship construction had achieved too high a degree of integration, calling for considerable workplace organization and teamwork, and Monday absenteeism could have an especially disruptive effect on production.[57] As early as 1546, the Senate tried to forbid the observance of Saint Monday by arsenalotti, ordering that any master who failed to come to the shipyards on the first day of the work week would not be paid for the rest of the week either.[58] For a long time this disciplinary measure was not conscientiously enforced, however, and any master who could offer a believable excuse to his timekeeper could expect to be paid on whatever day he might show up at the shipyards. The rule was definitely relaxed for the caulkers in 1622, as part of a move by the Senate to get masters who still worked only half time in the shipyards to come in as much as possible.[59]

Such a relaxed state of affairs lasted only as long as production demands remained relatively low, and the general tightening up of work requirements in the Arsenal during the 1630s also provoked a resurrection of the 1546 edict. The campaign against Saint Monday was led by the two newly appointed Inquisitors of the Arsenal, who claimed that the reduced Monday workforce was resulting in certain tasks in the shipyards not being integrated properly, with valuable materials being spoiled through neglect or misuse.[60] Originally aimed only at the caulkers, the provision was reissued in the opening year of the Cretan War and included the shipwrights as well.[61] The three major guilds of the Arsenal attempted to get the edict rescinded, claiming that their members were often absent from their places on Monday mornings due to legitimate business; despite repeated petitioning to give arsenalotti freedom to come to work when they chose, the Senate proved to be stubborn on the issue. The only compromise which could be worked out was to exempt from the rule those masters who could present written excuses, countersigned by one of the Patroni, showing that they had either been sick or at work on state business outside the Arsenal.[62]

Such protracted disputes over workplace conditions make it clear that, despite the almost limitless legal authority which the Senate and Patroni technically enjoyed over stubborn arsenalotti, their punishments or threats for making masters come to work were in fact relatively mild. Wage reductions, temporary suspension, or outright dismissal describe the limits of the discipline imposed; only rarely does it appear that corporal punishment or personal humiliation were employed.[63] Such restraint is probably a good sign that the Venetian state of the 1600s was not actually in a very strong position when it came to disciplining reluctant or disobedient workers: the fame of arsenalotti as shipbuilders and the international demand for their skills would have undermined attempts to punish or blacklist the disobedient. Too many foreign princes were eager to hire emigrant shipbuilders, and generally offered them superior pay and working conditions as well, as the gang boss Giacomo di Colombin made plain in a petition of 1633. Arriving in Rome after escaping from enslavement in Tunis, Colombin had been granted an audience by the pope himself, who tempted the shipbuilder to enter papal service with 500 scudi a year and such blandishments as "a house in Civitavecchia and one in Rome, with a servant and a horse and the kind of food that is usually given to the gentlemen of the [Papal] court."[64]

The Venetian state also had a wide variety of more positive inducements to insure that masters would come to work at the Arsenal and not find other employment in the city or abroad. The very fact that Arsenal shipbuilders were highly honored by the Republic gave the Patroni considerable leverage over them, since the shame attached to expulsion was far greater than what might be felt by other guildsman. As Arsenal shipwright Stefano di Giacomo dei Grassi lamented when he petitioned for readmission: "I was therefore left dismissed through no fault of my own, and in consequence deprived

of that honor and of that merit which I had acquired with my Su-
preme Prince."[65] The state could also tempt those arsenalotti who
cooperated with rewards that would not have been the common
expectation of other artisans. To sweeten the edict that arsenalotti
put in 150 days a year at the state shipyards, the Senate offered
masters who willingly complied an exemption from the city's newly
imposed renters' tax, or *Quarto dell'affitto*.[66] Shipbuilders who did
perform their minimum required service at the shipyards could also
expect the support of the Arsenal if they ever petitioned the Collegio
for a *gratia*; in backing such petitions, the Patroni often made a
point of praising an applicant's steady work habits and many "anni
continui" of service.[67]

Whether using coercion or persuasion, the efforts of the Senate
and Patroni were evidently fairly successful in convincing arsenalotti that work in the Arsenal was a public obligation that out-
weighed either private employment or the pleasures of personal
idleness. The ratio of masters actually coming to work to the total
of those enrolled began to improve after 1640 and by the end of the
century had reached nearly 80 percent, a considerable gain over the
30–40 percent ratios of 150 years earlier (see graph 1.2).

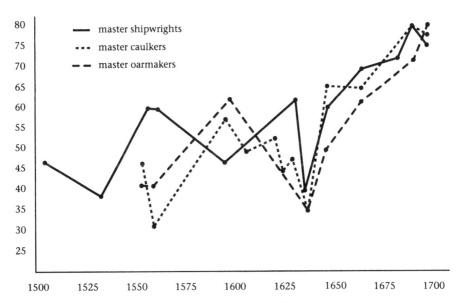

Graph 1.2. Ratio of actively working to nominally enrolled major guildsmen in the Arsenal, 1503-1696

Note: Derived from sources listed in Table 1.1

This long campaign to rationalize Venetian shipbuilders had clear benefits for the state, for it resulted in a total active workforce in the 1690s that was almost as large as the one from the boom period of the 1550s. At the same time, the total of master shipbuilders enrolled on the Arsenal's rosters had dropped by over 40 percent. The result was not only a more compact force of workers, the greater part of whom were familiar with Arsenal procedures, but a less expensive one in the bargain, since the number of masters whom the Arsenal was committed to support into old age and feebleness had been considerably reduced (see graph 1.3).

Wages and the Problems of Discipline

The Venetian government's long effort to persuade shipbuilders who were enrolled in the Arsenal to come to work there regularly would no doubt have been effected much more quickly if it had not been determined to pay them wages as low as it possibly could. Since all together the pay of the shipyards' workforce typically cost the Republic an average of about 150,000 ducats annually, the at-

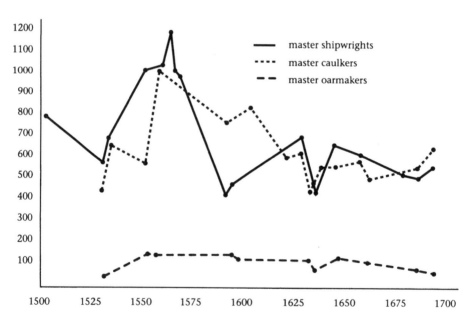

Graph 1.3. Total master shipwrights, caulkers, and oarmakers nominally enrolled and actively working in the Arsenal, 1536-1696

Note: From figures in Table 1.1. Generally, counts of active masters were based on daily averages taken from the Arsenal pay rosters

tempts of ministers to economize over the Arsenal labor budget are
hardly surprising, the more so because the notion was widespread
in the preindustrial world that workers who were paid too generously would only respond by cutting back on their hours of toil.[68]
The task of seeing that pay increases in the shipyards were kept
under control fell to the Colleggietto, and indeed when the board
was originally created it had been as part of a program to roll back
all earlier raises granted to masters unofficially. It was decided at the
time that henceforth all new masters would start in the shipyards at
the low wage of 6 soldi per workday and, after a six-year waiting
period, receive raises in stages up to a maximum level of 24 soldi.[69]
In the 1580s, most shipbuilders' base pay was jumped to 24 soldi,
and the ceiling was raised to 40 soldi per day.[70] If a master sought
any further raise beyond the maximum, he would have to personally
petition the Collegio.

The increase to 40 soldi was in fact the only raise granted in the
Arsenal wage ceiling over the entire three centuries between 1400
and 1700. Although a 66-percent jump from the 24-soldi maximum,
the new wage ceiling effectively only restored to arsenalotti the buying power they had lost over the previous century and a half of
inflation and devaluation. Soon even these modest gains would
evaporate as inflation heated up still more in the 1580s and 1590s.[71]
Arsenal masters were tied to a fixed wage structure with much less
flexibility than that of the private labor market of the city. In the
years just before 1560, master carpenters and masons in Venice's
construction industry had been paid a daily wage very similar to
that of arsenalotti—around 29 soldi per workday. The relatively free
labor conditions of the building sector, fueled by inflationary trends,
occasional sudden demand, and a fluctuating supply of workers,
soon drove up master builders' wages: from 38 soldi per day in 1580,
to 50 soldi in 1600, to nearly 68 soldi in 1630. From near parity
with these craftsmen, the arsenalotti pay maximum shrank to only
59 percent in just seventy years.[72]

The disparity between the wages of arsenalotti and those of independent artisans in similar trades was already bad enough by the
1590s to cause hundreds of shipwrights to give up the Arsenal for
good. But after the plague of 1630–31 the gap was still worse. While
shipbuilders were being forced to put in more time than ever at the
low Arsenal wages, other artisans were able to ask almost whatever
they wanted for their services: some master builders could hope to
earn over 100 soldi per day in this period, and as much as 150 with

an assistant. Independent craftsmen who ran their own shops could earn even more: master turners, guncarriage makers, and coopers were accustomed during the 1630s to make anywhere from 120 to 180 soldi per day.[73] By 1632, arsenalotti were complaining that other artisans were charging such high prices for goods and services that they themselves, with their rigid pay, could not afford to buy clothing or get their tools renewed. When the caulkers petitioned the Collegio for a raise, their bitterness against their fellow artisans was palpable: "all the others," they complained, "rejoice in their earnings . . . the workers of the city have found a remedy for their trouble [of inflation] by greedily demanding that others pay the costs."[74] Not that such options were not also open to certain arsenalotti as well: those masters with the best skills could hope to make 80–120 soldi a day in the private shipyards of the city, but to do so consistently they would have to risk the possibility of expulsion from the Arsenal registers and instead join the newly formed guild of the private ship-builders, or *squerarioli*.[75]

While the state insisted that its shipbuilders worked a minimum number of days in the Arsenal, it nevertheless also prevented them from working more than a certain amount. When there was no need for emergency production, the Arsenal closed its doors eight or nine days per month for Sundays and official religious holidays. This left only about twenty-two paid days a month for those arsenalotti who had no outside work, a cause of some complaint by many masters, who like the caulker Giacomo di Tomio lamented that "especially for the multiple holidays there are in the year," a 40-soldi maximum really only amounted to 29 soldi as a daily average; new masters had to scrape by on wages that in effect averaged out to a mere 18 soldi per day.[76]

Were such working conditions particularly unusual, however? Many recent scholars have concluded that preindustrial artisans and laborers typically worked even less than these shipbuilders, often barely half the year, when seasonal unemployment was added to a hundred or more holidays and religious festivals annually.[77] Yet for urban workers such estimates are derived largely from the construction trades, where, like the arsenalotti, craftsmen worked in visible and public sites that necessarily closed down on official holidays. Many other Venetian shopkeepers and craftsmen who ran their own shops could apparently choose to follow a much more liberal working schedule; the Senate repeatedly forbade artisans from doing business on holidays, and the Giustizia Vecchia frequently fined violators, but a long list of merchants and artisans were exempted from such restrictions and many more evidently imitated them, selling their products with their shop doors *socchiuse*.[78] Furthermore, crafts such as paper- and glassmaking needed a continuous cycle of production, and artisans who practiced them could only with difficulty break off for Sundays or feast days; many others, however, were only concerned with earning as much as they could. Even when they were observing public festivals, merchants and craftsmen usually managed to turn such events into enormous public fairs, their guilds taking advantage of processions before the public to display their wares.[79] The extent to which such commerce was tacitly allowed on holidays is not altogether clear, but the bitterness of some arsenalotti petitioners in referring to their own limited work schedules would indicate that shipbuilders were aware of this particular inequity between themselves and independent artisans.

Considering the attractive wages increasingly available in private yards, it is most likely that over time the best shipbuilders in Venice, if they could not find positions there as managers, would have largely abandoned the Arsenal to those who were more faithful, if less talented and ambitious. Prior to the mid-sixteenth century, when arsenalotti circulated more freely between private shipyards and the public Arsenal, Venetian shipbuilders were widely considered to be craftsmen of exceptional talent and innovation.[80] There indeed remained many capable masters in the city after Lepanto, but most of these tried to avoid Arsenal service if at all possible, working as much as they could for private shipbuilders. Those who continued to work in the Arsenal as ordinary masters soon became targets of sharp criticism: "There is no longer that good attitude that once there used to be; rather, if not all at least the greater part [of the current masters] are rascals, wretched men, and little more than villains."[81]

This decline in workforce quality was often seen as causing inefficiency and waste, topics of special concern to the Marine Secretaries of the Collegio. Several asserted after touring the shipyards that as far as the Arsenal labor budget was concerned, "the expenditure far exceeds the results"; having reported the Arsenal's 1683 labor budget to be 80,000 ducats, Vettor Grimani then went on to complain that "they [the masters] leave only 20,000 ducats of it to be enjoyed as the profit of their works."[82] Secretary Polo Contarini concluded his report of 1643 noting that "nearly two thirds of these people are useless, not doing more than picking up their pay."[83] The sentiment was often expressed that contemporary state shipbuilders had declined greatly in terms of morale and sense of purpose from the high levels maintained by their predecessors of the previous century. Most arsenalotti only came to work for completely selfish motives, they lamented: young apprentices showed up simply to get themselves noted in the pay books; having no intention to work or learn their craft, they just wandered around the shipyards all day. Those few mature masters who did report for work would come and go from the Arsenal whenever they pleased, often stealing goods as they left. The worst, however, were the older arsenalotti, complained the secretaries, for in their conduct they showed little gratitude for the state's charity that let them keep coming to the Arsenal even though they were useless as workers; instead of contributing the wisdom of their years, these veterans only distracted other masters and passed their idle days thinking up ways to carry off the shipyards' useful wood.[84]

Working in the state shipyards certainly did not promote self-discipline. Many masters did not even bother to bring their tools (*ferri*) with them to work; it often seems that they had sold them. Unable to do anything about the yards, such men either just idled about or borrowed the tools of others, leaving those workers idle in turn.[85] More than one secretary made the connection in their reports between masters' lack of training in their craft and the waste of time and materials; Polo Contarini warned of the potential cost to the Arsenal:

> The most aggravating thing is that those men [of the workforce] are a long time in the Arsenal and for ignorance or laziness have not learned their craft; from whom, beyond the little work that is received, [there] also results considerable damage in it, since that which they work on turns out to be poorly done, causing harm and destruction in their bad work, with the useless consumption of materials.[86]

Complaints about the arsenalotti are certainly in keeping with the overall gloomy air that pervades most of the Marine Secretaries' reports on the Arsenal, but they were not without foundation. Masters were often found doing jobs of their own while supposedly working at the shipyards: one shipwright was even dismissed for making shoe heels on Arsenal time with public wood; others were chided for continually bothering the Patroni for permission to leave the shipyards "under various pretexts of private business."[87] Several times during the seventeenth century, edicts were issued against masters who spent their working day meandering about the shipyards hawking food or drink to their fellow workers.[88] The Patroni also complained that many arsenalotti habitually arrived late to work, but managed to persuade their timekeeper to enter them in the paybook for the day anyway; once inside the shipyards, a number of masters just wandered about all day and if accosted, claimed to be on special business for one of the Arsenal foremen.[89] The Patroni tried, though without great success, to forbid arsenalotti from hiding themselves in the many wooden tool sheds, or *camarelle,* between the yards and sleeping away their shifts.[90] At the end of the day, the rush to leave was tremendous, despite the fact that many arsenalotti had apparently already managed to slip out early. So great was the hurry to leave that the "poor, old, bereft masters of the Arsenal" once petitioned for the privilege formally "conceded to the old ones of all the guilds in the Arsenal to be able to leave a half hour before the regular hour in order to avoid all the pushing and shoving and other torments employed by young masters [as they leave]."[91]

Poor workplace discipline in the Arsenal must certainly have been due in part to the excessive consumption of wine. Watered wine was distributed free to the masters, a daily ration that the government considered essential to keeping up production levels in the shipyards; occasionally the Senate ordered that masters engaged on special or difficult duties be give an extra daily allowance of undiluted *vino puro* to stimulate their efforts.[92] Few arsenalotti seemed to exercise much restraint in their drinking, however: in the late 1630s, the Inquisitors of the Arsenal complained that the 1,400 or so masters and laborers who regularly frequented the shipyards were managing to consume over 650,000 liters of wine each year.[93] Although the Arsenal cellarer, or *canaver,* was supposed to distribute the wine ration on a regular schedule, presumably by sending around the appropriate quantity to each work gang, in practice many masters went themselves to the cellars with large tubs (*mastelle*) and simply made off with all the wine they could carry.[94] For arsenalotti the pleasures of drinking must have been an attractive alternative to the regimentation of their workplace, and shipbuilders made the cellars a kind of social center, always finding some excuse to come and hang around the wine vats and socialize with one another or with visitors who came by to drink and to see the Arsenal's celebrated wine fountain.[95] Marine Secretary Grimani described the results:

> Especially in the summertime, a very considerable number of people of other occupations [besides shipbuilding] drink the public wine and do not sweat for the public benefit . . . these layabouts, uniting and fraternizing with the masters assigned to work, add the temptation of amusing companionship to [the masters'] natural tendency to avoid labor, dedicated [as they are] more to their pleasure than to their obligations, caring more for their companions than for public service.[96]

Yet the wine of the Arsenal's vats and fountain played an economic as well as a social role in the shipyards, functioning as wages in kind worth about 5 soldi per day. Although Marine Secretaries might advise the Collegio to do away with the cause of so much disruption, the masters successfully opposed the idea, even when it was suggested that they be given a cash substitute: not only were arsenalotti unwilling to surrender one of the pleasures of their work, but they probably also realized that wine, unlike the coin of the day, was safe from the inroads of inflation.[97]

The wine ration was only one of several inducements which the state offered shipbuilders to make the Arsenal attractive despite the low wages. Traditionally, younger or poorer masters could also expect help from the state in buying themselves new tools, with the Arsenal advancing them the cash for such equipment and then deducting the costs from their wages on a weekly basis; a regular allowance was also made available to master caulkers to help them with the cost of renewing their caulking chisels.[98] In another paternalistic gesture that may well have been unusual for the time, the Arsenal also gave the arsenalotti four paid holidays a year as a privilege of their enrollment: Christmas Eve, Fat Thursday, and Holy Thursday and Saturday.[99]

In addition, since the Arsenal did not demand very long working hours from its shipbuilders during the winter (as little as six hours per day, compared with nearly eleven in the summer months), it was possible to attract more shipbuilders from private yards during this off season by offering masters overtime. An extra quarter to a half was added onto a master's daily wage when he worked from sunrise to sunset ("dal levar fino tramontar" or "da prima marangona . . . fin'all hore 24").[100] The actual amount of overtime available depended on the needs of the state shipbuilding program: sometimes the Senate asked the Patroni to permit overtime only to the best workers and sometimes the offer was general.[101] During much of the War of Candia special large work gangs of shipwrights and caulkers were organized to finish and outfit large frigates and warships used for transport; masters in these gangs were paid an extra half pay for every long day's work, with the requirement to stay in the shipyards during lunch.[102]

Arsenalotti also enjoyed a privileged tax status among Venetian artisans, although it was not a position without certain burdens. Non-noble Venetians generally were expected to contribute to the support of the Republic's fleet of galleys, whether by personal service at the oars or (much more often) by buying themselves off through paying the regular galley tax *(tansa insensibile)*. The arsenalotti could not be exempted from such service, however, since they were the men who routinely served with the fleet as ships' carpenters, caulkers, and petty officers; therefore in compensation they were freed of the *tansa,* which would cost the typical Venetian artisan at least several ducats a year.[103] To encourage them in volunteering for sea duty, the state went further and promised arsenalotti who completed an entire voyage an extra 4 soldi raise onto their pay.[104] As already noted, the arsenalotti were also excused from paying the city's renters' tax, on the rationale that anyone who worked all his required hours in the Arsenal was necessarily so poor that he should be classified with those others of the city's poor, indigent, and *miserabili* who were exempted from the tax. So at least argued the Arsenal guilds, and the Senate evidently agreed, having also decided that it would be cheaper to treat the arsenalotti as impoverished wards of the state than to give in to their demands for a general raise in pay.[105]

Taken all together, the tax privileges and customary bonuses associated with Arsenal enrollment probably meant that most arsenalotti were paid at a rate considerably higher than the official 40 soldi daily wage ceiling of the shipyards: most mature shipbuilders were in fact probably earning the equivalent of around 55 soldi in cash and kind per workday. But although these various forms of income may have defined a special, paternalistic relationship between arsenalotti and the state, they certainly did not in themselves bring enrolled shipbuilders up to anything like income parity with the similar artisans in the city. Probably at best, in the years after 1630, income from the Arsenal brought a shipbuilder only 70–80 percent of what he could expect from working regularly in the private yards of the city.

If many shipbuilders faithfully continued coming to the Arsenal during the seventeenth century, it was certainly not simply on account of the real income it provided. It was quite clear to every master that enrollment in the Arsenal meant a promised security for the future: the state's guarantee of lifelong employment was one of the most alluring prospects that any craftsman could imagine, and probably a more than adequate reason to accept decades of inferior wages. Shipbuilders who persevered in state service could certainly expect to continue collecting their Arsenal pay well past the age when any private shipyard would still employ them at all: it was an option available to very few other artisans, either in Venice or elsewhere in preindustrial Europe. The importance of their privilege to them is underscored by the tenacity with which masters were determined to keep on taking advantage of it: many kept coming in years after they had evidently ceased being able to do any useful work at all and were indeed barely able to move themselves; often into their eighties or nineties, crippled or even completely blind, still they came to work, though they had to pay others to row or carry them back and forth to the shipyards every day.[106]

The New Factory Worker

The stability of the Arsenal workforce was thus achieved, but at the cost of a certain loss in quality, as the renowned independent shipbuilding community of the Republic was gradually converted into a hereditary workforce of state dependents. In good part this was due to the rigid wage structure of the yards, which was bound to attract masters who preferred lifelong, steady work with lower pay to a more erratic (and possibly more challenging) but higher-paying employment as private *squeraroli*. Yet wages alone were not the only factor shaping workforce quality. Despite a century of repeated warnings and complaints from Marine Secretaries about the degraded state of the *arsenalotti*, the question of improving the workforce or recapturing some of the talent that had distinguished earlier generations of Venetian shipbuilders was no longer so important an issue after 1600. The Senate itself was much more concerned about maintaining the stability of workforce numbers and developing strategies for keeping masters at work: in its eagerness to fulfill these goals, the Senate showed itself noticeably less interested in keeping up traditions of craft training and experience in the shipyards.

Typical in this regard was the state's attempt over the years 1605–25 to increase the number of caulkers *da fizer,* the craftsmen responsible for planking and building the superstructure on galleys. Since boys enrolled in this branch of the guild served longer apprenticeships for slightly lower pay than did those of the caulkers *da maggio* who did the actual caulking, enrollment in the caulkers *da fizer* was never popular.[107] The Senate attempted in 1609 to do away with the problem by combining both branches of the guild into one: masters of each guild were ordered to learn the skills of the other, a process that the Senate judged would take a mere four months to accomplish. Such a time limit, however, set off a *grandissima commotione* among the masters, who claimed that such a move would "slaughter" their guild; eventually they forced the Senate to back down, simply by all refusing to take the required master's examination of the other branch.[108] In time, the Senate tried again, after finding that the number of enrolled caulkers *da fizer* had dropped by nearly half in less than twenty years. In 1622, all master caulkers were once more ordered to take the other examination of their craft.[109] This time they were allowed only three months to do so, even though the Patroni themselves had warned that probably fewer than two thirds of them would be competent enough to pass. On this occasion, however, the Senate also offered the caulkers several positive inducements, such as wage increases and the abolishment of summer and winter pay differentials, and eventually most masters fell in line with the new system.

To assure its supply of caulkers of both specialities, the Senate had been willing to accept a notable decline in their training. Caulkers with almost no experience in the other branch of their craft were hastily certified as competent anyway. Significantly, the terms of apprenticeship for future caulkers were also to be altered. Previously, boys had trained for six years before taking the master's examination of the caulkers *da maggio* or eight years for that of caulkers *da fizer.* After the two branches were combined, however, a young man studied each branch for only four years, still completing his apprenticeship in a total of eight years. For older masters the result only seems to be caulkers who were not especially skilled in either branch of the craft. Veteran caulker *da fizer* Cristofolo di Zordan grumbled in 1624 that he had been told to complete a rush job planking a galley frame, "in spite of the fact that they had given me 'modern' caulkers, who had done the examinations in both crafts and who did not

know how to begin to drill a hole, [but] with my valor I did everything, which came out excellently."[110]

The policy of cutting back on apprenticeship training in order to
produce new masters quickly was also applied to the oarmakers and
shipwrights. When masters of these guilds were judged in short
supply, the Senate could order the Patroni to select out promising
young men from the apprentices and give them their master's examination, even though they might lack a year or more of their
normal eight years training period.[111] The practice was expanded in
the 1630s, not only to increase the Arsenal workforce quickly, but
also in the hopes that more masters would volunteer for a tour of
duty with the fleet and take their sons along as well: to encourage
apprentices to accompany their fathers or to enlist on their own, the
Senate voted that any of these young men (the so-called *maestran-
zette*) who made an entire tour of duty on a Venetian galley could
then cut as many as three years off their training period and take
their master's examination upon their return.[112]

This manipulation of apprenticeship training periods to further
the goals of the state had already been undertaken in the sixteenth
century: to replace the masters that had sailed off with the fleet to
Lepanto, the Senate had shortened the service of many apprentices.[113] Between 1620 and 1670, however, it appears to have become wholesale practice, so much so that young men themselves
started requesting shorter apprenticeships. Many pled poverty as
their reason; some said they were sons of arsenalotti who had died
while in state service and had left them as masterless orphans.
Young Iseppo di Battista, apprentice caulker, admitted that he had
worked at the shipyards for only 918 days (at least 1,200 were required, at 150 days per year), but claimed that he needed to become
a master in order to support his widowed mother, younger brothers,
and nubile sisters.[114] Other young men were well aware that normal
training schedules would be sacrificed if the need for masters
seemed to warrant it. Nicolò di Steffano, although an apprentice
pulleymaker for only three years, thought he still might be allowed
to take his master's examination early, "the more so since the Arsenal has considerable need for such masters, many of the best having
died in recent years."[115]

Regardless of whether young men served a full apprenticeship of
eight years or managed to get their required time reduced, it seems
that many did not receive especially diligent training. The imper-

sonal nature of construction in the shipyards, where most masters labored together in gangs, did not favor the traditional apprentice-master relationship. Many young men ended up completely abandoned by their masters, who often decided to sign on with outgoing ships or otherwise search for better wages outside the Arsenal. Such youths were routinely reported idling about the shipyards, a particular problem at the times when apprentices were being enrolled in large blocks, for they became even more difficult to control. Concerned that they should not wander aimlessly (*non vadino vagabondi*) about the shipyards, the Senate ordered such masterless boys to be rounded up daily by their guild foremen, who were to assign them on a temporary basis as laborers to one of the work bosses of their guild: a solution that kept apprentices occupied but hardly promoted their training.[116] One of the Senate's announced aims in establishing the baptismal register of the arsenalotti was in fact to put a stop to this situation and insure better training of apprentices: it was assumed that a master would pay more attention to his own son or grandson than to more distant relatives or complete strangers and would take more care that the boy learned the skills of his craft.[117] In this case, the Senate appears to have been too optimistic, however, since some years later the Marine Secretary Francesco Sanudo observed that among the boys always seen idling about the shipyards were to be found many sons of absent masters.[118]

Regular apprentices in the shipyards were known as *fanti minuti* and were normally enrolled with the Arsenal at the age of about ten or twelve.[119] When the Senate shaved a year or two off the training period of individual boys, the result was some masters of lower skill, but the overall impact on workforce quality was probably not critical as long as not too many were hurried through in this manner at the same time. But if the Senate decided to open the Arsenal rosters to special older apprentices, the so-called *fanti grossi,* the effect on the workforce was much more marked. At times when a number of masters was needed in very short order, a block of such youths of around eighteen to twenty-two years old would be enrolled and paid a wage of 12 soldi per workday, the pay which a regular apprentice was given only in his final years. Being so much older, *fanti grossi* were expected to complete their training and pass their master's examination within just two years instead of the normal six or eight. The practice was popular with arsenalotti, both because a master could enroll an overage son or more distant relation as his apprentice and even more because after he had gotten his *fante grosso* past his examination, masters were awarded for life the youth's 12-soldi daily wage in exchange for overseeing the accelerated training.[120]

The practice of enrolling older apprentices was not unique to the Arsenal: probably the majority of Venetian guilds took on overage youths, especially during the 1620s and 1630s when labor was in short supply.[121] Yet the Arsenal shipyards operated on an altogether different scale than the workshop of a single craftsman in the city, and serious problems could arise in training these apprentices. Being older, *fanti grossi* were generally more difficult for their masters to control than regular apprentices, and far from studying diligently to learn their crafts in the limited time available, many of them took advantage of the lack of close supervision typical of the Arsenal to waste their days wandering about the yards looking for amusements. Many never finished their training period at all, but left the shipyards for better-paying work; those who did complete their required two years were still often considered to be poor workers and ignorant of their craft.[122]

The impact of *fanti grossi* on the Arsenal was especially great in the seventeenth century because of the practice of enrolling them in large lots, thus allowing a considerable number of poorly trained young men to reach the level of master shipbuilder at the same time.[123] In 1616, the Patroni were ordered to enroll sixty *fanti grossi* "of twenty years and up" for the caulkers; in 1618, one hundred youths of sixteen to twenty were to be quickly trained as shipwrights, and a few more were added in 1621.[124] As this crop of youths matured and took their examinations in the 1620s, they probably came to represent about 15 percent of all enrolled masters. After the plague of 1630–31, their influence would be much more marked: in short order the Senate enrolled another 170 *fanti grossi* in an Arsenal workforce that amounted to fewer than 400 active masters.[125] By the 1640s (when the Arsenal would be called upon to sharply increase production), probably around half of all its shipbuilders had received reduced training, either as *fanti grossi* or as regular apprentices with shorter service.

The overall quality of the Arsenal workforce was also lowered by long-standing traditions which dictated that elderly Venetian sailors of merit should be accepted in the shipyards, usually as caulkers *da fizer* or as pulleymakers, since these were the lightest tasks available. When this custom originated is unclear, but it was continued in the seventeenth century largely in the hope of attract-

ing more young men into the declining seafaring trades.[126] In petitioning for a place, most sailors made no pretensions about having
any real training as shipbuilders; they simply wanted the working
pension which the Arsenal could offer them. Some, as a result, were
rather vague as to what they would actually do once they had arrived at work: one, named Vicenzo di Bernardin da Pirano asked for
"a worker's place in your Arsenal, as caulker, shipwright or . . . pulleymaker, as will please Your Serenity."[127] Sailors could be quite
frank that their motives for seeking enrollment among the arsenalotti did not include hard work. Iseppo Chiocca asked for a place as
pulleymaker so that "after having toiled at sea, I could find some
rest for myself in the Arsenal." Santo di Zulian requested admission
saying, "now already made old, I long to settle down in my own nest
at the Arsenal."[128] More than one Marine Secretary complained that
the practice only cluttered up the shipyards with inept old men:

> For a favor there are often admitted into the Arsenal useless or unfit
> men, rather noticeably harmful, as is often the case with much of the
> enrolled workforce. This especially happens with sailors, who are
> accustomed to be introduced into [Arsenal] service by the patronage
> of others, not by their own merit. So harm comes to the merchant
> marine, so necessary to this *Serenissimo* Domain, and at the same time
> to the Arsenal itself, where they draw their pay, and being unfit, they
> do no work.[129]

In most Venetian crafts, a minimum level of competence among
masters would have been insured by the traditional master's examination given to candidates for admission to the guild. Logically it
would therefore seem that even poorly trained *fanti grossi* and sailors must have possessed at least enough skills to pass the examination *(prova)* for the shipbuilding guild which they desired to join,
since this was likewise required of all who would work in the Arsenal. This might well not have been the case, however, given the
extent to which the state intruded into the examination process. It
had been decided as early as the fifteenth century that the Arsenal
should administer its own examination of candidate shipbuilders, in
addition to the guild examination itself, to insure that masters
whom the *gastaldi* of the shipbuilding guilds had passed were in fact
fully qualified.[130] The eventual rise of the Arsenal to dominance in
the Venetian shipbuilding industry would have meant that the state
examination became in time the only test that really mattered: it is
entirely possible that before the 1600s the two separate examina-

tions had been absorbed into one, and that all shipbuilders in the city (with the exception of the private *squeraroli*) would expect to be judged by both guild and state.

Under such conditions, the Arsenal master's examination was hardly a *prova* like any other, with candidate shipbuilders demonstrating their skills in the traditional guild manner: exhibiting a masterwork or carrying out an assigned task before the assembled *banca,* or governing board, of their guild. Since one of the Patroni and the candidate's foreman also sat in on the examination to make sure that the interests of the Arsenal were represented, the nature of the Arsenal *prova* could in fact be quite different than those of other craftsmen in the city.[131] Having a larger vision than ordinary guild officers of the Republic's particular needs and policies, these two powerful state officials also probably had the decisive voice in judging a candidate: if the Arsenal shipbuilding program demanded a large influx of new masters or if maritime policy required the admission of worthy but unskilled sailors to the shipyards, the Patron and foreman could see that the criteria for mastership were lowered and standards sufficiently relaxed to quickly admit new candidates. In addition, many sailors wishing to become masters had taken the precaution of first petitioning the Collegio for admission; with that board's approval already behind them, their chances of impressing their guild *banca* must certainly have improved considerably.[132]

There survives little evidence of what Arsenal master's examinations were actually like, but it is possible to infer at least something of their reputation from the petitions of men who wished to take them.[133] Certainly they could be daunting for those who were completely unprepared: on occasion the Senate noted that apprentices were avoiding their master's examination for fear of failing them.[134] Nevertheless, it would not seem that the examinations were especially difficult either. Sailors were willing to confront the shipwright's examination with just the knowledge about ship's carpentry which they had picked up during their voyages. Some unlucky petitioners had received a bit of training as shipwrights when enslaved by the Turks, but many others simply claimed to have acquired shipbuilding skills through their own efforts.[135] Many who petitioned were turned down, but their suppliche in any event help reinforce an impression of the generally low opinion that such men held both of the rigors of the Arsenal examinations and of the skills required of workers in the shipyards. Several of the Arsenal office clerks and pages, along with a multitude of elderly supervisors and other nonmanual employees, wrote that they had mastered the arts of ship-building simply by keeping company with arsenalotti.[136] Only one of these, Steffano di Camillo, claimed to have actually done any real shipbuilding ("the profession which has always delighted me"); this he did by imitating his arsenalotti relatives, from whom he felt, "I was able to learn what there is to the profession of shipwright."[137]

It is tempting to conclude (as several scholars have) that the lowering of skills represented by its slackening of training and ad-missions standards was both a factor in and evidence of the general decline of the Arsenal as a manufacturing center.[138] Such a conclu-sion should be made warily, however, for despite all the complaints of the Patroni and Marine Secretaries, it is not at all clear that the Senate and the Collegio saw a talented and innovative workforce in the shipyards as necessary, or even desirable. In part this can be blamed on the creeping conservatism that generally stifled Venetian leadership during the sixteenth century. The aristocracy of the Re-public became steadily less involved and thus more timid in naval matters, rarely providing any encouragement or financial support for craftsmen promoting alterations in ship designs; the Venetian light galley was in any event widely considered already perfect. It would seem that such craftsmen still flourished in Venice, but their offers of new technical or stylistic approaches to shipbuilding gen-erally went unheeded; even when improved designs were finally ap-proved, decades could pass before a project might be actually real-ized.[139] By the later seventeenth century the Republic would have hardly been in a position to buy the services of the best local ship-builders. Pushed deep into debt by inflation and the Candia War, the state had little money to spare, either to improve the training of shipbuilders or to raise wages high enough to prevent the loss of talented workers to the private market.[140]

Nevertheless, genius in shipbuilding or indeed in any sort of manufacturing could be said to lie as much in the organization of production as in the art of design, and while the Arsenal by 1650 clearly no longer had the kind of talented designers at its disposal that had been so evident 150 years earlier, in the days of Marin Sanudo, these may not have seemed so necessary if all that mattered was to maintain the legendary Venetian efficiency. The improved integration of production at the Arsenal indeed demanded a differ-ent sort of worker than the traditional independent craftsman. Ap-prentice shipbuilders up through the sixteenth century had been taught a wide range of skills appropriate to the many tasks they might expect to perform in the private shipyards of the city. Their relatively long training periods would have been necessary just to give them the experience in every type of shipping which these yards commonly produced, from gondolas and small work boats (*peote*) to large merchant ships and galleys, many ordered to unusual specifications or requirements.[141] Shipbuilding in the state Arsenal was altogether a different matter: the independent shipwrights, caulkers, and oarmakers who had received their training in the private *squeri* of Venice were likely to find themselves overqualified for much of the work that would be expected of them once they enrolled in the Arsenal. Already by the 1550s and 1560s the state had begun to limit its ship production to very large numbers of just a few types of galleys, galleasses, and armed cutters (*barche armate*), built to only a small variety of designs.[142]

If anything, this process of standardization was intensified in the seventeenth century, possibly as part of an effort to maintain consistent output from a reduced workforce. Arsenal administrators pushed rationalized ship production further by instituting a new stratum of worker managers: the gang bosses who were charged with commanding squads of ordinary masters in all matters of construction. Much of what little planning there was and all of the technical decisions would be in the hands of such bosses, leaving the mass of ordinary masters to carry out only the routine and repetitive tasks in the yards. Several Marine Secretaries complained that much of the work which masters were doing in the Arsenal was in fact so simple that it rightly belonged to unskilled laborers (*facchini*), who were to be paid only half as much.[143] With most arsenalotti serving on such well-directed work gangs, skilled masters with six or eight years' apprenticeship in their crafts were simply no longer necessary.

Thus, it is not surprising that the Collegio and Senate were willing to accept a general lowering of standards in the Arsenal, the more so since such a quality of worker would almost inevitably have been the result of the state's tight-fisted paternalism anyway. There are indeed signs that from the government's point of view, docility and willingness to work were characteristics more likely to be rewarded among its shipbuilders than were skill and a high degree of training. In supporting a master's petition to the Collegio, the Patroni often singled out the traits of obedience and dependability for praise; Arsenal managers and bosses backed them up with *fedi* attesting to the worker's proven willingness to follow their orders.[144]

By the end of the seventeenth century, the emphasis in the shipyards was on a master's steady work habits and his capacity to function as part of a team, without disturbing others by his grumbling or disobedience; the most prized worker would be one who through obedience, loyalty, and regularity was able to adapt himself well to the demands and rhythms of the Arsenal's factory-style production.[145] A check list of questions used by members of the Colleggietto to quiz the admiral and foremen of the Arsenal about individual masters in the late 1600s indicates the balance of qualities and attitudes which the Venetian state sought in its shipbuilding workforce by that time. The managers were asked to respond about the workers:

1. if they are capable in their craft
2. if they obey their bosses
3. if they work willingly or only under duress
4. if they swear
5. if they are honest and honorable
6. if they are diligent in the labors of the Arsenal
7. if they are quiet or grumblers
8. if they instruct the apprentices under them well
9. if they make bad use of the wood that they employ
10. if they work the required hours or if they go wandering about the Arsenal.[146]

A workforce with modest skill levels was essentially one that insured its own stability. Masters who were poorly trained would be less able to find employment in the outside shipyards; with few options beyond their steady if rather menial work in the state shipyards, they would therefore be less willing to risk being fired through misconduct than had been the independent shipbuilders of the previous century. This indeed appears to have been the result: most master shipbuilders in Venice managed over the course of the seventeenth century to leave behind their independent craft traditions and adjust themselves to the factory organization of the Arsenal, where the gang boss system increasingly was in force and where obedience was the characteristic most prized in workers. The transition was not accomplished without difficulties, for like any workers coerced into converting from independent artisans into factory hands, Venetian shipbuilders experienced severe dislocations in the process of becoming arsenalotti. In the late sixteenth and early seventeenth centuries, wage riots and mass desertions from the Arsenal were the result. Eventually, the shipbuilders accepted their new status, largely because of the state's considerable skill in tying them to the shipyards. The efforts of the state to forge independent shipbuilders into government arsenalotti were not simply coercive, however, and through the establishment of such customs as direct petitioning to the Collegio and the Arsenal baptismal register masters were given a positive sense of their special status in exchange for their loss of independence and skills. Indeed, arsenalotti in time won an entire range of honors and duties in both the Arsenal and in the city—particularly Venetian roles which set them apart as a community and which served to counterbalance the weight of the disciplined manufacturing routine under which they labored by the late 1600s.

The Arsenal
Worker Managers

One of the most distinctive features of the Venetian Arsenal was the way in which it was administered. Among the earliest and largest examples of state capitalist industries in modern Europe, the Arsenal presented the Venetian government with particular management problems which had yet to be encountered by other western nations. Although most of these difficulties would eventually have to be faced by administrators elsewhere—first by state bureaucrats and then by private capitalists—the Venetian way of managing a centralized, large-scale, state manufacturing complex is of particular interest. The Republic's approach to running its shipyards has indeed been one of its most studied aspects to date, perhaps in part because the Venetian state registers are so rich in useful material on Arsenal management: scholars interested in the institution's administration have found themselves well supplied with many detailed lists of its offices, their hierarchies and functions.[1] The subject of Arsenal management is not merely one for students of economics and factory production, however, since the daily administration of the shipyards was in fact the business of the arsenalotti themselves and thus a key factor in shaping their social world. On the one hand, the involvement of the arsenalotti in running the Ar-

senal has a clear impact on what kind of workplace the state shipyards would be and how production would be carried out there; on
the other hand, their self-governance of the yards gave hierarchical
form and continuity to the shipbuilders' own worker community
outside the Arsenal walls.

Growth of the Hierarchy

In a list of the Arsenal managers that he compiled at the end of
the seventeenth century, the Marine Secretary Francesco Cornero
enumerated offices of fully 112 foremen, administrators, and supervisors in the state shipyards. Of these, 27 were nonmanual posts that
belonged to members of the *cittadini* class of Venetians (and were
generally concerned with the bookkeeping or supply aspects of
shipbuilding), while the remaining 85 offices were held, or at least
exercised, by Arsenal shipbuilders. Since at the time about one thousand masters were coming regularly to work in the shipyards, this
management cadre represented at least 8 percent of the overall
workforce in the Arsenal; if a number of decidedly minor but still
distinct supervisors whom Cornero left out of his list were included,
the proportion would have been still higher.[2]

In earlier centuries, the Arsenal had been directed by a far
smaller group of managers. During its first years after being founded
in 1104, when still functioning largely as a storehouse for naval supplies, most of the institution's day-to-day direction was in fact in the
hands of noblemen rather than artisans: indications are that at least
as early as the thirteenth century the oversight of operations in the
Arsenal was assigned to a board of patrician *Patroni all'Arsenale*. The
three Patroni, serving in overlapping, thirty-two-month terms, divided among themselves the responsibility for locating, buying, and
guarding the various naval stores which the Arsenal accumulated.
Since nearly all Venetian shipping, whether merchant vessels or war
galleys, was built in private shipyards around the Lagoon, the problems of technical direction could be left up to local builders to work
out on their own. Only a few artisans were needed at the state Arsenal, mostly to equip and disarm warships; on the occasions when
the Patroni or the state needed expert technical advice, they could
hire one or two of the better local shipbuilders on a temporary
basis.[3]

This at least is the most plausible explanation of how the hierarchy of Arsenal worker managers had its gradual beginning. The
first managers who appear in documented references were the two

protomaestri, or foremen, of the shipwrights and caulkers, and the *Ammiraglio,* the Arsenal Admiral who served as general superintendent of the state shipyards. Very likely, in its early years these men worked only part-time in the Arsenal and still found the time to devote to their private businesses as well. But the state's need of such directors became more urgent and permanent with the expansion of the Arsenal to include a shipbuilding division in the 1320s; to these initial three managers were soon added the services of two others, one foreman in charge of masts and spars and another to direct the workers in the Arsenal's oarmaking shop.[4]

These few officers formed the original managerial core of the Arsenal administration. To them were also added by the late fifteenth century between two and four appraisers, or *stimadori,* who were responsible for judging the quality of all products purchased by the shipyards, as well as inspecting finished galleys. All together, the foremen, Admiral, and appraisers were often referred to as the *salariatii,* for they were distinguished among other Arsenal managers and workers by their receiving a monthly salary rather than a daily wage.[5] From the state's point of view, this was a sign that such top managers were expected to devote their entire efforts to running the Arsenal, rather than trying to combine state employment with private activities, as many masters did at the time. To make doubly sure that they undertook their obligations seriously, the government eventually would expressly forbid these men from holding any employment elsewhere.[6] Violators could face a stiff fine: in 1652 the foreman of the caulkers, Giacomo di Grassi, was charged 54 ducats (his base pay for six months) after he was reported absent from Venice without express license.[7]

To the few salaried worker managers in the Arsenal were in time added an entire hierarchy of wage-earning officers. The process of expanding the shipyards' management cadre was already under way by the mid-fifteenth century, but to a large extent this was probably no more than a reflection of corresponding growth in the workforce and the shipyards themselves. A second major phase of building and expansion began in the shipyards around 1450, and the number of masters frequenting the Arsenal had jumped from the dozen or so that had been typical a century earlier to well over a thousand.[8] The expansion of the Arsenal's management hierarchy was also promoted by two additional trends during the period. As the affairs of the shipyards became steadily more complex, the Patroni began to withdraw from the daily supervision of shipbuilding and concerned themselves much more with the business of planning, procurement, and finance. Even though by the late 1400s the Senate had created an auxiliary board of three noble *Provveditori all'Arsenale* to represent the Patroni before the Collegio and to thus free them from the need to be away from the shipyards, the business of these patricians was increasingly seen as financial and political rather than technical; by the fifteenth century the Patroni appear to have become quite accustomed to depending on the worker managers for the day-to-day direction of the Arsenal.

At the same time, there was a strong tendency toward specialization by managers themselves, and offices began to multiply in number while taking on more precisely defined responsibilities.[9] This trend was clear by around 1500, and can be linked not only to the increasing output of the shipyards but also to a growing desire on the part of the state to standardize the production of the many parts and fittings that went into making up a galley. Previously, the technical business of running the yards had been the essential responsibility of the foremen of the shipwrights and caulkers, who were in overall charge of matters pertaining to shipbuilding proper, and of the Admiral, who was responsible for problems of outfitting, launching, stores, and repairs.[10] With the increased and rationalized production of the 1500s, however, there were too many processes under way for just three men to supervise each activity personally, and the responsibility for the fabrication and preservation of many of the galleys' component parts was in time delegated to a host of underlings. Thus, the Admiral administered the various Arsenal storehouses through a number of supervisors, or *sovrastanti*, who guarded the materials in their care and doled them out to authorized workers. By the mid-sixteenth century he also had under him two officers delegated to command the laborers *(facchini)* in the shipyards, as well as subforemen for the blacksmiths *(favri)* and the masons *(mureri)*, and the headmistress of the women who sewed sails *(vellere)*. The foreman shipwright had in his department three subforemen: one *alle banche*, who supervised the construction of benches and deck furnishings, another *ai tagieri*, who oversaw pulley making, and one who directed the twenty or more Arsenal sawyers, the *proto alle sieghe*. To a certain extent, he also gave orders to the appraisers and to the foremen of the mast and oarmakers. Under the foreman caulker were the subforemen *da maggio* (for caulking) and *da fizer* (for planking) as well as four supervisors in charge of oakum, pitch, and large and small hardware (see Appendix 2).[11]

These positions of supervisors and subforemen appear to have been created by the state itself, in recognition of the increasing management needs of the shipyards. Very likely, however, top managers also furthered the growth of the Arsenal management hierarchy themselves, particularly by appointing their own personal assistants, known as *sottoproti* or *aiutanti*. Some foremen were naming assistants as early as 1500, although apparently without government approval. Although the Senate attempted to keep the practice from becoming an established custom for about another century, eventually each foreman needed to have his own assistant, not only to help carry out the growing number of duties assigned to him but also to lend his office an appropriate stature.[12]

Assistants were necessary to fill in when a foreman was called away from the shipyards to personally oversee such work as tree cutting or ship repairs abroad. Since major foremen held their positions for life, many became in time too old and feeble to actually carry out their offices; one of the benefits of a foreman's position was to have an assistant appointed at such a time to take over his duties (but not his salary, which he continued to enjoy).[13] Significantly, his position did not guarantee an assistant the right to take over when his superior died: of seventeen Admirals and principal foremen in the shipyards during the seventeenth century, only four had previously been helpers. Assistants served as a kind of executive officer for their superior, seeing that his orders were implemented and providing him with a greater range of control over the masters and lesser managers who were often scattered all about the Arsenal.[14] As the responsibilities of foremen expanded in the seventeenth century, so did the relative importance of their assistants. In the early seventeenth century the foreman of the oarmakers had to beg the Patroni to order the masters in the oarmakers' shed to obey his helper, but by the 1660s the authority of such officers was far more secure: the foreman shipwright (and perhaps other foremen as well) had two assistants with specialized functions, and some assistants even had a personal helper, or *aiutante,* of their own.[15]

Many other Arsenal managers served in a disciplinary rather than a technical capacity. In the Middle Ages, the task of keeping an eye on the Arsenal workers had fallen mainly to one of the Patroni, known as the *Patron delle maestranze,* and to the foremen of each guild. As the shipyards grew, however, and the foremen were increasingly engaged elsewhere, other offices were created to control and discipline the masters. A few positions, such as the four door-keepers *(portoneri)* who watched over those entering and leaving the shipyards, were held by men from outside the workforce; most of the others, at least when first created, were instead especially destined for arsenalotti themselves. The earliest such post to develop appears to have been that of the timekeepers *(appontadori)*: first mentioned in 1501, by 1560 there were three in the shipyards.[16] Each responsible for one of the major guilds, the three took up their post every morning at the shipyard gates and made note of which masters and apprentices of his particular guild came to work. Workers who failed to show up, like those who arrived late or left early, were crossed off the list and received no pay that day.

Although the timekeepers were effective enough in checking which masters had actually come to work in the shipyards, they alone could not insure that work discipline would be maintained. Since their principal duties kept them all day at the Arsenal gates, they were unable to be of much use in keeping an eye on the masters once they were inside the shipyard walls. After the great influx of newly enrolled workers began in the 1530s and 1540s, the problem became more acute: with shipbuilders scattered in yards all over the Arsenal, guild foremen and the *Patron delle maestranze* could no longer hope to keep so many masters and apprentices busy at work if they were to still fulfill their other duties. Furthermore, most of these shipbuilders had originally been attracted from their employment in private yards precisely because enrollment with the Arsenal would guarantee them lifetime employment. Once inscribed on the Arsenal rosters, many masters apparently considered themsleves safe from any threat of dismissal, with little incentive to do any work beyond showing up every morning and getting their name checked off by their timekeeper; they could then pass the day within the shipyard walls doing whatever they pleased. To see that arsenalotti kept at their duties assiduously, a new disciplinary office was created in 1566, evidently on the suggestion of a master himself, who offered to take on the task of ferreting out shirkers and loafers and striking them off the daily rosters of their timekeepers. In time this position of workforce overseer became a fixed one, known as the *revisor delle maestranze*. The art of the job, according to one who later held it, evidently lay in being able to spring out unexpectedly *(sopragiungendo immprovisamente)* on unwary malingerers, reporting them before they could hurry back to their work.[17]

A single officer could hardly hope to cope with two or three thousand masters and apprentices, however, and so by 1600 the Senate had added three more overseers, known as the *despontadori delle maestranze*. Chosen for life terms, each of these overseers was responsible for the masters of one of the major guilds, with the overseer of the oarmakers also keeping an eye on all the miscellaneous workers who were not part of the ordinary workforce.[18] Forming a link between masters laboring in various yards and the officers at the main gate, the guild overseers each day received from their corresponding timekeeper the morning's list of arsenalotti who had come to work; going to each worksite in turn, they then made sure that the masters and apprentices who had been marked as present were in fact on the job. The job was arduous, as one guild overseer complained in 1628, for it was necessary each workday to hunt up every master on the list, in whatever corners of the shipyards they might be working.[19] Workers who were caught red-handed while loafing offered all sorts of excuses, and if these failed to impress their overseer, they might well attack him: one overseer noted in a petition that an earlier officer had been murdered, another had been "wounded to death" (that is, injured very seriously), and his immediate predecessor had resigned out of fear.[20]

As the experience of the guild overseers indicates, masters sometimes disobeyed orders and committed acts of violence; on occasion they stole Arsenal goods. Outsiders also might illegally trespass within the shipyards to steal, hide out, or sell food and drink to workers.[21] To deal with such criminality, the Patroni decided to elect a Captain (*capitanio*) of the Arsenal from among the most trusted arsenalotti. Serving as a combination police chief and jailor for a three-year term, this officer was charged with watching out for thefts and other forbidden acts and with carrying out "all the executions and arrests occasionally necessary . . . lest for such an omission many criminals might go unpunished and their crimes be forgotten as in past times."[22]

The Arsenal's sharp expansion in output and workforce after the 1530s not only stimulated the creation of new posts for technical and disciplinary supervisors but also provoked a general overhaul in the directing of production methods themselves. Until the late sixteenth century, shipbuilding in the state yards was carried out with much the same sort of informal organization that had characterized it in the Middle Ages. The foreman shipwright (or his assistant) directed the work on each galley under construction, delegating temporary bosses to carry out his instructions in coordinating the workers on hand. When many ships were under construction at once, however, the attentions of the foreman shipwright could be stretched very thin: masters wandered off to work in other yards as they pleased, and materials were improperly and unevenly distributed to the worksites.[23] In the early 1500s, the foreman shipwright Leonardo Bressan attempted to direct personally the construction of eight light galleys and one galleon at the same time; while some were completed quickly, other ships languished in their yards for years.[24]

As a result, the practice was adopted by the mid-sixteenth century of using a kind of intermediate manager in the Arsenal, to improve the organization of production by providing closer technical and disciplinary supervision of masters at the worksite. Called *capi d'opera,* or gang bosses, these managers evolved over the course of the century from those shipbuilders known as *fabricanti di navi* who had for years built much of the state shipping on contract, working in either their own private yards or in the Arsenal itself. Since at least the early fifteenth century it had been customary to arrange for some ships or hulls to be constructed with payment by the job instead of by the day, with contracts awarded by the Patroni and Senate to masters experienced in constructing galleys to their own design *(al proprio sesto)* and offering the lowest bid.[25] When construction was to take place in the Arsenal, these independent contractors would be assigned a dock of their own and usually allotted the required lumber and hardware as well; they were expected to hire and pay their own team of masters to assist them, although the Arsenal might supply a gang of porters when it came time for launching.[26] Their power over their workers was like that of any private shipyard owner, and since they generally paid masters better than the Arsenal did, they could freely fire inefficient workers, and expect to quickly hire others. *Fabricanti* who had sufficiently demonstrated their abilities could win successive contracts for several years at a time; some were rewarded by the Senate with a special wage bonus to keep them coming to the Arsenal to work as regular masters even when the state had no contract work to offer them.[27]

By the mid-1500s, some of these contractors appear to have had enough experience directing other masters that they began to emerge as permanent managers in the Arsenal: in 1560, around twenty such bosses were counted among the carpenters and another three among the caulkers. Such a system allowed the delegation of technical authority from the foremen of the carpenters and caulkers to a management level closer to actual production. As long as these bosses continued in their informal status in the shipyards, however, their importance in production was largely limited to their personal ability to bid for and carry out building contracts. Still essentially temporary managers, bosses came to work very much when they pleased, often abandoning the Arsenal for years at a time when they found better paying work elsewhere. Regular masters tended to flock to join gangs directed by the best known or most generous contractors, leaving less fortunate bosses to work almost alone in their yards, like "a captain that thinks himself to have a company with one soldier only."[28]

Beginning around 1569, the state set out to strengthen the gang bosses and make the work gang system more effective, choosing the best leaders from existing bosses and ordinary masters and putting all ship construction under their personal direction, with all other workers made subordinate to them.[29] Boss shipwrights were reduced from twenty or so to fourteen (later briefly to ten), while somewhat later gang bosses of the caulkers were increased from three to eight; those who were selected could expect a 50 percent increase in their daily wage as a bonus (called the *caposoldo*; only 25 percent for the caulkers). In exchange, it was expected that bosses would devote their full time to the state shipyards and, eventually, also see to some of the paperwork involved in construction.[30] To avoid an unequal distribution of shipbuilders between the various yards, masters would henceforth be divided up into squads each morning and apportioned by their timekeepers among the active gang bosses. The authority of the bosses themselves was strengthened by granting them the power to discipline with wage reductions or other punishments those masters who refused to keep working or stay at their yard. The result appears to have been a much more efficient use of both technical skills and available labor in the shipyards. Gang bosses led their gangs more or less independently and at their own speeds under the general, overall direction of their foremen; some evidently also took on their own personal assistants, or *vicecapi,* thus creating yet another management level in the shipyards.[31] Skilled themselves in the details of ship construction, these bosses were also close enough to the workers they directed to provide an essential link between the technical and disciplinary branches of the Arsenal management.

Wages and Honors

Whereas rank-and-file masters had some limited freedom to work outside the Arsenal when the state's production requirements were normal, shipyard managers always needed to be available. It was therefore necessary for the state to tie these managers to public service with stronger inducements than were generally necessary for ordinary arsenalotti, especially since the men chosen to run the Arsenal were often the very same ones whose talents and connections would also have assured them the most success as private shipbuilders.[32] As the system of production began to rely more heavily on the initiative of managers than on the individual creativity of masters, the kinds and amount of rewards offered to secure the service of foremen and bosses were naturally increased apace. As a result, Arsenal managers not only became more powerful as a group, but they also grew more distinct from the rest of the workforce, both in terms of their pay and in the status they enjoyed.

In the century after Lepanto, Arsenal managers appear to have generally done well for themselves economically, despite the fact that the pay of management positions was officially no more flexible than that of regular arsenalotti. Work bosses, it is true, could expect their raise in real wages upon assuming office, but subforemen and supervisors were elected with no more than their ordinary master's pay. Worst off of all were the top managers, the *salariati* whose official base pay remained unchanged over the entire two centuries after 1500: the salaries of foremen lagged so far behind the times that by the 1600s some established bosses found that upon election as foreman they were actually rewarded with a cut in pay.[33] This rigidity of managers' pay in the Arsenal was more apparent than real, however, for it was increasingly the accepted custom for officers to supplement their official income with personal *gratie,* or wage bonuses, from the Senate. In the seventeenth century the great majority of managers enjoyed such *gratie,* given either for services rendered or sometimes for sheer longevity, and often piled one on top of another until they could effectively more than double their position's official pay.

Arsenal officers further prospered, however, because they managed over the course of time to establish for themselves various money-making prerogatives in the shipyards: income they could expect on a regular basis in the course of their work or extra benefits that they enjoyed more irregularly (that were thus known as *in-*

certi). The most straightforward of such extras were the piecework contracts for galley building, largely the monopoly of experienced gang bosses. Just in the year 1639, ten such contracts for building or refitting were awarded to masters, and eight went to gang bosses: a boss could be paid between 425 and 650 ducats for just two months work; his principal expense was in hiring assistants, since the Arsenal generally supplied all the materials.[34] A few gang bosses also enjoyed the paid work of inspecting and evaluating the ships that served the Arsenal; three of them once complained that they could count on *incerti* "of only around 4 to 5 ducats a year," a sum nevertheless equal to two weeks' pay for an ordinary master.[35] Gang bosses and supervisors were also usually the first arsenalotti to be granted a *fante grosso* when the Senate decided to expand the Arsenal work force with the special apprentices.[36] When the young men passed their master's examination, the managers would receive a 12-soldi daily raise; the Admiral and four principal foremen were permanently assigned two apiece, bringing them an extra 36 lire (nearly 6 ducats) per month.

Like the gang bosses, almost all other officers could expect to enjoy the profits of concessions specific to their positions. Many supervisors and all of the major foremen could expect a steady income from writing the *fedi,* or testimonials, that ordinary masters constantly needed to back up their petitions and requests, a practice that the Patroni and the state apparently took for granted. The four appraisers of the shipyards also expected "to receive some acknowledgment [that is, bribe] from those who bring lumber to the Arsenal," a custom that evidently made the Patroni more nervous, since they once complained about how "the import of this [bribe] cannot be found out"; on the other hand, they seemed perfectly content that the officer in charge of opening and closing the two bridges adjacent to the Arsenal should be paid 8 soldi by every passing ship which required his services.[37] This supervisor's colleague who saw to the bridge by the Tana and raised the Arsenal flags (linen on workdays, silk on holidays) on the two *stendardi* in the Campo dell'Arsenale was granted another sort of extra with his office: the privilege of running a bread, dried fish, and cheese concession in the Campo "for the convenience of the workforce."[38]

Perhaps the most significant extra which was allotted to worker managers, however, was that of free housing. As part of state policy since the earliest days of the Arsenal, the government had aimed at forming a management nucleus near the shipyards "in order [for managers] to always be at all hours ready to contribute to the public service as is incumbent to . . . [their] positions."[39] Three houses had been constructed as early as the fifteenth century for the use of the Patroni, to insure their constant presence on the scene; by 1640 there were forty such houses, twenty-two of them granted to worker managers along with their offices.[40] The houses were large, many of them several stories tall with balconies, large rooms, kitchens, walled gardens, and sometimes a rooftop sundeck (*altena*). The state considered the houses worth the equivalent of about 50 ducats per year on the city's rental market, and indeed they were often the subject of petitions from both minor managers and ordinary arsenalotti who hoped to receive one in recognition for special services.[41]

With so many sources of earnings, some open but irregular and others largely clandestine, it becomes quite difficult to even guess at the real income of most worker managers in the shipyards. Very likely the principal foremen of the Arsenal routinely increased their incomes by selling their personal influence and patronage on behalf of others, just as they no doubt made a comfortable amount every year through selling the excess of their enormous allotments of wine and old sailcloth (*fustagne vecchie*) that were their annual due according to ancient custom in the shipyards.[42] Nevertheless, it is possible to at least assess the importance of a top manager's multiple sources of (licit) income relative to one another, thanks to a surviving account of the earnings of an Arsenal Admiral of the early decades of the eighteenth century. In the 1720s, the Admiral Pasqual Bisson's official annual salary was still fixed at the 150 ducats where it had been set over two hundred years earlier, but this represented a mere 22 percent of his actual yearly income of 636 ducats. Another 20 percent derived from personal *gratie* previously awarded him by the Senate, while another nearly 30 percent came from the regular benefits of his office.[43] The remaining nearly 30 percent of the Admiral's total income, however, came from commissions and *provvigioni:* that is, *incerti.*

His income of over 600 ducats yearly certainly would have placed this Admiral securely in the ranks of the comfortable classes of Venice, along with lawyers, notaries, and other professionals.[44] Likewise, even though all the various *incerti* and special benefits that managers enjoyed may remain unknown, it is clear that from just their salaries, wages, and personal *gratie* alone, many officers were quite well rewarded for their work. Several foremen earned over 240 ducats per year, and some made as much as 300; the wages and *gratie* alone of an experienced gang boss might easily bring him anywhere from 150 to 200 ducats annually.[45] It would also appear that the earnings of many managers grew more quickly than those of ordinary arsenalotti: this is especially true of the salaried foremen, appraisers, and the Admiral, whose average income from stipends, wages, bonuses, and other extras in the mid-1600s more than doubled from a century before (see table 2.1).

Their more quickly increasing pay meant that in the century after 1560 managers were to be separated from ordinary workers by a widening economic gap. In the mid-sixteenth century, the arsenalotti pay ceiling had represented 56 percent of the average salary of foremen and 69 percent of the typical wages of gang bosses; one hundred years later this had shrunken to 38 percent and 61 percent, respectively. In the sixteenth century, the Arsenal's rewards of wealth or honors had been showered on only a few special shipwrights—technicians whose design skills had earned them particular riches compared to most masters; one hundred years later, nearly the entire management cadre would belong to this select group.[46]

The growing distance between managers and rank-and-file workers in the state shipyards can be measured in more terms than simple income. Baroque Venetian society found enormous impor-

Table 2.1. Comparative Wage and Salary Increases in the Arsenal

	Average Wage/Salary plus Extras		
Position	*1560*	*1650*	*% Increase*
Salaried managers	97 du/year	229 du/year	136
Gang bosses	42 s/day	80 s/day	90
Subforemen and supervisors	35 s/day	60 s/day	71
Ordinary masters	29 s/day	44 s/day	52

Note: Management salaries and wages of 1560 from Lane, *Venetian Ships and Shipbuilders,* 161–63, 244; mid-seventeenth century averages from suppliche, *fedi,* and the Senate edicts awarding the petitions. Figures for ordinary masters derive from the Arsenal pay maximum plus a 4 soldi average as typical for the extra sea pay or other *gratie* enjoyed by most workers, but not including tax benefits, wine ration, or other benefits given to wage-earning managers as well. Wages in ducats per year or soldi per day.

tance in position, family, and status, and the prerogatives and precedence granted to Arsenal managers by their offices were at least as valuable in personal terms as any wage the posts may have carried. The quest for status was of course intimately connected with remuneration, since pay was itself a point of honor, and managers or those who coveted office made their concern with rank plain in their requests for economic benefit.[47] Gang bosses petitioned the Collegio for their boss's bonus using the argument, "in work I'm not inferior to any of the others who enjoy the benefit," and complained that without the bonus they would be only receiving the wages of "any ordinary master."[48] The craving by such technical managers for some distinction did not stop at simple raises, as the Senate clearly recognized, when it honored bosses whose work was particularly appreciated with the award of a special gold medal.[49]

The top managers in the shipyards were visually marked out by their rich brocaded robes, which they purchased at their own expense. The distinctive gowns of the Admiral and principal foremen were signs of an exclusive and public honor, which set them among the middle to higher *cittadini* officers of the state (see Figure 2.1).

Figure 2.1. The Arsenal foreman (left), work boss (center), and admiral (far right)

It was an honor that they sometimes might have to defend from the encroachments of lesser managers, however: in 1621, the top Arsenal managers appeared before the Patroni protesting that the five subforemen were not only usurping ceremonial activities reserved for them, but were also dressing in long robes that were too similar to their own.[50] The Admiral and top foremen combined forces to protest the award of old sailcloth, complaining that by including too many lesser supervisors and bosses among the recipients the Patroni had degraded the gift.[51] Top managers were just as sensitive about questions of honor among themselves, as when the foremen oarmaker and mastmaker came to the Patroni in 1667, arguing over which had the right of precedence over the other.[52]

In the sixteenth-century Arsenal, it had been technical ability, often given only part time, that gained shipbuilders wealth and honor from the Venetian government. A hundred years later, in a much more highly bureaucratized workplace, such rewards derived largely from a manager's proven devotion to the state shipyards and the extent to which he linked his personal and family ambitions with Arsenal offices. Domenico di Zuane, a gang boss of the caulk-

ers, could assert with pride, "to have never abandoned the Arsenal by going to work outside and giving myself to another profession, as some of the others have done"; while the Admiral Zuane Luganegher boasted more than once how "well known [is] the true worth of our house, rendered in hundreds of years [of service to the Arsenal]."[53] The Admiral and principal foremen stressed the honor they received in having their personal fortunes linked with the Arsenal: "We ministers of the Arsenal . . . are singled out as most faithful servants of Your Serenity and privileged with a mark of particular affection: that of not having other sustenance or savings than that which by the highest generosity of Your Serenity is paid to us in recompense."[54]

This personal linkage of managers to the shipyards was a key factor in their unique social status: by the seventeenth century, the Arsenal was the repository of over 500 years of tradition and excellence, and office holders in the shipyards were especially invested with the grandeur of the venerable institution which they served. It was inevitable that worker managers would become the arsenalotti who most symbolized the Arsenal to the greater Venetian public, those best suited to present the shipyards to visitors from the outside world who came to see their marvels. Indeed, both technical and nontechnical officers evidently spent a good deal of their time showing the shipyards to a seemingly endless stream of foreign visitors. Most of these were ordinary gentlemen enjoying the sights of the Republic, but there were also princes, cardinals, duchesses, and

Table 2.2 Distribution of the *Donativo* of Frederick IV, 1708

Position	Share (ducats)	% of Annual Nominal Income
Admiral	150	100
Major foremen	13–19	14–20
Subforemen	3–6	4–7
Supervisors	3	4
Timekeepers	2½	3
Gang bosses	3	2.5
Rank-and-file	1	1

Note: Annual nominal income here is considered the base salary or wages received by a worker, not counting personal bonuses, extras, or *incerti:* MC:ms Gradenigo 193 II, ff. 118r–119v.

other notables who came as much to judge the military potential of
Venice as to amuse themselves with a tourist's curiosity.[55]

Since the officers of the shipyards were the workers who "most
exerted themselves in serving, accompanying, and honoring the
princes and other personages who come to see the Arsenal," it was
only natural that they should also expect some of the honor and
profit that would come from sharing in the *donativo* expected of
departing guests—an "honorarium" that could be demanded so in-
sistently that it sometimes made visitors uncomfortable. Although
at one time these donations had been reserved only for the gatekeepers, the responsibility of managers and supervisors for guiding
visitors through the yards, workshops, and storerooms under their
personal authority was eventually recognized, and it was decided
that they too should have the honor of an allotment.[56] With characteristic Venetian thoroughness and practicality, a ranking system
was thereupon worked out whereby each officer and worker would
receive his due, in a sense putting the question of the relative stature
and importance of every worker manager in the hierarchy on a cash
basis. When an exceptionally generous *donativo* of over 1,600 ducats
was left behind by the King of Denmark in 1708, it was decided to
give a portion to every worker in the Arsenal. A list of recipients
was therefore made up, along with their shares; from it we can quan-
tify the relative status and public honor enjoyed by different ranks
of worker managers (see table 2.2).

Elected Managers

Little direct evidence remains to show what guidelines were
used to choose Arsenal managers, although some idea of the varying
processes employed in selection can be inferred from the petitions
written by the different sorts of officers. Of the three broad groups
of worker managers, the thirty or more gang bosses of shipwrights
and caulkers appear to have been those whose selection was most
closely based on training and shipbuilding skills alone. When one
of these positions became available, the Patroni usually invited all
interested masters to apply, in a competition that required candidates to demonstrate their skills as *fabricanti* in a formal examination.[57] Among the shipwrights, candidates were required to demonstrate possession and familiarity with their own set of shipbuilding
plans and templates, that is, the *sesti* used by builders to organize
construction; they might also have had to produce models before
the assembled Arsenal board, to show the range of their competence

and training. Some evidence from petitions indicates that candidates might also be called upon to carry out some actual ship construction, which would then be inspected by the foreman shipwright and the foreman of the caulkers.[58]

Although the selection of gang bosses was based on open competition, such a system did not necessarily insure that candidates were chosen on the basis of their skills alone. Masters who felt that they had been passed over might try going around the Patroni and petitioning the Collegio directly for the next available position; others tried to get one of the top officials in the Arsenal to intervene on their behalf.[59] And indeed, foremen did occasionally approach the Collegio with gang boss candidates of their own, hoping to fill a vacancy or even suggesting that a certain existing boss was too old to carry out his duties and should be replaced by their willing protégé.[60]

Such attempts to manipulate the selection process were not the only factors weighing against simple talent in the choice of Arsenal gang bosses, for the training necessary to make a good boss was not equally available to every master in the shipyards. Mastering the use of building plans and gaining the authority for command were experiences generally available only within certain families. That this was so was taken for granted by both popular and cultured Venetian tradition, which assumed that with shipbuilders (as indeed with every skill), excellence was inherited as much as taught, and that only certain lineages could be counted on to produce quality *fabricanti*. A certain undefinable "genius" was seen to play a key role in shipbuilding, especially in the laying of the keel and construction of the hull, the success of which largely depended on the sensitive guidance of the work boss. The idea of inheritable skill was reinforced by the tacit and widespread belief that the designing and constructing of galleys was an art whose secrets were best transmitted within the family, from father to son, rather than taught systematically to students in professional schools.[61] Despite a high degree of standardization in Arsenal galley production, the correct accomplishment of the initial stages of galley building still depended largely on the "eye of the master" (*l'occhio del maestro*) to select the proper curve of oak ribbing from the Arsenal's tangled piles of specially forked logs (*stortami*) and to shape them correctly for maximum speed and manageability in the water.

Thus, in the Arsenal it remained customary that work bosses be trained by a father or uncle who was also a boss. The apprenticeship

of these boys was set at three years longer than that for ordinary
masters, and indeed they were customarily taken on at the age of
seven, instead of at the normal ten.[62] When they graduated to be
masters, they were already well on their way to a place in the ranks
of the work bosses, like Marco d'Antonio able to claim that "[my
father] instructed and trained me in the shipwright's craft and he
also taught me the way to build from my own pattern (*sesto*) the
galleys and other sorts of ships that are normally made in the Arsenal."[63] Once such an apprentice had passed his master's examination, his chances of becoming a boss in his own right were quite
high. Sometimes these privileged young men had to wait a few years
before they were chosen, building a galley or two under their old
master or finishing vessels started and abandoned by other bosses.
A few were so esteemed, however, that they were made a boss virtually from the moment they had taken their examination, perhaps
at the age of only eighteen or nineteen.[64]

This restriction of a boss's skills and secrets just to certain lineages inevitably meant that the positions themselves went to only a
few families. The diffusion of these skills became even more limited
after 1650, when the institution of the arsenalotti baptismal register
formally forbade any master or boss from signing on as an apprentice any boy not his own son or grandson. As a result, the same
family names occur repeatedly on lists of gang bosses in the 1600s,
with sons and grandsons following fathers across the century; several sets of near relatives served at the same time, including five
members of the Gramolin family, brothers, sons, and nephews, all
of whom were working together in 1660.[65] Those unfortunate
enough to be born outside an established family of *fabricanti* were
thus quite unlikely to receive the training necessary to become
bosses themselves. Nor would they have had much hope in competing for a place among the foremen and subforemen, since these technical posts were in turn generally drawn from the ranks of gang
bosses. For the particularly talented or ambitious, there remained
only the possibility of making oneself a name as an independent
builder, competing with other masters for Arsenal galley contracts
in the expectation that recognition might eventually lead to election
as a gang boss.[66]

Other positions for technical managers in the Arsenal were also
filled by election, but the process was not always so obviously based
on skills and training as it was with the gang bosses; indeed, it is
not even always clear which of several government boards—the

Patroni and Provveditori (the *Banca all'Arsenale)*, the Arsenal Col- leggietto, the Collegio, or the Senate—actually would assume the responsibility of electing the various officers.[67] For the posts of sub- foreman and warehouse supervisor, patronage connections within the shipyards appear to have played an important part in winning election by the Patroni. The most valuable patronage would have been that of the foremen, who inevitably had the strongest say on who was best qualified to hold subordinate offices in their own de- partments; occasionally a foreman might suggest the creation of an entirely new office, also proposing his own choice to fill it.[68] Fore- men nevertheless could not expect to replace subordinates with oth- ers more to their liking when they themselves took office, and a subforeman or even a foreman's own assistant could openly quarrel with his superior without risk of dismissal. So firmly was the prin- cipal of life-tenure established in the shipyards that these lesser technical offices, like most in the Arsenal, were granted to their holders for life and could not be taken away except for senility or gross incompetence.[69]

The Patroni were also sometimes guided by social considerations when choosing supervisors for the Arsenal warehouses. Requiring few skills beyond tenaciously protective instincts, such positions seem to have been customarily reserved for aged or disabled mas- ters, as a kind of compensatory reward for past service or injuries sustained on the job. The ex-shipwright Anzolo di Zamaria Tasso benefitted from this tradition after sustaining a chest injury ("that I will feel as long as I live") from an accident in the yards: as compen- sation he was appointed by the Patroni to be supervisor of the Ar- senal's mud and rubble barges.[70]

Yet another set of criteria appear to have functioned in the choosing of the highest technical managers in the Arsenal, the Ad- miral and the principal foremen: these officers appear to have been selected primarily on the basis of reputation and personal connec- tions. Certainly a previous foreman in a candidate's family back- ground must have often influenced the *Banca's* decision: sons were selected to succeed to the offices of their fathers and brothers took over from brothers five times over the course of the seventeenth century (see table 2.3).

Competitive examinations were rare, probably because few ship- builders would have been seriously considered for a foreman's post before their technical reputation was already firmly established in the Arsenal and they were well known both to the Patroni and to

Table 2.3 Admirals and Major Foremen in the Arsenal in the
Seventeenth Century

	Years	Age upon Election (years of age)
Admirals		
Biasio di Martino	1589–1618	63
Gasparo Gagio	1619–30	61
Horatio di Zuane	1630–35	51
Zuane di Domenico Luganegher	1635–61	40
Marco Fasoi	1661–80	
Stefano Antipa	1680–83+	
Nicolò Antipa	in 1696	
Foremen Shipwrights		
Zuane dal Moro	?–1611	
Domenico di Zuane Luganegher	1611–19	60+
Zuane di Domenico Luganegher	1619–35	24
Vicenzo di Pasqualin "Vice"	1635–50	51
Zuanfrancesco Lazari	1650–60	73
Zorzi di Zuanfrancesco Lazari	1660–83+	46
Zuane di Michiel	in 1696	
Foremen of the Caulkers		
Francesco Picolo "Chiozotto"	1601–07	
Marco di Andrea Santorini	1607–13	
Nicolò di Giacomo	1613–33	
Giacomo dei Grassi	1633–58	52
Filippo di Francesco	1658–61	33
Francesco Cavazzina	1661–83+	
Pietro di Zorzi	in 1696	
Foremen of the Oarmakers		
Christofolo di Zorzi	?–1604	
Marin di Nicolò	1604–23	72
Zorzi di Christofolo	1623–51	36
Lorenzo di Nicolò	1651–63	52
Michiel di Nocolò	1663–1703	
Bortolo di Battista Picoli	1703	
Foremen of the Mastmakers		
Pasqualin di Rado	?–1601	
Gasparo Gagio	1601–19	43
Zorzi di Pierantonio Grandi	1619–66	29
Domenico di Fulcentio	1666–96+	32–34

Sources: ASV:TA, passim; ASV:CRD suppliche, various petitions of Admirals
and foremen; and parish archives of S. Martino, *libri di morti e battesimi*.

the other foremen. Thus, it was customary that the foremen caulker and shipwright were drawn from among the work bosses of their respective guilds: a candidate's record as a work gang leader would have been sufficient to give the *Banca* a clear sense of both his technical abilities and administrative talents. The selection process was evidently more difficult for the foremen of the mast and oarmakers, since these Arsenal departments were too small to have either gang or work bosses. With only thirty or forty masters in each guild, the Patroni and Provveditori might find they had only one candidate for whom to vote; on one occasion it was necessary to forbid shipwrights from putting their names in the competition. On the other hand, should three or four candidates decide to vie for leadership in one of these small guilds at the same time, the *Banca* might well end up deadlocked by their inability to find one candidate clearly more qualified than the rest.[71] Not surprisingly, the only record of an actual foreman's examination *(prova)* given in the Arsenal was that taken by three competing candidates for the post of foreman mastmaker in 1619.[72]

Considering the tenacity with which the gerontocratic tradition was maintained in the Republic, it is somewhat surprising to find that the Arsenal's top managers were by no means all elderly when elected. Admirals, it is true, tended to conform to the Venetian supposition that considerable age was a primary qualification for office; since the position included a number of ceremonial duties along with technical requirements, it was probably considered desirable to select a candidate combining appropriate age and dignity with expertise.[73] Such was not apparently the policy followed with major foremen, however, and indeed the Patroni seemed to prefer vigorous and active craftsmen to masters whose greater wisdom and experience might have been offset by their being past their prime. Foremen were after all expected to take an active hand in the construction work; some even sustained serious injuries while carrying out their duties.[74] Based on those ages available (see table 2.3), foremen averaged something over forty-six years old when elected to their posts. Two foremen were in fact chosen when in their seventies, but the technical direction of the Arsenal was also entrusted to some surprisingly young managers. Thus, Zorzi di Christofolo was only thirty-six when he was chosen as foreman of the oarmakers and his successor Filipo di Francesco was thirty-three; Zorzi di Pierantonio Grandi was twenty-nine when elected foreman of the mastmakers, and Zuane Luganegher succeeded his father as foreman shipwright in 1619 at the age of only twenty-four.[75]

One factor that may well have distinguished successful candidates for top foremen positions was that, unlike the run of other gang bosses and supervisors, they had enjoyed a wide range of previous experience working outside the Arsenal. Those chosen to be foremen had often seen unusually extensive service at sea compared to other bosses, some of whom never went abroad at all. After completing his master's examination, Zorzi di Christofolo had indeed spent almost no time in the Arsenal, but had served instead for over twenty years with the fleet, coming back to Venice only a year before he would be elected foreman of the oarmakers; Francesco di Alessandro Cavazzina, chosen as foreman of the caulkers in 1661, had likewise earlier distinguished himself in two long voyages to Corfù and the Levant as a gang boss in charge of a squad of masters sent to refit the fleet.[76] To win election as Admiral of the Arsenal, extensive service with the fleet was indeed considered to be virtually obligatory, far more so than having previously served as foreman shipwright, as several scholars have maintained. The *Banca* made its selection from among candidates whose main qualification was consistently one of lengthy naval experience: five of the seven Admirals elected in the seventeenth century had reached the highest possible non-noble rank of *ammiraglio dell'armata,* or admiral of the fleet.[77] Having passed the greater part of his life in active sea duty, the newly elected Admiral was often a comparative stranger to the Arsenal—something of a drawback in directing a socially close-knit workforce, but necessary if the state were to have expert supervision in launching and outfitting vessels. On one occasion, the *Banca* actually elected an Admiral who was not even enrolled with the Arsenal, but instead was away serving with the fleet. This difficulty was overcome—his brother was a master and could serve in his place until he returned—but there were loud objections raised about a later Admiral who was suspected of not being from arsenalotti stock at all, but instead was said to have been only an orphan raised in the local foundling hospital.[78]

It was important for successful candidates for top offices to have distinguished themselves with services beyond those routinely expected from ordinary arsenalotti and minor managers. Some foremen when younger had been responsible for inventions or ideas which had proven useful in the Arsenal; others had shown their excellence in salvaging or repairing wrecked ships, or had been especially active in directing the cutting and management of Venetian forests in Istria and the Dolomites.[79] Some foremen had also gained practice and reputation at serving the Arsenal through holding lesser offices when younger: sometimes they had purchased the position themselves, sometimes it had been granted to them by the Patroni.[80]

Successful candidates for places as top managers in the Arsenal also appear to have had a wider network of support than other arsenalotti, particularly enjoying strong connections with noble households that held sway in the Senate, Collegio, and other high magistracies. Even ordinary masters probably enjoyed more familiarity and closer dealings with patricians than did other Venetian artisans: when serving at sea, the masters' importance to the ship was considered such that they could claim a regular place at their noble captain's table.[81] The opportunities for gang bosses and foremen for involvement with patricians and with the arts of patron and client that so ruled social life in the Republic were still greater, however. These were the men who personally oversaw galley production, and noble commanders were forever seeking them out, hoping as a favor to get some change in the standardized design of the warship they would command or to speed up its production.[82]

As a result of such services, at least some arsenalotti families managed to form special cliental relationships with particular patrician lineages that lasted for generations. Ottavio Cesani, grandson of a common shipwright who became chief stores officer at the Arsenal, recalled how his brother had recognized the Cesani family's connection with the noble house of Ciuran: "at the first sign from the *Illustrissimo* Francesco Ciuran, *Governatore delle navi*, Martin Cesani quickly got ready to obey and serve him as his ship's overseer, in order to continue the ancient servitude that we hold with that most illustrious house." Such services might expose a master to personal danger (Ciuran and Martin Cesani in fact both died when their ship was wrecked), but a noble patron could also be depended upon to act as his advocate either in the Senate or when promotions or honors were being voted upon by the Patroni. Some top managers attempted to extend their family networks with the Venetian nobility beyond a single lineage, possibly assuming that the larger the number of Senators with whom they had connections, the easier time they would have in securing social patronage or a *gratia*. [83] The ideal social position would seem to have been that of Zuane di Do-

menico Luganegher (elected as foreman shipwright at twenty-four
and Admiral at forty), for the Patroni could write of him: "our nar-
rative would only serve to confirm rather than attest to Your Serenity the faithfulness, aptitude, and talents of the subject . . .
[since] You yourself and a great many very important Senators have
had occasion to know the accomplishments and quality of this minister in action."[84]

The godparent relationship was another cementing point in the
social networks that flourished between Arsenal foremen and the
Venetian nobility; it also provides an indicator of the lengths to
which many managers would go in cultivating such ties. Foremen
were especially keen on arranging that the godfather for their children or grandchildren be a patrician, probably less as a future pro-
tector for the newborn than as a means of establishing or reaffirming
a patron-client relationship between the godparent and themselves.
When Zorzi di Christofolo presented himself as a candidate for foreman of the oarmakers, it was certainly important to the Patroni that
his father had once been foreman as well, but it was also no doubt
helpful that he had been held at the moment of his baptism by the
young nobleman Gerolamo Ciuran; the foreman caulker Francesco
Picolo had men of the Querini and Pisani families stand as godfather
for a grandson and granddaughter in 1601 and 1602; Zorzi di Pierantonio Grandi, foreman of the mastmakers, used his family's connections with the Contarini to have one of their scions serve as
godfather to his son and niece, while a nephew was held by one of
the Foscarini.[85] The best connected and most accomplished of all
Arsenal managers at spreading his patronage net, however, appears
to have been foreman caulker Francesco di Alessandro Cavazzina,
who managed to enlist noblemen to stand as godfather to no fewer
than eleven of his twelve children between 1662 and 1678.[86]

Venal Offices

Nontechnical offices in the Arsenal evolved in a very different
direction than did those of foreman or gang boss. Since positions
such as timekeeper and guild overseer did not require any particular
craft skills to be carried out well, they did not come under the same
sort of scrutiny by the Senate or Collegio as did the top technical
posts. Up through the early 1600s, the criteria employed by the Patroni when they came to elect such disciplinary officers were fairly
limited. The primary requirement was that candidates be actual
masters of the Arsenal, if only because other arsenalotti might well

refuse to tolerate an outsider in a position of authority over them.[87] The government also ordered that any master elected to such an office be debt-free at the moment of his selection, lest his creditors someday try to impound the position (which after all was legally a personal possession of the officer) to settle their claims.[88] For offices such as timekeeper and overseer, a certain amount of literacy was required; in addition, the overseers, like the Captain of the Arsenal and the leaders of the gangs of porters, also presumably had to be fairly robust in order to protect themselves in disputes with the workers they were charged to supervise.[89] The Patroni were concerned about a candidate's reputation for honesty as well: officers caught cheating the state shipyards (although not necessarily those who defrauded other arsenalotti) were subject to dismissal and often heavy punishments. After one particularly flagrant case of time sheet falsification in 1596, three of the timekeepers were even put to death.[90]

It had also long been customary that office holders were expected to be competent enough at their jobs to carry out assigned duties themselves, rather than have to hire a substitute to do the work for them. After the 1620s, however, the state's attitude about substitutes began to change. Despite the Senate's occasionally voicing disapproval, it became almost commonplace for the Patroni to appoint the same masters to serve in two or even three offices at the same time, possibly as part of rewarding shipbuilders in their own clientage networks and perhaps also because after the plague of 1630–31 there simply were not enough well-qualified arsenalotti to go around for all the management posts available.[91] Whatever the reasons behind appointing managers to multiple offices, the practice almost by necessity demanded that such managers be allowed to take on substitutes, if only because many would have to abandon one position for months at a time while fulfilling another. Thus, by the 1630s, the Patroni were permitting many office holders to hire replacements; to keep the quality of substitutes from falling too low they could only insist that office holders pay them adequately, by turning over their position's entire income to whoever actually carried out its duties.[92]

Such a permissive attitude toward allowing substitutes to do a supervisor's or overseer's real work made it all the easier to sell the positions themselves. In 1636, pressed for hard cash, the Senate decided to have another of its periodic auctions of most Venetian public offices and (evidently for the first time) put many supervisory positions in the Arsenal up for sale as well. Since such offices demanded only a few skills, it was indeed not difficult to convert their selection process from one based on merit (or the social considerations of the Patroni) to one that was almost purely monetary. Once a position was purchased, it would become its owner's private property, to exercise personally if he wished, or to rent out to someone else.

The right to award nontechnical offices in the shipyards was thus in effect taken away from the Patroni and given instead to the Provveditori and Deputati of Public Funds, the magistrate in charge of auctioning off government posts.[93] At first the Patroni tried to insure that the sales of Arsenal offices would at least be limited to arsenalotti alone, essentially trying to continue earlier policies that restricted shipyard management to the masters but now conceding that shipbuilders would be made to pay as well if they wished to hold offices. It appears that some arsenalotti were wealthy enough to respond to these new conditions: auction records show masters paying small sums of 50 or 60 ducats for a post as warehouse supervisor, up to as much as 550 for the office of timekeeper.[94] Indeed, before long such sales began to spread to skilled offices as well, much to the distress of the Patroni and many Marine Secretaries. In 1641, an appraiser's office was sold, in 1659 the magistrate over Public Funds even tried to sell the post of foreman caulker, although in the end they were prevented by a vigorous protest on the part of the Patroni.[95]

Even if not all positions were allowed to be sold, the variety of those that were available was considerable, and at a wide range of prices: over thirty offices ranging from overseer to forest supervisor to accounting positions, costing from as low as only 20 ducats to well over a thousand. For those arsenalotti who could afford it, the Arsenal management hierarchy became a virtual marketplace of opportunity, with jobs of every sort accessible by purchase for anyone who could pay their prices. Some observers, it is true, protested the loss of the Arsenal's social function that venality represented, for supervisory and other guard posts were no longer available to be doled out to deserving or infirm masters. The Patroni felt that when desirable posts went up for sale to any master who had the cash, many other arsenalotti would lose an important incentive to keep coming to work at the shipyards, and in turn the Arsenal would surrender an important means of channeling the ambitions or restlessness of talented workers.[96] Nevertheless, the policy of allowing arsenalotti to buy offices at the shipyards was not an altogether negative one. By selling these offices, the state had greatly opened up the management hierarchy, freeing it from the domination and patronage of the Patroni and just a few well-connected families, in effect turning over the election process to the candidates themselves. Venality of such positions not only stimulated and encouraged masters' vested interest in the welfare of their own workplace, but also introduced those who bought or sold offices and hired substitutes to cash and market activities, in effect making them petty capitalists.[97]

Any possibilities which venality might have offered for opening up the Arsenal's management hierarchy to new or younger masters were never fully realized, however. As soon as these offices began to be put up for sale in 1636, they attracted the attention of Venetians outside the Arsenal who realized that they could be profitable investments. At first the Patroni resisted their incursions, rejecting some buyers precisely because they were not members of the workforce.[98] Indeed, on one ticket *(polizza)* for the auction of the position of timekeeper of the oarmakers in 1639, it was written, "Not to be bought by others than those of the House of the Arsenal."[99] In time, however, investors' insistence and the state's continual need for money wore the Patroni down. Nontechnical offices became generally available to outside bidders by the 1650s; even technical positions such as appraiser and head stores supervisor were soon on the open market, despite the Patroni's alarmed warnings that allowing merchants such as timber dealers and hemp suppliers to buy the very offices that were designed to oversee the quality of their products was an open invitation to corruption that would quickly render the positions meaningless.[100]

The attraction of Arsenal offices to both arsenalotti and outside investors was due less to their actual pay (which might be quite low) than to the side benefits and irregular forms of income *(incerti)* which might be worth several times a position's stated wage.[101] It was evidently quite easy for such investors to find someone in the Arsenal who would carry out the actual duties of the position at a fraction of its nominal wage; in fact with many offices substitutes could readily be found who were actually willing to pay well for the privilege of renting them. The Patroni asserted that for posts such as doorkeeper and timekeeper, where the possibilities for graft and corruption were very high, office holders could demand as rent not only their position's entire yearly wage, all other wages in kind and *incerti,* and the house that might go with the job (thus obliging the renter to live elsewhere, although this was forbidden), but also as much as 40 ducats a year, just for the right of tenancy. According to the Patroni, those who rented the office (and many were arsenalotti) could thus never make a living off its legitimate income, but expected instead to offer favors for any sort of bribe they could possibly solicit.[102]

In a sense, the spread of outside office seekers into the Arsenal was a kind of economic colonization, in which investors from the city eventually took over much of the management of the state shipyards from the arsenalotti who had once exercised it and then rented it back to these same workers at whatever the job market would bear. The greater wealth of outside bidders further had the effect of soon driving up the prices of venal positions in the Arsenal, and many arsenalotti were forced to pay dearly if they wanted a management position or even had to abandon the office market altogether. To buy the office of Captain of the Arsenal, a sea captain named Andrea Moro was able to outbid by six to one a shipwright who was competing for the post; when the office of head stores supervisor was offered in 1648, Ottavio Cesani had to put up the substantial sum of 3,040 ducats in order to beat out rival *cittadini* bidders.[103] The office had been granted free to Ottavio's father in 1633, simply on the basis of merit and connections.

The eventual impact of this outside competition on the Arsenal management hierarchy is clear from Francesco Cornero's 1696 list of offices and their holders. The four timekeeper posts, the Captain, the workforce overseer, all the gatekeeper positions, several of the warehouse supervisors, and virtually all the bookkeeping offices in the Arsenal belonged to outsiders—including one nobleman, six noblewomen, and two nuns. Few outside office holders could have expected to exercise their posts personally, and indeed most of them would never have been allowed to do so anyway, for reasons of age or sex. The policing office of Captain was held for several decades by a woman named Anzola Bombella, who had received it (perhaps as a dowry) from her ship captain uncle Andrea Moro. The office of workforce overseer was sold in 1641 in the name of a three-month-old boy; and the clerical position of stores bookkeeper, or *scontro alle porte,* had been granted by the Senate to the four young children of the nobleman Marin Pisani for his past services.[104] Ultimately, the lively demand for Arsenal offices appears to have shut out all but the wealthiest arsenalotti families, those of foremen and other well-off shipbuilders, who had in any event begun to closely resemble this same investor and rentier class in terms of both wealth and social standing.[105]

Management, Innovation, and Production

Over the sixteenth and seventeenth centuries, the involvement of Venice's governing elite with the state Arsenal became both more bureaucratic and more nominal. The government created certain patrician offices in the shipyards and strengthened others, but no noble with wide authority was ever entrusted to direct the Republic's ship production in the yards themselves for any extensive period of time. The annual visits of the doge to the shipyards continued (they were one of the stated conditions of his oath of office) but by the seventeenth century they were noticeably perfunctory and ceremonial affairs. Even the Patroni themselves appear to have only rarely visited the actual yards and construction sites of the Arsenal.[106] It is true that Secretaries of the Marine were sent by the Collegio to investigate the state of the shipyards, to count their stores, judge their productivity, and to punish or reward workers; once their reports were filed with the Senate, however, the nobles who had drawn them up went on to other posts. The actual running of the Arsenal remained in the hands of those who stayed behind: the permanent administrators and worker managers of the shipyards.

Compared with its durable management hierarchy, the nobles who administered the Arsenal were indeed only a transitory presence. Patroni were elected by the Senate to serve for thirty-two months, the Provveditori only sixteen, and the Inquisitors and the Marine Secretaries just for the six months or so that it took them to draw up their reports. By contrast, tenures of the Admiral and principal foremen during the seventeenth century averaged more than nineteen years apiece.[107] Over the course of the century, while twenty-one different doges ruled in Venice and nearly 150 Patroni came and went at the Arsenal, only four different foremen of the oarmakers and three foremen of the mastmakers ran their respective departments in the shipyards.

The turnover of worker managers was so slow in good part because of the Patroni's tendency to elect relatively young masters to the positions. The custom clearly had the advantage of bringing men in their creative prime into posts of command, but when such managers continued serving into their sixties or seventies, their ideas and technical skills might become increasingly out of date. Giacomo

dei Grassi was elected foreman of the caulkers probably in part be- The Arsenal
cause while still a young gang boss he had come up with some useful Worker
technical innovations in caulking and in reclaiming ship's hardware. Managers
When as a foreman he later petitioned the Collegio for a raise, these
were the same two creative accomplishment which Giacomo repeatedly cited as his main justification for a *gratia*. It is striking that
though a foreman for several decades, Giacomo continued to stress
only these and other youthful achievements in his petitions, as if he
had done little worth mentioning to the Collegio during most of his
tenure in office: in his final petition, the most recent innovation he
chose to recall was one he had instituted some seventeen years
earlier.[108]

The long tenures of most foremen and other worker managers
in the shipyards may help to explain the relative stagnation and lack
of new ideas in the Arsenal during the seventeenth century, a pre-
carious situation when rapid technical advances were taking place
in other European shipbuilding centers.[109] The Arsenal saw only two
periods of even limited innovative activity during the century, and
both were preceded by abrupt and major turnovers in the ranks of
the top managers. Between 1619 and 1623, a new Admiral and three
foremen were elected, with an average age of thirty-seven; in the
years that immediately followed, the Arsenal undertook its first serious attempts at rejuvenating its workforce since the 1570s. It was
probably also no coincidence that between 1660 and 1663, when
once again the Admiral and three major foremen died and were replaced, Venice elected to begin a long-delayed conversion of the Arsenal from the building of galleys and galleasses to the construction
of ships-of-the-line.

Conservative and thoroughly entrenched top managers could fit
in well with a state policy which, as has already been seen, was
strongly inclined to squelch new ideas and creative responses to
shipbuilding problems. The Admiral and principal foremen were
quite able to keep to a minimum any innovative activities of their
subordinates that the state might deem unnecessary or disruptive,
thanks to their powers of patronage and reward, powers to bestow
offices and favors within the shipyards themselves. Positioned at the
top of patronage pyramids, foremen were very well placed to reward
underlings who supported them or to freeze out those of whom they
disapproved. They had a hand in every stage of a master's working
life and were easily able to promote the careers of those they favored, whether in suggesting a preferred candidate to the Patroni

for a minor office, in judging the finished ships of a gang boss, or sitting in on the guild boards that administered the master's examination to apprentices.[110] As long as patronage networks continued to flourish in the shipyards, the Arsenal's administration of production remained at the personal rather than structural level of organization, and a conservative foreman could provide an especially powerful deterrent against novelties fostered by his subordinates, even on those occasions when the state actually sought to promote innovation.

Tendencies toward stagnation and unresponsiveness in the Arsenal's management hierarchy were furthered by the nature of job tenure itself. The strict identification between office and man that was fostered by the lifetime ownership of management positions resulted in a keen awareness on the part of officers of the precise obligations and limits of their posts and a great unwillingness to go beyond them without extra reward. Security of tenure was for many managers a license to perform the minimum possible amount of work; even simple competence in carrying out duties appears to have struck some as grounds for claiming a bonus.[111] When the state attempted to alter a manager's obligations, protests were the inevitable result; some, like the warehouse guard Alvise Moscatello, felt that any increased responsibilities soon justified a request for extra wages. A manager who had worked out an innovative approach to his duties considered the procedure as much his property as his office. Having no automatic obligation to divulge it or put it into effect, he was rather more likely to keep his innovation to himself, hoping, like the appraiser Zuane di Gerolamo Fantebon tried to do in 1640, to eventually sell it to the state.[112]

Even if the management hierarchy of the Arsenal were hardly geared ideally for running the shipyards with flexibility and creativity, it could nevertheless still be perfectly adequate in the business of regular and sustained production. Manufacturing galleys at a consistent and dependable rate depended especially on a workforce that was obedient and responsive, and the Arsenal's patronage system, which personally obligated ordinary masters and lesser officers to top managers, was particularly successful in this regard. The state protected the powers that managers held over their underlings, and took care when workplace discipline was intensified in the later seventeenth century that it was done so through the agency of these officers. The workforce overseer was directed to embellish his payroll book with "distinct descriptions" of all masters so that he would be better able to recognize and denounce shirkers. Work bosses, as the officers closest to both the workforce and actual shipbuilding, were given broader disciplinary powers over the masters who worked under them. It was further ordered that each master upon coming to work was to be issued a chit (*polizza*) by his foreman which assigned him to a particular gang boss.[113] The bosses in turn began keeping their own work books, based on these chits, in order to more rigidly control the masters who had been ordered to their squad; those workers whom they considered slack in their work could be struck off. Even elderly masters, who had once been left largely to wander much as they pleased about the shipyards, were put under direct control of their foremen, with the mission to spy out and report on masters who had evaded their bosses or who were otherwise malingering.[114]

The power of worker managers to run the Arsenal workforce as they thought best was further enhanced by the state's decision to give them rights over workers that resembled those of military commanders. In 1662, with the declared intention that "everyone [must] satisfy his own duty as required and obligated," the Patroni ordered that all managers (*ministeri*) should "be without exception given the respect due to the incumbency of their positions, such that no one should dare either in deed or word or in any other imaginable way to annoy them." Workers who questioned the orders of their superiors could henceforth be "banished, imprisoned, sent to the galleys, or banned from the Arsenal."[115] Masters who tried to wander from their assigned places were to be forced back not only by the threat of a pay cut, but also by overseers who would henceforth go armed on their rounds, a decision which the Patroni expected would "repress the temerity and pride of these workers . . . so that given in this way some awe and fear . . . they might then abstain from their transgressions and give the obedience and respect [which are] due to their officers, for the good direction and the necessary care of the Arsenal."[116]

The level of personal power which top Arsenal managers assumed or were granted was probably necessary for maintaining control over the workforce of largely low-skilled shipbuilders which was to be found in the shipyards by the seventeenth century. The result was certainly a less creative and experimental workplace than that of a hundred years earlier, but it could nevertheless still be counted on to produce a few carefully designed and familiar types of shipping. In this regard, the seventeenth-century Arsenal could be said to have succeeded in reaching virtually the same productive capacity as that of the sixteenth, when it gained its fame for marvels of shipbuilding.

This is best demonstrated with vessels as standardized as the light galley *(galia sotil)*—for centuries the mainstay of production in the shipyards, and so similar to one another that as early as the 1400s one observer had called them "as alike as two swallows' nests."[117] By the middle of the sixteenth century, after several decades of intense experimentation with design and materials, a few particularly successful models had been selected and made the official standard of the Arsenal. Henceforth, until they were finally phased out in the early eighteenth century, there appears to have been little attempt on the part of the state or Arsenal managers to alter the basic design of the light galleys, which was evidently accepted as ideal.[118]

Since available information on the Arsenal's light galley production before the 1600s consists only of tallies of vessels under construction or launched at various moments, it is difficult to establish what the shipyards' capacity might have been in terms of a yearly rate of output. Some figures for galley launchings may look quite impressive: one was outfitted (or built from scratch, according to some sources) in a single day in 1574 to entertain the visiting King Henry III of France; one hundred fully armed galleys left the Arsenal in less than two months before Lepanto; fifty frames were completed in only ten months in 1537. Unfortunately such figures say little about actual output, since massive launchings may well have been made up mostly of refurbished galleys or of hulls and frames that had been built years before and left in storage until needed for a hasty outfitting and arming.[119] Figures for new construction are likewise not very informative about long-term production rates, although they do reconfirm the fluctuations in sixteenth-century building activity that have already been noted. Thus, although forty-six light galleys were under construction in 1503 and no fewer than sixty in 1560, during four other years in which construction figures are available, an average of fewer than twenty were being built.[120]

A more useful range of production figures is available for the seventeenth-century Arsenal, however. There continue to be counts of galleys under construction, tallies which indicate that, despite long-held assumptions to the contrary, shipbuilding in the Arsenal during the mid-1600s compared very favorably to that of a century earlier, with twelve light galleys reported under construction in 1645, twenty-eight in 1651, and thirty in 1660.[121] Yet there are also long-term figures of Arsenal output of the kind that are not available for the sixteenth century (see table 2.4).

Supplied by the Patroni, one of the Marine Secretaries, and the Admiral himself, these figures indicate just how well the managers who ran the Arsenal were capable of keeping up a sustained production in the shipyards: nearly 350 light galleys were in fact turned out in the space of just fifty years.[122] In contrast to the erratic construction rhythms of the sixteenth century, in these years the Arsenal not only produced steadily but still had the reserves to sharpen output at the beginning of the Cretan War, increasing its rate of construction from an already fairly respectable seven galleys per year in the 1630s to over ten the following decade.[123]

That the Arsenal could maintain such a substantial output of light galleys throughout the middle seventeenth century is a particular testimony to the worker managers who ran the yards. Not only

Table 2.4 Light Galley Production in the Arsenal, 1619–1669

Date	Number of Years	Number of Galleys	Galleys/ Year
1619–25	5	90+	[a]
1619–39	20	123	6.5[b]
1635–39	4	24	6.0[c]
1619–46	27	194	7.2[d]
1639–46	7	71	10.1[e]
1645–60	16	112	7.8[f]
1645–69	29	149	5.1[g]
1619–69	50	341	6.8[h]

[a]"New and restored." ASV:SM, filza 254, 4 Nov 1626.

[b]Production during Zuane Luganegher's term as foreman shipwright ASV:CRD suppliche, filza 30, 17 Oct 1639.

[c]Ibid., Luganegher's production as Admiral, 1635–39.

[d]ASV:SM, filza 386, 24 Aug 1646.

[e]Luganegher's production figures of 1619–39 subtracted from those of 1619–45.

[f]ASV:Collegio V (Segreta), bu. 57, relazione of Piero Mocenigo, 1660, f. 2r.

[g]ASV:SM, filza 576, 29 Sept 1670.

[h]Luganegher, Mocenigo, and the Patroni's figures combined, less 14 galleys for one and a half years' overlap.

were the ordinary masters of the Arsenal generally less capable craftsmen than they had once been, there were also often fewer of them actively working than in the previous century—in some years barely half as many. The fact that galley production continued at respectable levels in spite of this decline contradicts the assertion that efficiency in the Arsenal declined together with the number of masters working there: indeed, the drop in the workforce appears to have spurred both state and managers to increase efficiency, mostly by simplifying masters' duties and tightening their discipline.[124] In so rationalizing the production process in the Arsenal, the Venetian state apparently offers a preview of what would be commonplace in later industrial centers, where output could be enhanced through a workforce that was both more atomized and more regimented. The condition of rank-and-file arsenalotti, trained in the workplace for increasingly simplified tasks and held to an inflexible level of wages, has a striking affinity with what would be the lot of factory workers of the industrial era. Interestingly, however, in furnishing its management cadre with greatly enhanced personal powers, the Republic drew not so much on this "rational" mode of workforce organization, but rather on older traditions of office holding that derived from Medieval and Renaissance public administrations. Secure in their monopolies of technical knowledge and disciplinary powers, Arsenal officers became steadily more distinct from the mass of arsenalotti and increasingly identified with the privileges and status of their position. The houses, bonuses, *incerti,* and traditional trappings and prerogatives of the offices they owned only served to underscore the ties of quasi-feudal dependence that bound many managers to the shipyards and to the state. Ironically, the worker managers charged with reorganizing the Arsenal masters into a disciplined factory workforce were themselves increasingly identified by the symbolic values of an earlier era.

The Community
of the Arsenalotti

The area around the state shipyards was the distinctly "Arsenal" zone of Venice, given a characteristic atmosphere by its resident shipbuilders much in the same way that other districts in the city were distinguished by their own enclaves of weavers, fishermen (*nicolotti*), or glassworkers. At the same time, however, the arsenalotti community of Venice was peculiar even in comparison with these other artisan neighborhoods in the city, conditioned as it was by the looming industrial presence of the Arsenal in its midst and by the force of the state, which was forever intervening in the lives of its residents. To a considerable extent their territory in the city is still recognizable as a worker enclave today. Especially once beyond the main gates of the Arsenal, proceeding into the sprawling parish of San Pietro di Castello, the signs of a once extensive artisan zone are clear: low and relatively modest houses set in orderly rows, their lines of plain facades only rarely broken by the ornate marble windows or balconies of a patrician palace. Few of the large *campi*, or public squares, which are so distinctive in other Venetian parishes, exist to focus the social activities of the district; more commonly the small neighborhoods turn inward on their individual *campielli*, tiny squares where a few narrow alleys meet and where now as during the seventeenth century there is room enough only for hanging laundry or setting up simple outdoor workshops.[1] Although landfill and apartment construction undertaken since the fall of the Republic have considerably altered the area, much of its sense of isolation and separateness from the Rialto and Piazza San Marco is still evident. As in the seventeenth century, these neighborhoods are not oriented toward Venice's cosmopolitan center but look for their focus instead toward the Arsenal in their midst and beyond to the islands of the Lido and the world of the open sea.[2]

The Formation of the Community

In the seventeenth century, the Venetian shipbuilding community had many social and economic characteristics in common with the so-called company town of the Industrial Revolution: a uniformity of worker occupations which overwhelmingly depended on a single employer, geographic and social isolation, little diversity in available services, and a general although not extreme poverty. Unlike later factory towns, however, this community was also marked by its stability and a relatively leisurely pace of development: far from mushrooming like the company towns of industrializing England, the Arsenal district was in fact several centuries in forming.[3] Although as many as 6,000 shipbuilders may have worked in medieval Venice, they did not all live together in a single occupational enclave but were instead for the most part scattered about the city and its *dogado*. Prior to the fifteenth century the Arsenal had rarely needed more than a hundred masters at a time, and therefore shipbuilders simply had no particular reason to live nearby, in this remote and only partially built-up area of Venice. Instead, the masters appear to have been fairly evenly spread about the city, just as were the private shipyards where the majority still earned their living at the time.[4]

The development of a recognizable shipbuilding community near the Arsenal only began with the expansion of the state yards in the late fifteenth and early sixteenth centuries. Masters responding to the Republic's promise of enrollment and guaranteed work flocked to the area and settled at the far seaward end of the city, in the four parishes of Santa Ternità, San Martino, San Biagio, and San Pietro di Castello. The Venetian government was apparently aware of this migration and to some extent encouraged it further in 1471 by founding a charitable home (*hospedale*) there to care for elderly sailors and homeless shipbuilders.[5]

Little documentation survives from this period to reveal just how this newly expanded workforce settled the area around the Arsenal walls. It is likely that the arsenalotti moved into whatever empty housing or vacant land they could find or afford, and considering their generally modest incomes, this probably meant underdeveloped areas which bordered on the open Lagoon. Indeed, around 1520, the Procurators of San Marco (who oversaw much of the state's property) were complaining about a troublesome number of squatters who were occupying recently reclaimed mudflats along the outer edges of San Pietro parish.[6] A tax census (condizioni di decima) taken six years later indicated that the majority of these new residents were either arsenalotti or sailors, men who with their families had erected simple wooden shacks near the edge of the water. In time, the Senate decided to let the squatters stay on the land they had settled and essentially deeded them full title to their plots of ground (including the right of inheritance) in exchange for paying the Procurators a nominal annual rent. The wooden shacks were eventually replaced by more substantial, if not much less humble brick houses, and the neighborhood, known as the Secco Marina, became in time the core of a much larger arsenalotti community. Compared to other worker neighborhoods in Venice and to the rest of the arsenalotti community itself, an unusually high percentage of the shipbuilders and others who lived here owned their own homes, one factor in the stability of the neighborhood.[7] This donation of low-cost living space to workers was an example of state paternalism that resembles the operation of progressive factory towns of the Industrial Revolution at their best.[8] Having perceived the necessity of maintaining a stable workforce in the shipyards, the Venetian government elected to encourage its establishment in an isolated and undeveloped area of the city, where not coincidentally the private lives of workers could be better managed and controlled in the public interest.

At the opposite social pole from the humble neighborhood of the Secco Marina, there grew up another center in the Arsenal district, in the parishes of San Martino and San Biagio. Concentrated around the Campo dell'Arsenale and its adjoining alleys were around forty state-owned houses which were given out by the Arsenal to the more important bosses and managers of the shipyards as one of the prerequisites of their positions. State policy was to give a residence (nearly all of which lay within only a few steps of the main shipyard gates) to every officer "whose commitment and continuous presence in the Arsenal renders him worthy to receive [it]."[9] The placement of so many important officials around the Campo dell'Arsenale had the effect of making the area into a kind of management enclave, concentrating all the shipyards' most powerful figures in one neighborhood and effectively making the Campo the social as well as the institutional hub of the arsenalotti community. Most of the residences were fairly grand: large enough to accommodate several servants and a virtual retinue of occupants; the foreman shipwright Vicenzo Vice lived with an extended "family" of four boys, two girls, five adult women, and four other men, including the nobleman Alessandro Priuli, ex-podestà of Chioggia, and an unspecified foreigner.[10] The social importance of these residences for the community was reflected in the large number of marriages and baptisms held within them: a good many of those rituals, according to the parish registers, involved members of the shipbuilding community who were not directly related to the occupant, but who evidently enjoyed some other social ties with him.

The concentration of important managers around the Campo dell'Arsenale no doubt contributed toward making the area the primary ceremonial center for the arsenalotti community. Here proclamations and edicts concerning the arsenalotti were posted so they would be seen by the 2,000 or more masters and apprentices passing through the Arsenal gates every day. When the doge came to make his periodic inspections of the shipyards, his barges—crowded with attendants and foreign guests—glided alongside the campo on their way into the Arsenal. On those rather less festive occasions when convicted arsenalotti or other unfortunates were ordered by the Patroni to be hanged, the sentence was also carried out in the campo, next to the two *stendardi,* or flagpoles, that displayed the banner of San Marco before the main gates of the shipyards.[11] In times of emergency, the Campo dell'Arsenale was the rallying point for arsenalotti: when the alarm bell rang in the Arsenal tower, the masters were expected to form ranks there before heading off into the shipyards or the city to confront fires or other crises.[12] Even on ordinary work days, the campo had its official use, for the Patroni licensed two Arsenal supervisors to run food concessions there, selling such edibles as cheese, bread, and preserved fish *(salumi),* "for the convenience of the workforce."

The campo also functioned as the religious center for the arsenalotti. On the *fondamenta* of the canal flanking the campo was the shipyards' own chapel, the Beata Madonna dell'Arsenale, built in the early sixteenth century to house a miracle-working image; ship-builders on their way to work habitually stopped off first at the cha-pel to pray.[13] Down a short fondamenta was also the parish church of San Martino, considered (at least by its own priest) as "the church of the Arsenal": when guests of the Arsenal and distinguished for-eign visitors completed their tour of the shipyards, they often at-tended mass at San Martino.[14] Likewise, after their election, new Arsenal foremen were invested with their offices in the church with a religious ceremony that was evidently designed to give sacred le-gitimacy to the officers' new hierarchical status.[15]

By the seventeenth century the community of shipbuilders around the Arsenal had essentially achieved its full extent. While small enclaves of these artisans continued their crafts on the outer islands of the Lagoon, only a few remnants of Venice's own once citywide diffusion of shipbuilders still remained, and these were rap-idly being absorbed into the concentration near the Arsenal. Thus in 1624, there still was a colony of seventy-six shipbuilders' house-holds (most of them caulkers) found on the Giudecca in the parish census (the *anagrafi dei piovani*), but by 1642 this enclave had al-ready declined by nearly 30 percent; most of the other arsenalotti households which the 1624 census had recorded scattered about the city had almost completely disappeared in the census taken eighteen years later.[16] Shipbuilders were in fact under continuous economic and social pressure to quit their old and familiar neighborhoods and to relocate closer to the Arsenal, a point that the arsenalotti from the opposite side of the Grand Canal made clear in a petition they submitted in 1628:

> We live in our traditional homes [which are] very far from the House of the Arsenal so that often we have to put up with those discomforts that Your Serenity can imagine, but more important, living at such a distance we cannot manage to arrive [at work] at the required hour, which often results in our loss . . . furthermore, at the ringing of the bell we cannot serve You, either at [putting out] fires or in other re-quirements . . . nor can we be ready at the command of the Patroni. Therefore . . . we petition You to concede us a gracious license to rent out our houses, so that from the income we will make from them we can pay the rent on other homes as close as possible to the House of the Arsenal.[17]

Although in general the concentration of Venetian shipbuilders around the Arsenal was too gradual to leave sharp traces, its course can at least be charted by the long-term movements of the workers' devotional and charitable groups such as the *scuola dei calafati*. This confraternity of the caulkers' guild was originally founded in the thirteenth century, at the church of the Carmini, in the *sestiere* of Dorsoduro. In 1454, however, the guildsmen chose to transfer their meeting place across the Grand Canal, to Campo Santo Stefano in the *sestiere* of San Marco, a location which would appear to have been equally convenient for both the caulkers' community on the Giudecca and that in Castello. With the decline of the former group, however, it was decided to move the *scuola* again, first to San Francesco della Vigna, and finally, in 1684, the caulkers settled down for good in the parish church of San Martino, directly across from the Arsenal walls. The *scuola* of the oarmakers traced a similar, if somewhat shorter route drawn by the increasing concentration of the city's oarmakers around the Arsenal; since the shipwrights' *scuola* had been founded already fairly close to the Arsenal, at Santi Giovanni e Paolo, it alone remained fixed throughout its life (see map 3.1).[18]

While other enclaves of shipbuilders were diminishing in Venice, the arsenalotti community around the Arsenal was growing with a corresponding vigor, even in the face of two particularly devastating plagues in 1576–77 and 1630–31. The latter epidemic struck the Arsenal district especially hard: the overall population of the four parishes dropped by two-fifths, and the *parocco* of Santa Ternità listed over one-fifth of the houses in his parish as empty in 1633. Nevertheless, an impressive number of shipbuilders from elsewhere in the city and Lagoon soon poured back into the area. In 1624, 549 arsenalotti families had lived in the four parishes of Santa Ternità, San Martino, San Biagio, and San Pietro in Castello; immediately after the plague, this had dropped to just 390 households, but only nine years later the arsenalotti community had grown back to 688 resident families, an increase of nearly 20 percent from the pre-plague figure.[19]

The census of 1642 provides a good index of the extent and relative importance of the arsenalotti in these four parishes. Their households consisted of roughly 3,200 family members, including around 855 working-age men (that is, over eighteen), almost all of whom were probably enrolled with the Arsenal. With the exception of the diminishing enclave of caulkers on the Giudecca, these households were by 1642 the only significant community of shipbuilders left in Venice, very likely accounting for as many as 80–90 percent of the enrolled masters of the Arsenal.[20] Such a high concentration also made arsenalotti a dominant occupational group in each of these parishes, representing as they did 11 percent of the *popolani* households in Santa Ternità, 23 percent in San Biasio and San Martino, and nearly 40 percent in San Pietro (see maps 3.1 and 3.2).[21]

The dominance of the Arsenal in this district was even stronger than these percentages would indicate, however, for many other *popolani* who lived there also found work in the state shipyards. Thus, in Santa Ternità in 1642 there was a colony of eighteen sawyers (*siegadori*) and their families, mostly immigrants from Bergamo or Trento who made their living in the sawpits of the Arsenal. In the parishes of San Martino and San Biasio were quartered fifty porters (*fachini*) who lived in two large, barracks-like houses and who served as laborers in the Arsenal during the daytime and as a fire-fighting force at night.[22] In San Pietro parish there were to be found 171 households headed by sailors (*marineri*) in 1642; rather than earn their living at sea, many of these men worked full-time in the Arsenal launching or moving galleys. The parish of San Pietro di Castello was in fact the heart of the city's nautical community, for in it there flourished every sort of craft connected with ships and the sea, with nearly 60 percent of the resident *popolani* families there working as arsenalotti, ropemakers, sailors, sawyers, porters, boatmen, private shipbuilders (*squeraroli*), pilots (*peoti*), and ships captains, not to mention hundreds of apprentices in the process of mastering these same trades.[23]

The arsenalotti had an especially strong attachment for their local neighborhoods and for each other, ties which gave their community the resilience it needed to weather the losses of warfare and the plague. In many ways, arsenalotti were artisans set apart from the world of Venetian workers. They were said to have their own private jargon, a *"linguaggio arsenalesco"* which marked them out in a crowd as distinctive residents of the Arsenal district; as indeed so did the long pigtails which they habitually wore.[24] In their travels around Venice and its empire, arsenalotti usually preferred to stick together in their own groups, to the extent that men from one small neighborhood of the district might still keep close company with one another even while serving in a distant outpost like Corfù.[25]

It thus comes as no surprise that the residents of the arsenalotti community also tended to marry within the limited confines of their own geographic community. Arsenalotti sons and daughters in fact showed a very high degree of marriage endogamy, evidently having

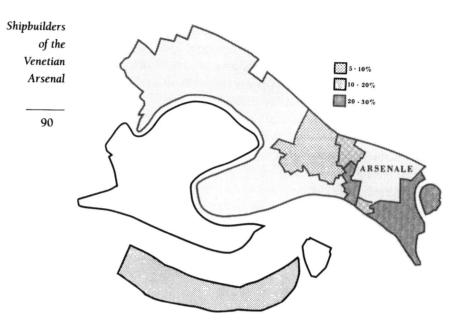

Map 3.1. Distribution of arsenalotti households in Venice in 1624

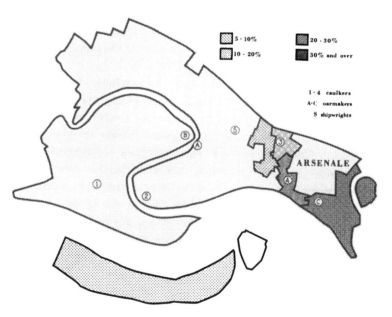

Map 3.2. Distribution of arsenalotti households in Venice in 1642 and movement of Arsenal *scuole picciole,* 1300–1700

little interest in seeking a spouse beyond the boundaries of their parish or in many cases even from much further away than their own street.[26] Shipbuilders living in the moderate-sized parish of San Martino (441 *popolani* households, or roughly 2,000 residents in 1642) managed to wed within the parish boundaries about 46 percent of the time during the mid-seventeenth century; nearly a third of all their marriages took place between men and women living on the same street or campo. In the much larger and more remote parish of San Pietro di Castello their endogamy rate ran still higher: perhaps as high as 65 percent, although the available evidence is too incomplete to fully judge.[27]

Profile of a Company Town

By the mid-1600s, the on-going consolidation of the arsenalotti community had given the four parishes adjoining the Arsenal a sufficiently strong social and economic conformity that it is reasonable to deal with them together as a distinct zone in the city. This "Arsenal zone" was demographically one of Venice's most distinctive areas; its anomalous features can perhaps best be seen by comparing these four parishes with other, nearby parish clusters that also shared the administrative district *(sestiere)* of Castello.

Admittedly, using parishes as units of social analysis has not met with much acceptance among scholars of Republican Venice. The city has generally been presumed to have been too uniform socially, and its seventy-six parishes have been dismissed as little more than administrative abstractions, both too small and too arbitrary to serve as useful units of social research. Nevertheless, the Venetians themselves relied almost exclusively on the parish as their basic unit for tax and census purposes, with the result that this imperfect abstraction still remains one of the primary sources for any quantitative study of the city. Fortunately, when parishes are treated in groups, rather than individually, they can be made to describe a kind of Venetian mosaic, one which highlights the demographic and economic variety flourishing under the surface uniformity of the city. For most Venetian *popolani*, life would have been largely played out just within the confines of one such enclave or another, like so many urban villages each with its own special character and its particular dense webs of social, economic, and occupational networks bound together by the limits of daily, personal interactions.[28]

From the three surviving seventeenth-century parish household censuses of Castello and the district's 1661 tax *decime,* there is

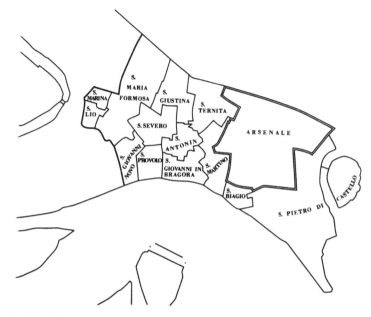

Map 3.3. The parishes of the *sestiere* of Castello

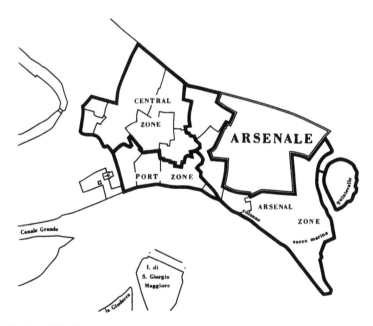

Map 3.4. The three zones of the *sestiere* of Castello

enough information on occupations, family structure, and property ownership to show that the *sestiere* in fact broke down into three zones, each with its own special and distinctive characteristics. Besides the Arsenal district, there was also a well-defined "port zone" in Castello, that of the three parishes of San Giovanni Novo, San Provolo, and San Giovanni in Bragora, along with a piece of the waterfront area of San Martino parish. The remaining parishes of the *sestiere*—Santa Maria Formosa, San Severo, Santa Giustina, Sant'Antonio, Santa Marina, and San Lio—were characterized by the mixed population and economy more typical of the urban center, and indeed had more in common demographically with other parishes near the Rialto and Piazza San Marco than with the more specialized and peripheral zones of Castello itself. Thus, it is convenient to consider these six parishes as part of Venice's "central zone," and as an area that can provide a standard of comparison with the port and Arsenal zones (see maps 3.3 and 3.4).[29]

By their very structure, the *anagrafi dei piovani* provide an immediate means of comparison between the city's zones, since in printing up the census forms the state divided the lay population of each parish into the three categories of *nobili, cittadini,* and *artefici.* This last category of *artefici* (that is, *popolani*) accounted for about 77 percent of the Venetian population overall, and indeed the six central parishes of Castello had only slightly more than this figure, with an average of around 79 percent of all households occupied by *popolani*. In the port zone the frequency of *popolani* households jumped to 88 percent, however, and it was still higher in the Arsenal district, where each of the four parishes had over 90 percent *popolani* households. Such a figure was typical of what Beltrami has termed the "peripheral zone" of the city, and indeed was only matched by the percentage of *popolani* households on the relatively remote islands of the Giudecca (Santa Eufemia parish). This concentration of worker households (or rather the absence of patrician families, whether noble or *cittadini*), was in marked contrast with the central zone of the city, where all social classes tended to intermingle.[30]

The Arsenal zone was thus a worker community with a high degree of social homogeneity, a feature which was reinforced by its relative scarcity of foreigners. Not surprisingly, foreigners were fairly common in a trading center such as Venice. With their varied cultural backgrounds and the links which they maintained with wider, international networks, exotic visitors and residents were very much a part of the city's social landscape, giving it much of its worldly and cosmopolitan air. In 1642, parish priests had noted 325 such *forestieri* living among 4,318 *popolani* households in the *sestiere* of Castello; they also wrote in 140 household heads as having foreign antecedents, presumably using names such as *Dimitri grego, Zuan francese,* or *Anzola schiavona* when unable to identify the principal tenant as they did with most Venetians, by father or guild occupation.[31] On the average, resident foreigners were to be found in Castello at about one for every nine *popolani* households, the ratio generally maintained in the central parishes of the *sestiere,* although reaching as high as one in every five hearths in the parish of San Severo, where large Greek and Armenian colonies had established themselves.[32] As might be expected, a high incidence of foreigners was one of the main distinguishing features of the port zone: they averaged no fewer than one for every 2.5 *popolani* households. Only a few streets away and closer to the Arsenal, however, foreigners turn out to have been quite scarce; in San Pietro the census of 1642 recorded just twenty-seven individuals scattered about the entire parish, only one for every forty-eight households.

Earlier Venice's shipbuilding industry had been noticeably more cosmopolitan: during most of the 1400s and 1500s, foreign nationals as well as various Greeks and Dalmatians from the Empire had been among the most important shipwrights and designers in both the Arsenal and the city's private shipyards. The decline of foreign residents in the area was apparently spurred by an increasing xenophobia on the part of the state (and possibly the arsenalotti as well): indeed, by the seventeenth century every effort was being made to keep the shipbuilding community as purely Venetian as possible, on the assumption that, "as natives of Venice they are more inclined toward love of their fatherland."[33] The Council of Ten kept a close watch over both its shipyards and the community which surrounded them: sabotage was always a possibility and foreigners found in the vicinity of the shipyards were bound to fall under suspicion. By edict of the Senate, those who could visit the shipyards were restricted: Jews, Jesuits, Capucins, and third-order religious (*romiti*) were banned altogether, and only those foreign visitors who had received the necessary permission (*licentia*) to visit the Arsenal were likely to be seen in the surrounding district.[34]

Many of the foreigners or transients in Venice preferred to stay where lodging and food were available and cheap, and since these outsiders concentrated in the port parishes, a number of rooming houses flourished there as well. Around 150 *popolani* residents of these parishes either ran inns *(locande)* or simply let rooms; the average for the district was around one rooming house for every thirteen households—a density that prefigures the Venice of today. By contrast, rooming houses were much less frequent in the central zone of the *sestieri*, evidently because transients were less common: only about one for every forty *popolani* households. But even this was high compared to the worker neighborhoods of the Arsenal district, where such accommodations were found in an average of fewer than one in every 150 *popolani* households. This may likely have been a reflection of the often relatively small and probably already overcrowded housing of the area, which would have offered scant room for foreign lodgers; it certainly reinforces the impression that the area was not one where transient outsiders were likely to be met.

Craftsmen and retail merchants were also unevenly distributed about Castello, and the district around the Arsenal was in every case less well served than were its two neighboring zones. Small shopkeepers and makers or sellers of notions, trinkets, and other items of everyday use represented only about 2–3 percent of the *popolani* households near the shipyards. By contrast, in the three most central parishes of Santa Maria Formosa, Santa Marina, and San Lio, these sorts of petty craftsmen accounted for over 10 percent of the working population; the variety of goods they produced was correspondingly greater as well. The disparity between center and periphery was even greater in what might be termed the "luxury trades" of the period. Master printers, goldsmiths, painters, musicians, and teachers made up less than 1.5 percent of the *popolani* households in the parish of San Pietro, while in central parishes such as San Lio or Santa Marina, near the commercial hub of the Rialto and the Mercerie, their numbers exceeded 15 percent of all worker families. Textile trades were also almost wholly absent from the Arsenal zone: families who made a living at carding, weaving, dying, or spinning tended to live across the Grand Canal, in the *sestieri* of Santa Croce and San Polo. What textile activity there was in Castello was concentrated instead in its central zone, where as many as one household in seven in some parishes was headed by such workers.

The absence of luxury craftsmen, with their self-conscious artistic pride and greater frequency of contact with wealthy or foreign customers, was certainly a factor in making the Arsenal zone one of the less cosmopolitan parts of the city.[35] The area's parochial character was also furthered by its shortage of shopkeepers of the more humble sort, for it had little in the way of commercial activity that might bring about economic or social contacts with the outside world. Ironically, although sailors and arsenalotti were by the seventeenth century probably among the most widely traveled of all Venetians, their community was nevertheless probably the least worldly of any of the city's neighborhoods, integrated neither into the city's own economic fabric nor into the larger marketplace of outside nations. Along with the absence of nearly every other sort of retail trade, the Arsenal zone was also poorly served by food merchants, which is surprising considering its large number of resident workers and the considerable distance which they lived from the city's major fish and produce markets at San Marco and the Rialto. Yet food merchants were nevertheless distributed about the *sestiere* of Castello in much the same pattern as were other shopkeepers: retailers and peddlers were most common in the three parishes of the port zone, where they accounted for over 15 percent of all *popolani* households; most of them probably made their living hawking ready-made food and drink to the transient crowds around the harbor. In the central parishes food sellers represented around 7 percent of all worker families, a somewhat lower figure than for the city overall in these years, but still far more than in the Arsenal zone, where they accounted for only 3.5 percent of all *popolani* households: a total of just 79 families to feed the remaining 2,167.[36]

What few shops there were in the Arsenal district tended to be clustered in one particular neighborhood. This was along the Rio di Castello, a long, straight canal which ran through the center of San Pietro parish and was flanked on both sides by *fondamenta*, or quays. Here were located sixty-eight of the eighty-six shops listed in the 1661 tax *decime* for San Pietro di Castello (another twenty-three retailers served San Biasio and San Martino parishes). Appropriately for the *popolani* character of the district, the shops offered only relatively limited goods and services. Generally, they gathered along the *fondamenta* in clusters, each group featuring more or less the same few trades and evidently aiming to serve the same simple needs of residents of the two or three alleys which were immediately adjoining. Most clusters thus included a barbershop, tailor, cobbler (*calegher*), and a dry goods seller (*marzer*); often there would also be found vendors of fruits and vegetables (*frutarioli*), sausage dealers (*luganegheri*), and the spice dealer/pharmacist (*spicier*). Rather more widely scattered along the quays were some shops not found in every cluster but which probably sought their trade from more than just a few neighboring streets: besides three bakers, there were also a pair of beef butchers *(becheri)* and a hardware dealer. Two coopers *(botteri)*, two pulley makers *(tagieri)*, a tub maker *(masteller)*, and a blacksmith *(favro)* had also set up shop on the Rio di Castello; they very likely supplied the local shipbuilding industry, producing specialized goods to meet the needs of the dozen or so private ship-yards operating nearby.[37]

The Community of the Arsenalotti

97

Thus particularly in its demographic profile, the Arsenal zone had much in common with the company town of the later Industrial era. Located on the extreme edge of the city, the district was a large residential expanse of inexpensive, modest dwellings occupied by a socially and occupationally homogeneous population. Peripheral to the Venetian cityscape, resident worker families were also poorly furnished with most essential retail services. With the exception of the double *fondamenta* on either side of the Rio di Castello, the four parishes had none of the busy commercial shopping streets, or *sali-zade,* where most Venetians normally did their business and shop-ping.[38] Few retailers troubled to establish themselves in this periph-eral corner of the city despite its dense population, a good indication of the relative poverty of the area: certainly artisans in the luxury trades of Venice could expect little custom in a district which was both heavily inhabited by *popolani* and only infrequently visited by wealthy foreigners.

The Arsenal zone's peripheral location suggests another reason why such shopkeepers as retail food sellers should be in short supply. Since the district lay at the edge of the city, a good deal more vacant and exploitable land was at hand than in the central parishes of the city. Indeed, a large number of residents in San Pietro parish (seventy-two in 1624) listed their occupation in the censuses as "market gardener" *(hortolan),* and evidently were able to scratch out a living growing vegetables either in the waste lands out past the Secco Marina (in the so-called Swamp of Saint Anthony: the *paluo di Sant'Antonio),* or on adjacent islands of Lido, Vignole, or San Erasmo. A certain amount of their produce they no doubt sold di-rectly to their neighbors, tying up their open boats *(peote* and *cao-line)* at the quays in San Pietro parish to carry out their business (as they still do today); such producer-retailers may well have ac-counted for a good share of local grocery sales, helping to explain why so few retail food shops appear in the censuses.

Yet the Arsenal itself was also almost certainly a major factor in shaping the commercial climate for small retailers in the community. The fact that two Arsenal supervisors were granted concessions to sell cheese, bread, and preserved fish to the masters and their families could hardly have encouraged other food retailers to set up shop nearby. Bakers were indeed rather less common around the Arsenal than elsewhere in the *sestiere* of Castello: in 1642 there averaged only one baker for every 185 *popolani* households in San Pietro parish, compared to one in 103 households in the central parishes of Santa Marina and San Lio, or one in every 40 households in the three port parishes.[39] It was much the same with cheese sellers (*casaroli*), except that there were none at all doing business near the Arsenal. The state also distributed as much as 6,000 liters of watered wine to its shipbuilders daily, unquestionably a factor in the stunted local retail wine trade. In all of San Pietro parish there were in fact only four wine dealers and a few clandestine, unlicensed taverns (*bettole*).[40] The fact that the parish also boasted four sellers of grappa, however (that is, *acqua vita*)—compared with only five in all the rest of Castello—seemingly indicates that the alcohol distributed by the Arsenal hardly made shipbuilders tired of drinking, but only gave them a taste for something stronger than wine.

The Arsenal wine ration was considered necessary both to make masters more energetic at their work and to produce a thirst-slaking beverage which would be safer to drink than straight water.[41] The bread and cheese concessions in the Campo dell'Arsenale were also justified on practical grounds, as a matter of convenience for the workers; in awarding them, the Patroni were careful to specify that the sellers could only offer foods "of the usual quality and prices, subject to our inspection."[42] It thus appears that while the state was running something of a company store for its workers' food needs, it was motivated by paternalistic instincts rather than a desire to profit from its captive market of isolated shipbuilders. Although perhaps quite agreeable to many shipbuilders themselves, such policies would likely have had negative long-term effects on the masters' freedom of action. The receipt of their daily necessities from the state was just another connection of dependence tying the shipbuilders to a government that trained, employed, housed, and pensioned many of them. At the same time, this ability to buy or receive their food and wine from the Arsenal only furthered a relative isolation as a community from the rest of the city's artisan society and public marketplaces.

Private Wealth

To what extent should the worker community around the Arsenal be considered one of the "poor" parts of the city? Many artisans were of course quite impoverished, even in a wealthy city such as Venice. Thus has Braudel judged the lot of preindustrial artisans generally, and indeed, such has been the conclusion of several modern historians of Venice after examining the personal death inventories (giudici di petizioni inventari) of many of the city's workers. Judging by the few goods they had piled up over the years, most of these workers had passed their lives on the edge of subsistence: their small dwellings typically yielded for the notary's record little more than a few rickety pieces of furniture, battered pots, and old pine trunks with their collection of rags and old clothes of dubious value—"strazze da niente," according to one inventory.[43]

With over 90 percent popolani households, the parishes in the Arsenal district would certainly then have been poorer overall than areas where patricians were more in evidence. Poverty in the community was indeed furthered by the state itself, and not simply through its policies which discouraged tradesmen settling in the area. As land beyond the Secco Marina was being reclaimed during the sixteenth century, the government established a number of charitable houses and hospedali there as well for the city's indigent. These ranged from the massive Case di marinarezza (more popularly known as the Colonne), with sixty apartments overlooking the Bacino of San Marco, to several blocks of twenty-five to thirty-five charitable dwellings which the Procuratia di citra operated in various parts of San Pietro parish. Here retired sailors, elderly arsenalotti (as long as they had made at least one complete voyage as far as Corfù), or their poor female relatives could have lodging for previous service (per merito) or for charity (per l'amor di Dio) and live out their days on slender pensions.[44] The government was particularly interested that the area develop as a haven for retired sailors and shipbuilders, to the extent that retired seamen who lived in other public housing in the sestiere of Cannaregio were actively encouraged to move over nearer to the Arsenal.[45]

Under these circumstances, it would be reasonable to expect the Arsenal district to be an especially poor part of the city, and indeed, this has long been the consensus of both popular and scholarly traditions in Venice.[46] Yet there are also numerous indications that the arsenalotti themselves—who were after all the social and economic mainstay of the community—often enjoyed far more than a life of bare subsistence and as individual workers could in fact be quite well off. What few remaining arsenalotti death inventories survive indicate that when notaries opened up shipbuilders' wooden trunks and sea chests, they found extensive collections—indeed, hoards—of material goods. A shipwright named Antonio Trivisan of the Giudecca left behind six pine trunks containing eighteen shirts, three pairs of sheets, four paintings, and twenty-four plates when he died in 1635. Another inventory describes the possessions of one Alvise, an oarmaker of the Arsenal, who lived on the Corte Nova in San Pietro parish. Clearly better off than Trivisan, when Alvise died in 1633, he left to his widow six trunks containing no fewer than forty-three shirts, twenty-five sheets, sixty-three assorted table cloths or napkins ("tovaglioli di diverse sorte"), and fifty-three handkerchiefs, along with eighteen chairs, a table, two bedsteads, seventeen pictures, and 105 pewter plates.[47]

Far more numerous than the half dozen inventories are the surviving wills of shipbuilders and their wives and daughters: these also show the arsenalotti living and dying in the midst of personal worlds filled with material goods. Their wills describe in particular detail the variety of furniture in their households, which generally included a bed (or sometimes two), usually completely equipped with a frame *(littiera)*, two mattresses *(stramazze* and *pagliarizzo)*, a feather cover *(letto di piuma)*, sheets, bolster *(capezzale)*, bedspread *(coltro)*, and a variety of large and small pillows *(cussini)*. Most shipbuilders also had a generous collection of kitchen goods to leave behind, including as many as several dozen pots and pans, numerous fire tools, and various vases and buckets. Being Venetians, it is not altogether surprising that some also had forks and spoons of silver or pewter, although this was at a time when the fork was still almost unknown among the north European gentry.[48]

Furthermore, many arsenalotti seem to have been well enough supplied with ready cash. Their wills often include large bequests of coin or state bonds, left either to survivors or for the care of their own soul. When Arsenal appraiser Andrea di Zuane Chiodi died in 1678, he had 1,100 ducats invested with the *Ufficio del Sal* and another 100 left over to give to the church of San Martino for masses for his soul. Likewise, the caulker Giacomo di Nicolò died in 1647 with 800 ducats invested in a state fund at the *Zecca* ("500 ducats at 5 percent and 300 at 7 percent").[49]

The extent of the shipbuilders' liquid wealth is also revealed in other ways. As already noted, many were able to produce sums equivalent to several times their yearly wages to buy a position in the Arsenal management: most offices were auctioned for around 150 ducats, but at least one ordinary shipbuilder managed to come up with 800 ducats in cash to buy himself an especially desirable post.[50] Furthermore, arsenalotti families were regularly able to produce similar sums (although only with some difficulty, according to their petitions) in order to free male relatives who had been enslaved by the Turks: ransoms of 300 ducats or more were typically demanded for a shipbuilder's freedom, and although there were local *scuole* and *hospedali* dedicated to raising ransom money, these rarely paid everything.[51] Dowries were also customarily given by arsenalotti to their marrying daughters, and here too it would seem that shipbuilders had the available wealth when it was necessary. As a rule, of course, the dowries exchanged between most *popolani* families or among the poorer *cittadini* were not enormous, having grown relatively slowly into the seventeenth century and escaping the sorts of social pressures that had swollen patrician dowries to 10,000 or more ducats.[52] Nevertheless, the dowries paid by arsenalotti for their daughters were certainly substantial in comparison to the sort of income these workers could expect from the shipyards. Ordinary masters, whose yearly wages and bonuses would have rarely amounted to more than 90 ducats, still managed to come up with dowries averaging around 200 ducats. As befit their greater wealth and higher status in the community, top managers in the shipyards could pay much more: 400 ducats seems to have been fairly typical.[53] By way of comparison, when the Venetian *Scuole grandi* awarded charitable dowries to orphan or indigent girls of *cittadini* families, just 15–25 ducats was considered sufficient to secure them a suitable husband; poor artisan-class girls could expect the *Scuole* to give them only half as much.[54]

These substantial dowries consisted not only of cash, but also of goods, and indeed, it was quite likely that the hoards of household items which shipbuilders and their wives laid by in their family trunks were destined for just this use. Thus, when the caulker Tomaso di Alvise left to his daughter Calidonia fifty-eight men's and women's shirts (twelve of which were still new) along with forty-three assorted tablecloths ("of different sorts, small and large, with lace and without"), and a large collection of fur cloaks and skirts of expensive materials, he was passing along what had probably once been his own wife's trousseau; it would be his daughter's to pass on in her turn, for fashions among workers changed only slowly. Likewise, when Angela, wife of the shipwright Zorzi di Iseppo, willed to her daughter her bed complete with changes of sheets and bedding, along with six women's shirts ("of the best that I have: delle migliori che io habbia"), six aprons, and eighteen tablecloths, she would have been leaving a trove of family goods which she had received as a girl and increased with her own needlework throughout her life.[55]

Such hoards of material goods also served arsenalotti as a kind of bank account, an insurance against possible sickness or personal disaster. Unlike cash, material wealth was not eroded by inflation, and the fairly high cost and resale value of items such as clothing insured they could be sold or pawned for a substantial return: a pair of sheets could be given as the barter equivalent of 4 scudi, or around sixteen days' wages at the Arsenal; a good man's shirt was worth about 4 lire, or two days' work. Hoards like that of the oarmaker Alvise noted above could thus be worth several hundred ducats, but trips to the used-clothing dealer (*strazzarol*) were not made lightly. The wives of five caulkers, whose husbands (all brothers) had been imprisoned, lamented in a petition that losing their breadwinners would soon force them to start liquidating their family possessions; nevertheless, they pronounced themselves ready to "sell the best that we have," if that would pay a fine sufficient for their husbands' release.[56]

The ability of arsenalotti to pile up such quantities of cash and goods is more remarkable in the light of the almost inflexible wages on which they were kept by the state. Long-term inflation steadily eroded the buying power of the fixed Arsenal pay and even when their wage maximum was nearly doubled from 24 soldi to 40 in the 1580s, it could hardly compensate for an even greater rise in the prices of grain and other staples during the same period.[57] Indeed, even after 1600, when the price of grain had finally begun to level out, the politics of baking in the city continued to drive up bread prices, forcing artisans to keep on paying higher prices for their bread.[58] The Arsenal 24-soldi wage maximum in the 1570s was typically worth the equivalent of around 4.2 kilos of white bread; fifty years later, the 40-soldi maximum could buy only 3.1 kilos.

Trapped between rigid wages and surging inflation, those arsenalotti who did not choose to desert their craft altogether had only a few options, if they hoped to pile up the hoards of cash and possessions that would serve them to buy offices or dower their daughters. One option, as will be seen, was to take advantage of various special paid duties about the city and Empire which the state made available only to shipbuilders, and which allowed many masters to collect extra pay for both nights and holidays. Workers could also hope to pocket the slender wages paid to their sons apprenticed at the shipyards or the earnings of their wives and daughters.

Nevertheless, it was still necessary for arsenalotti families to be extremely frugal. Beef *(manzo)* at 18 soldi a kilo was probably rare at a shipbuilder's table; capons, costing 30 soldi apiece, were no doubt almost unknown. Instead, arsenalotti, like most Venetian workers and indeed many patricians, satisfied themselves with fish: usually dried *(salumi)* or salted; when it was fresh fish, it was most often the heavily flavored *pesci azzuri* such as mackerel (2 soldi apiece) or sardines (8 soldi per kilo). Even bread, although constantly in demand by Venetian workers, was often replaced by wheat or cornmeal mush *(polenta),* supplemented with an onion or a few olives.[59]

The resulting frugal diet was, not surprisingly, much like Venetian popular fare today. Hardly luxurious, it would have nevertheless been sufficient to provide shipbuilders with a minimum supply of daily calories, especially when supplemented with the additional liter or two of wine allotted by the Arsenal. Most important, it would have been affordable, representing only a third of the 29 or so soldi per day that the Arsenal 40-soldi maximum amounted to when averaged out over the month (see table 3.1).

Frugality also meant restricted housing, and most arsenalotti appear to have lived in fairly cramped and shabby circumstances; indeed, Arsenal masters as a group paid less for the homes they rented than almost any other artisans in Venice. In 1661, over a quarter of the shipbuilders living in San Pietro parish paid rent of 8 ducats or less per year; by the standards of the times this almost certainly meant no more than a single room with perhaps a tiny kitchen (or a wooden shack in neighborhoods like the Secco Marina).[60] Many of these arsenalotti could of course afford no better, especially those beginning masters who would be paid only 24 soldi per workday for their first six years at the shipyards. Yet not all those who lived in only one or two rooms were impoverished. Antonio Trivisan and Alvise, whose inventories have already been noted, lived in just one and two rooms respectively; the caulker Francesco di Antonio of Santa Ternità parish, whose goods were inventoried in 1615, also had lived in a single room, which he had filled with a complete bed and three trunks packed with a hoard of clothes, linens, rags, and kitchenware.[61] Such shipbuilders would seem to have been less interested in renting comfortable housing than in maintaining or extending their material wealth.

Probably the most important factor in shipbuilders' ability to pile up wealth, however, lay in their right to continue receiving their wages for as long as they were physically able to show up at the Arsenal. Having reached the end of their active working lives, most Venetian artisans could only look forward to living on the slender charity of their guilds and would thus be forced to start pawning and selling the goods they had acquired over a lifetime. Thus, when the sea captain Zorzi di Bortolo fell on hard times, he was reduced to an all-too familiar state where "the tightness of life forced me to sell even my own bed and clothes to survive."[62] Shipbuilders who had kept up their registration with the Arsenal could instead continue collecting their 40 soldi plus bonuses per workday into their seventies or eighties, well past the time they could have done paying work on the outside. Out of sixty-two arsenalotti from San Martino parish who died in the 1660s, twenty-six were over seventy at the time of death; no fewer than fourteen were over eighty.[63] When these workers finally died, they would not have done so in a bare room with only a few *strazze da niente*, but with the possessions of a lifetime still intact to will to their heirs.

Arsenalotti hoards of material goods and cash were thus the product of both individual and generational efforts, and a good indicator of the social stability that the Arsenal itself made possible in their community. Work for the state may not have paid well, but it

Table 3.1 Sample Venetian Workers' Diet, ca. 1650

Item	Amount	Calories	Cost (soldi/denari)
Polenta	700 grams	ca. 1,500	5/5
Wine	0.7 liter	ca. 450	2/3
5 sardines	250 grams	ca. 400	1/9
Onion	100 grams	ca. 30	(—)/3
		ca. 2,500	9/8

Note: This sample diet modeled on that drawn up by Pinto, "Personable, balie, e salariati dell'Ospedale di San Gallo," 156–59.

did pay consistently, and what one generation was able to retain, it could pass on for the benefit of the next. For every young master who, "for the little money was not able to keep coming, but had to abandon the Arsenal," there were many others who would be able to maintain themselves in spite of their meagre starting pay, through the inheritance which their father or grandfather had been able to sustain through years of steady work into their seventies or eighties.[64]

The Role of Women

It is worth considering the position of women in the arsenalotti community at some length, partly because they were a distinctive part of local shipbuilding society, but also since to do so helps further explore the roles of women generally among urban, preindustrial workers. Although the Arsenal workforce was overwhelmingly male, adult women were in fact the dominant demographic force near the shipyards, outnumbering men there to a notable degree. The household censuses of the period show that on the average there lived around 128 adult women (that is, over eighteen years old) in the four Arsenal parishes for every 100 adult men. By contrast, there were only 102 adult women for every 100 men in the central zone in that year, while the imbalance was reversed in the port zone, with 108 adult men for every 100 women.[65] In actual numbers, this imbalance translated into around 580 more individual adult women than men in 1642, equal to about 12 percent of the community's roughly 5,100 adults. For contemporaries, this local excess of women must have seemed even greater than such figures would indicate, considering that many male household heads were regularly, if temporarily, absent from the district, although still counted in the census. Many of these were sailors (around 13–17 percent in San Pietro parish), but even more were arsenalotti sent abroad to serve the state aboard the galleys they had helped to build. In 1629, out of a total of 1,320 enrolled shipbuilders, 490 (or 37 percent) were away at sea; in 1645, the percentage was about the same—516 out of 1,366 masters—but with the Candia War, which began that year, over half the arsenalotti would be sent out with the fleet.[66]

The departure of so many shipbuilders and sailors to face the dangers of service at sea not only increased the local ratio of women to men, but also contributed to the abundance of households headed by widows *(vedoe)* in the community. Overall in Castello, females headed households about 21 percent of the time, but those who did so in the Arsenal district were far more likely to be widows than in the other two zones. In San Pietro parish households headed by widows outnumbered those run by nonwidowed women by more than three to one, while around the port this ratio was likely to be reversed, as in the parish of San Giovanni in Bragora, where twenty-six households were headed by widows and sixty by other women. This certainly was not simple coincidence, for in the sea duty it demanded of its workers the Arsenal virtually manufactured widows: with every winter in which the state sent two dozen or so shipbuilders out to refit the fleet, it could be expected that four or five of them would never return.[67]

Likewise, the very fact that so few households in the Arsenal zone were headed by nonwidowed women is also worth noting. Only a short distance away, at San Giovanni in Bragora parish, over 20 percent of the *popolani* households were headed by such women; by comparison, San Pietro di Castello had barely 5 percent. The great majority of the women in the port zone were foreigners and identified not by occupation but rather by their place of origin: "Orsetta *Trentina*," "Camilla *Bressana*," "Marietta *Pugliese*," or "Margarita *Frulana* [from Friuli]." The narrow alleys running behind the church of San Martino down to the waterfront were also crowded with women, most of whom were of Slavic or Greek origin. Most of these women lived without children; often two or three shared a house together. They were almost certainly prostitutes, as some no doubt wished to convey to their clerical census-taker when they gave him such professional-sounding names, as "Allegra" or "Fior d'Amor." A few priests elsewhere in the *sestiere* were sufficiently conscientious in conducting their census to mark down such women in their parish with an "M" (for *meretrice*); their efforts indicate that prostitution must have been one of the dominant occupations for nonwidowed women who headed their own household: eight out of eleven nonwidows in the central parish of Santa Marina (1624) and six out of nineteen in the port parish of San Giovanni Novo (1642).[68] The rarity of households headed by single women in the Arsenal zone thus would indicate that it was not an area favored by prostitutes, even though many lived very nearby. This is indeed borne out by a 1570 catalogue of Venice's 215 top prostitutes (one *scudo* and up), which indicates that in all of San Pietro parish at the time there was only one resident professional.[69] Such women may have avoided the district because of its residential nature or because it was too peripheral to promise reliable custom; in any event if the Arsenal district was not a profitable place for single women to ply the trade of prostitution, the large surplus of adult women who lived there must have made their way through other occupations.

In the household censuses can be found some traces of the kinds of work which women in the arsenalotti community did pursue, even if this certainly only represents a fraction of their actual activities. On its printed instruction sheets accompanying the census forms, the state asked the parish priests compiling the tally to list only one name and trade per artisan household, and almost inevitably they would write down that of the man in the family. Even when themselves household heads, women were only rarely identified by occupation; instead the priests were content to note their status of *vedoa,* place of origin, or simply their first name alone. With textile workers or other artisans who worked at home, the women of the family may quite likely have followed the trade listed in the census for their household, working alongside their husband or father.[70] Among arsenalotti such combined family employment was hardly possible, however, since shipbuilders did the greater part of their work in the state shipyards, rather than in household workshops: their wives and daughters certainly worked, like artisan women everywhere, but they necessarily followed occupations distinct from their male relatives.

A few women, it is true, actually found their work at the Arsenal: between twenty-five and forty women known as *vellere* worked under their own female overseer (called the *maestra di velle*), cutting out canvass for sails. In the mid-seventeenth century, they received 14 to 16 soldi per day, while their *maestra* was paid 2 additional soldi. Such a small number of seamstresses may appear woefully inadequate for the vast needs of the Arsenal (where over 4,000 yards of worn-out sails were given away yearly), but it must be remembered that most of the actual sewing of sails was carried out by several Venetian *hospedali,* which contracted with the Arsenal for the work. According to Arsenal records, another dozen or so women also worked in the shipyards as oakum rollers *(le donne stopere);* they were paid more than the sailmakers (roughly 30 soldi per day on a piecework rate) and were included on the paybooks of the regular male workforce, but were apparently less than fixed in their employment.[71] Other women pursued shipbuilding crafts outside the Arsenal. Thus, the censuses record one female oarmaker (*re-*

mera), a shipwright (*marangona*), and three women involved in the caulking trades (one *stopera* and two *filastope*, or oakum rollers). There were also a half dozen or so female sailors (*marinera*), women who quite possibly worked alongside the male sailors laboring in the Arsenal. Many of these women, like the three blacksmiths (*favre*) and three cask makers (a *cestera* and two *barilere*) in the district, had probably learned their trades while working in private shops alongside a father or brother, continuing on their own after his death.

Such women were the exception in a community dominated by the industrial presence of the Arsenal, however. Most arsenalotti wives and daughters pursued work that was completely distinct from the shipbuilding trades, especially engaging in the finer crafts as tailor (*sartora*), stationer (*cartolera*), ribbon maker (*passamanera*), rosary carver (*coronera*), musician (*sonadora*), and cobbler (*zavatera*); or as food sellers, retailing wine (*malvasia*), fruits and vegetables (*fruttarola*), biscuits (*scaletera*) and spices (*spiciera*), or running bakeries (*fornera*). Eight washerwomen (*lavandiere*) also appear as household heads in the censuses of these parishes, certainly only a fraction of all those who took in laundry. Their wages, while not especially high, could make an important addition to a shipbuilder's income.[72] Still more common was work as a serving maid (*massera*), although taking the post of live-in maid would almost certainly have meant leaving the community for one of the wealthier districts of Venice: the Arsenal district itself employed a disproportionately small number of such women.[73]

Women also frequently earned some income by renting or subletting rooms. Although the area around the shipyards was by no means as crowded with rooming houses as the port zone, the censuses of the district still show a total of forty households which at some time or other offered rooms. Of these, twenty-six were run by women: six were innkeepers, or *locandiere*, while the other twenty simply sublet rooms in their own houses. The remaining fourteen rooming houses listed a male artisan as family head, but it was more than likely the wife who saw to the rooms and lodgers while the worker pursued his craft. Six arsenalotti families also tried this method of earning extra income, and four of these were headed by sawyers. Since most sawyers in the shipyards were transient workers from the provinces of Bergamo or Trento, it is probable that the woman of the house specialized in putting up her fellow countrymen when they came to the Arsenal for seasonal employment.[74]

Clearly these household censuses can suggest only some of the variety of female occupations in the Arsenal community: in all likelihood they conceal more of women's actual work than they reveal. The clerical census takers appear to have routinely ignored much female economic activity as simply too commonplace to note down. Thus, the *anagrafi* are silent about the professional wet-nurse (*balia*), although certainly the occupation was of considerable economic importance to poorer families. For private nursing a woman could earn as much as 8 lire a month, only about two-thirds of a sail-maker's pay, but probably also less fatiguing. Public charities were an endless source of nursing income for local women, although they paid much less than private clients: the *Hospital della Pietà* could farm out as many as a thousand infants a year, giving perhaps 2 lire a month for their care. There is evidence that arsenalotti women did not consider it unusual to go to the *Hospital*—conveniently located nearby in San Giovanni in Bragora parish—and take away (*"pigliare"*) a baby for themselves to nurse.[75]

Other women worked as midwives (*levatrice*), and although only one appears in the district's censuses, many more of their names were noted in local parish baptismal records. Midwives were not only present to assist at the birth of an infant but also might put up a pregnant mother during her lying-in: parish records indicate that many arsenalotti wives actually went to their midwife's house to give birth. Inevitably, these women also frequently served as godmother (*comare*) at the baptismal ceremony, and indeed Venetians often used the word *comare* to signify both roles.

Some female occupations, however, would have remained hidden from clerical census takers because the women who practiced them were themselves aware that they were pursuing activities that were considered somewhat shady, if not actually forbidden. Records of the Holy Office indicate that the Arsenal district was one of the regions of the city particularly favored by cunning women, fortune tellers, and folk magicians: fifteen practitioners from the area were hauled before the judges of the Inquisition during the middle decades of the seventeenth century, compared with only one or two from the central zone of Castello; considering the relative disinterest in the Holy Office in such activities by this time, these unfortunate women probably represented only a small part of the total practitioners in the area. Diviners and wise women were so common in the area, according to one witness, that any outsider seeking their services just had to ask among the Greek and Slavic women who always hung around the small *campielli* behind the San Martino parish church, and he would be quickly led to the nearest and most suitable practitioner. To many Venetians, folk magic seemed more effective when performed by such foreign women, perhaps because of their cultural links to an Eastern, mystical tradition of healing and divination.[76]

It was not simply an accident that cunning women and folk healers especially flourished in this remote part of the city, for residents in the Arsenal district had particular need of their services. The three household censuses counted only five legitimate doctors *(medici)* residing in the entire area of nearly 2,500 *popolani* households (and none at all in San Pietro parish): the same number of physicians that were recorded for just the one central parish of Santa Giustina. For doctors, as for most Venetian *cittadini,* the worker district around the Arsenal would in the main have seemed too poor to bother with: they left the care of the district up to its spice dealers, who in the seventeenth century served as a kind of poor man's pharmacist, and were quite common in this part of the city.[77]

Certainly many arsenalotti could not afford the services of a physician—several complained in petitions that a doctor's cure had "ruined" them—but shipbuilders and their wives who were sick also sought out cunning women because of the special cures which they claimed to offer, cures for illnesses due to a curse or black witchcraft. Legitimate physicians were not particularly interested (or were positively unwilling) in wasting their time on the vague complaints associated with witchcraft; probably even less when they were made by simple workers.[78] In 1646, Catharina, wife of a local ship's scribe, fell sick and believed that her illness was caused by the curse of a mysterious, masked woman, a factor she was unable to get doctors to take seriously. She finally gave up on them altogether: "The doctor said that I was not sick and that I was healthy as a fish, and yet I was afflicted with so many ills [that] when the doctor went away, the desire came to me to beat my head against the walls; [since then] no other doctors have treated me."[79]

When afflicted with illnesses like Catharina's, men and women in the arsenalotti community might seek out a wise women, someone skilled in combining folk medicine and popular forms of exorcism. One of the best known of these local healers during the mid-seventeenth century was a certain Laura Malipiero, who may have been part Venetian and part Greek. From a succession of houses in

San Martino and San Biasio parishes, Laura conducted her medical and exorcist practice for nearly thirty years before she was arrested by the Holy Office in 1649 and convicted of witchcraft. She seems to have particularly treated the wives and daughters of arsenalotti and sailors from the district, although she also found her clients from among the nuns of local convents and the Jews of the Ghetto; sometimes she even went aboard the ships anchored in the harbor in her search for new patients. Her treatments apparently often relied on special oils and unguents which she enriched with incense and various herbs; this she applied to the afflicted parts of patients' bodies while reciting prayers and orations (*orationi*—or spells, according to some) designed to counteract sorcery. Laura's folk cures seem to have enjoyed some success, probably at least as much as treatments offered by established doctors: several of her patients insisted on her curative powers when they were questioned by the judges of the Holy Office. She was evidently a respected member of the community and enjoyed the friendship and protection of such important figures in local artisan society as Lunardo di Pasqualin, a timekeeper in the Arsenal.[80] Perhaps because of her relatively high status (she was also said to be the bastard granddaughter of a nobleman), she did not sell her services cheaply. Once, it is true, Laura told a sailor that he should not feel bad if he could not pay her much, "because she also cured many just for the love of God," but this was only after four visits, when the man had already given her over 14 lire: around half a month's wages. In fact, Laura seems to have been about as costly as any legitimate doctor, and a course of her treatment might effectively reduce a patient to destitution. Lucia, the wife of a sailor whom Laura had treated for a withered arm, told the Holy Office:

> In the beginning she obtained from him a half *scudo* [about 4 lire] or a quarter *scudo*, but then at the end [she got] 4 *scudi* at a time, and also took a pair of sheets for 4 *scudi* (which she gave back when she got the money), another time four swaddling cloths of white linen and six lace napkins . . . for having bought oil and similar things, for which reason [he] did not go so often to her.[81]

Local priests, themselves schooled in tridentine reform, were generally no more willing than physicians to abet patients who believed they had been bewitched. Even after a caulker's wife had confronted her local cleric with the "proof" (in the form of charms hidden in her bed) of the witchcraft which had sickened her daughter, the priest only recommended that the girl be given "some syrups" (*sciroppi*) instead of agreeing to an exorcism. Angela, the daughter of shipwright Zanetto Vettori, was also disappointed by the protection offered by the Church: believing herself to be under a curse (*essere maleficiata*), she went and had herself blessed by a priest. When this proved to be ineffectual, Angela, like the caulker's wife before her, sought out a wise woman named la Franza, who lived near the Secco Marina and was skilled in defending against such curses with a combination of religious invocations and folk medicine.[82]

The work of wise women had a darker side as well. When someone—especially a small child—appeared to be incurably ill, his parents might seek to end his suffering rather than stand by helplessly. In the district there lived a specialist in bringing such lingering illnesses to a swift but sanctified end, a small, plump old widow named Isabella. Catharina, wife of the shipwright Francesco Mili, went to her for help with their sick daughter:

> [Coming to our house and] seeing our daughter, she said, "Be happy, because your girl will go to heaven," and she put a hand above her head, saying, "In the name of the Father, the Son and the Holy Ghost . . ." signing them on her forehead . . . saying cheerfully after these words, "Your daughter will go to heaven." After which words she said to me, "If you want that she goes to heaven quickly and with less suffering, learn these words . . . [and] sign her on the forehead once, reciting them, and also sign the heart . . . beginning from the right hand and then crossing to the left foot and then begin the cross again from the left hand to the right foot" . . . [this] effectively I only did once, because she died a short time later.[83]

The judges of the Holy Office suspected that Isabella was engaged in witchcraft (*strigoneria*) rather than simple folk medicine, and indeed much of the activity of local wise women went beyond just healing the sick.[84] As part of their repertoire of folk magic, many of these same women also performed various divinations and spells to find lost objects and persons or to promote love: so an arsenalotto's daughter might visit and pay 2 lire (probably a day's wages for her father) to a wise woman to find out if the man she lived with really intended to marry her.[85] The rituals necessary for this kind of magic relied on the sacred objects and rites of the Church even more than did medical cures; it did not matter that the women who performed them had no sacerdotal legitimacy, for the powers inherent in holy objects or gestures were considered available to anyone who understood their proper manipulation. Thus, orations were chanted as part of most divination rites: to Sant'Antonio and San Erasmo for winning a boy, to San Orsola to discover the condition of a missing husband. Local wise women, passing friars of questionable credentials, and assorted charlatans all availed themselves of the magic of the Church through the imitation of priests: by chanting prayers, signing others with the cross, or kneeling before books, candles, or images. Not surprisingly, a brisk undercover trade flourished in liturgical materials such as holy oil; Laura Malipiero was once accused of bribing her parish priest's servant to steal some from his rectory.[86] One wise woman claimed that her unguents based on holy oil could fetch "un scudo d'argento" for a small vial *(ampoletina)*, a price that was justified by the oil's power: according to a friend of Laura's, a *cortegiana* named Ziliola, it had "the virtue that touching people with it caused them to fall in love, and touching the robes of judges made them absolve crimes."[87]

This minor magic can largely be seen as the way in which local wise women tried to fill the gaps where official secular or sacred authorities fell short in fulfilling popular needs, much as herbalism supplemented the work of legitimate physicians. When Venetians from other parts of the city came to San Martino or San Giovanni in Bragora looking for a wise woman to help them in recovering lost or stolen property, they presumably had already tried the police but remained unsatisfied. The services of local diviners could run high, however: one wine merchant was willing to pay the Greek woman Maddalena 20 ducats if she could locate his missing treasure.[88]

Residents of the Arsenal district had a particular need of their own that drove them to visit local diviners: the wish to discover the location and state of health of a missing relative. Many arsenalotti and sailors who were sent out of the community on state service disappeared for years or never came back; they might have been killed in the course of their hazardous voyages, been enslaved by the Turks, or just decided to desert their family. The Venetian government seems to have had only limited ability to protect or even keep track of such men: so many masters failed to come back from their overseas service that the Patroni once had to admit they had no idea how many had died or been enslaved.[89] Communications with the East were painfully slow at best, and in any event good Venetian shipbuilders were such valuable property as slaves that their captors were often unwilling to free them no matter what ransom was offered.[90] The relatives that these arsenalotti left behind could face both emotional desolation and financial hardship: wives especially might find themselves in a delicate position, unable to discover if they were widows and thus able to legally remarry, claim back a dowry, or receive a pension. The questions such women asked of their local diviners were repetitive and poignant, sometimes about a single missing family member, sometimes an entire group of lost male relatives: was he (or they) alive or dead? was he free or enslaved? had he abandoned Christianity ("si faceva turco")? Armed with magical mirrors, smoke, or even a vase filled with holy water that conjured up images of a miniature Moor ("un hometto vestito da negro giovane, con un colar al collo"), the minor sorcerers of the community attempted (at 2 or more lire per session) to give their clients the reassurances that officials of the State, the Church, and the Arsenal were apparently unable to supply.[91]

It would seem that magic and witchcraft activities around the Arsenal often took place in a surprisingly casual atmosphere, and although many arsenalotti themselves harbored a certain distrust for the supernatural, their female relatives generally approached magic with a blend of innocent curiosity and easy familiarity, treating the healers and diviners in their midst much like any other tradespeople.[92] A woman might casually stop by a neighbor's house to see if she would like to come along to a divination session and ask, as one sawyer's wife put it: "whatever I wanted . . . [such as] who liked me or disliked me, and if they had made any curses against me." Someone might also ask to borrow a friend's young daughter, should the divination formula require the prayers of a virgin; a pregnant neighbor was once persuaded to attend a session, to fulfill the necessity of having a "pagan" (that is, her unbaptized fetus) there on the premises.[93] Their statements before the Inquisitors were naturally intended to stress their own ignorance and innocence about any events tinged with witchcraft, but such testimony nevertheless reinforces an overall impression of the casual and highly social way in which folk magic was practiced in the community. One woman claimed that she had only gone to a diabolical divination thinking it was going to be a palm reading; a teenage girl said she had attended a Greek woman's occult session under the impression she had been invited in for something to eat.[94]

Underneath this surface casualness there were evidently deeper currents of public dissatisfaction and local tensions, however. Clearly, clients of wise women felt that for them such services were often their only recourse in a community where the established social system often proved to be a disappointment: where doctors failed to cure, where priests ignored signs of sorcery, where the police had no success against robberies, or where the military was unable to keep track of the men in its service. Yet local residents' beliefs in the special powers of cunning women to fulfull these semi-legitimate needs was necessarily matched by a certain fear of magic itself, and indeed many in the arsenalotti community were uneasy or frightened about falling victim to curses or the evil eye. The Arsenal district was something of a village isolated on the edge of Venice, and the tensions of close and continuous contact that could sometimes scar village life readily flourished there. Antagonisms between near neighbors might easily erupt into noisy and public witchcraft accusations: when Perina, widow of an Arsenal gang boss, caught her neighbor Regina painting a sign on her door at four in the morning, she chased the woman down the street, screaming, "Ah, witch witch, you have come to bewitch me!"[95]

Such tensions may well have been sharpened and brought into the open by the surplus of women in the Arsenal district. It would not be unreasonable, in fact, to see the presence of too many women in such a closed community as a factor behind the antagonisms that led to witchcraft accusations; in the same way, an excess of adult men has been offered as the root cause behind the episodes of violence that tore through many medieval Italian cities.[96] Antagonisms between resident women could only have been worsened by the multitude of foreign women who crowded the community on every side—not only the prostitutes and female street vendors of the San Martino and San Giovanni in Bragora waterfronts, but also the foreign wives and mistresses of arsenalotti themselves, women brought back from tours of service abroad who further increased the sexual imbalance of the community. Such women could be a real social threat to the closed arsenalotti community, with its artisans' pretensions of respectability, and they were denounced to the Holy Office as much for their foreignness as for their witchcraft, for being, in short, women "unworthy to stay in a place where honorable people live."[97]

That the women around the Arsenal could produce such tensions provides another indication of the special qualities of isolation and even xenophobia which invested the arsenalotti community. Here, the otherwise largely cosmopolitan and socially heterogeneous city of Venice became instead strikingly uniform and closed-off. In this respect, it is true, the Arsenal district bore some resemblance to other peripheral perishes, such as Santa Eufemia on the Giudecca or San Nicolò and Angelo Raffaele, center of the fishing community. Yet the enormous state shipyards in their midsts made the social world in which the shipbuilders and their families moved a truly particular one. The Arsenal not only created a zone with a uniform economic focus but also effectively discouraged any other real or regular flow of commerce and trade in its immediate vicinity: tradesmen and merchants avoided the area as much for the direct competition provided by the institution's various concessions as for an insufficiency of wealthy customers.

Even more than as an economic force, the Arsenal affected the arsenalotti community socially, particularly in its function as an imperial institution, for which purpose both shipyards and community had after all originally been brought into being. For as will be seen the workforce of the Arsenal was by tradition intimately linked to the operation and maintenance of Venice's naval empire, and the masters were far more likely to be sent out for service abroad than were other Venetian artisans or indeed than the ship's carpenters and caulkers who labored in Chatham, Marseilles, or Amsterdam. During times of war or other emergencies, as many as half of all the arsenalotti were likely to be away at sea; indeed, those who refused to go were liable to be fired or even banished.[98] The arsenalotti community thus was given an element lacking in other peripheral regions of the city, from this continual shifting of its residents abroad, whence many masters came into contact with Greek, Slavic, and Turkish populations, bringing home wives and foreign habits; others vanished entirely, leaving the community with its potentially disruptive surplus of women. In these ways, the arsenalotti community was unlike any other in the city, or indeed possibly unlike any other worker enclave in early modern Europe: at once an urban village rich in folk beliefs and superstitions, just outside of the glare of the "high" culture radiating from central Venice's palaces and *campi;* and at the same time one of the city's most imperial zones, intimately connected by experience, labor, and sufferings with such eastern outposts as Spalato, Zante, Candia, and the anchorages of the Levant. Such a community was likewise essential in giving a distinct and particular form to a worker population unlike any other in the city, for the arsenalotti considered themselves a group apart in Venice: craftsmen separated by their particular communal experience from the crowd of ordinary workers, with a superior stature that bound them intimately to one another and to the state itself.

Arsenalotti as Agents
of Disorder in Venice

Out in the city at large, the Arsenalotti enjoyed a special position among Venetian workers generally. In part, this was due to the separateness of the shipbuilder community and the Arsenal workplace; also important, as the subsequent chapter will show, were the particular civic roles which the arsenalotti were given outside the shipyards: special duties which they carried out on behalf of the state and which gave them distinctive power over other artisans. Restricted in membership and enjoying a particularly close relationship with powerful patricians, the arsenalotti thus came to enjoy a special status among *popolani*, but their privileged position in the city did not necessarily mean that the shipbuilders always comported themselves as models of civic responsibility. It would indeed seem that the masters of the Arsenal were an arrogant bunch and a particular source of trouble and disruption in the city, routinely identified with murders, smuggling, theft, and violence: with almost every sort of disruptive activity except for actual labor unrest. Thus, the Venetian shipbuilders had a dark side as a social group, a somewhat unsavory place among the Venetian *popolani* that has not generally surfaced in their histories until now. And yet, this may well have been the side of the shipbuilders' public character that was most familiar to contemporaries: that of arrogant *bravi* and thugs who basked in the reflected power of the state and the institution where they worked.

Criminality in the Arsenal

Inevitably, it was criminal activity in the Arsenal itself where shipbuilders were most often implicated. Pilfering and minor theft by workers were constant problems in the shipyards and provoked innumerable complaints by the Patroni. Such workplace crime was of course not unique to the Arsenal but a commonplace of all manufacturing, especially when production was dispersed in the "putting-out" system, where pilfering represented an inevitable part of both an employer's cost of production and a worker's extra income.[1] Whereas worker theft from private shops could be handled within guilds or by the communal magistrates, such petty crime in the Arsenal was a more sensitive matter: the goods and materiel of the shipyards were state possessions, giving their theft a treasonable overtone. This particular aspect of Arsenal pilfering was well recognized by an anonymous informant of 1640, who denounced the blacksmith Antonio Trevelin to the authorities; Trevelin, according to his betrayer, had been coming to the shipyards "only with the aim to steal some hardware and assassinate his Prince."[2]

Despite the Arsenal administrators' often expressed conviction that thieves were motivated by malicious or treasonable intent, it rather appears that Venetian shipbuilders saw a certain amount of petty larceny as one of the unspoken rights of their employment in the Arsenal: a reflection of the traditional conditions and terms under which they served the state.[3] Antique custom did in fact hold that arsenalotti, unlike the great majority of Venetian artisans, were to receive a portion of their wages in kind, and thus in a sense had rights to certain goods of their workplace. All shipbuilders could enjoy the Arsenal's daily wine ration, which effectively increased a master's pay by at least 15 percent. Other benefits in kind were more selective: some aged arsenalotti who had served at sea could expect an allotment (*peso*) of bread or ship's biscuit as a kind of pension; others whom the Patroni considered especially worthy were given a periodic donation of used, but still valuable sailcloth (*fustagne vecchie*).[4]

The distinction between goods given as wages in kind and goods that were simply taken could often be unclear, as was underscored by the Arsenal's long-standing dispute over free firewood. Arsenalotti had a traditional right to bundle up and carry off woodchips, known as *stelle,* from the construction sheds; in the medieval Arsenal this practice may well have amounted to a form of supplementary wages in kind. With the expansion of the Arsenal and its workforce, however, it became increasingly difficult for managers to supervise masters as they collected their woodchips. Thus, the suspicion increasingly spread that good wood and even possibly Arsenal hardware were being wrapped up and concealed inside the bundles of scrap; the Patroni were parsimonious enough to also worry at one point whether in taking off the scrap shipbuilders might not be using good, public twine to tie up their bundles. Fearing that the custom was too open to such abuses and concerned that masters would not leave enough wood behind for the fires used to melt pitch, the state moved as early as the mid-fifteenth century to forbid the practice of taking *stelle.*[5] The ban was reissued in 1589 and subsequently reiterated in an ever harsher form: in a 1613 edict, workers found taking firewood were being threatened with a 4-soldi reduction to their wages, but by 1665 the Patroni were promising them "the galleys, banishment, prison, and corporal punishments" if they were caught.[6]

In Venice, as in many early-modern states, such attempts to challenge popular custom with government regulation could easily arouse tenacious resistance, however, and even relatively honest artisans might prove remarkably stubborn in practicing activities that their government had declared illegal.[7] The arsenalotti's persistence in making off with wood chips was such that the Patroni were compelled to republish their 1613 edict no fewer than twenty-two times and the 1665 ruling nearly as often. It would seem that most arsenalotti simply failed to comprehend their government's yardstick of justice, remaining impervious to the notion that they were actually committing a crime. Many shipbuilders must also have felt that there were good economic reasons for continuing to carry off as much wood as possible: the value of a bundle has been estimated at around 7 soldi, or nearly a third of what many younger masters could expect to receive for a day's pay.[8] Under the circumstances it was hardly surprising that the edicts failed, for shipbuilders were largely charged with policing their own workplace and thus were in a good position to make a mockery of any regulation which they did not support. An etching of arsenalotti going home for the day published by Giacomo Franco just after the 1613 edict shows how much effect the Patroni's efforts actually had: among the departing masters

Figure 4.1. Arsenalotti leaving work from the Arsenal gate

are seen a number of shipbuilders carrying large bundles of the state's wood on their shoulders, leaving their work with perfect nonchalance (see fig. 4.1).[9]

If arsenalotti removed goods such as wine and firewood from the shipyards as part of their customary work rights, they also plainly stole other materials with the clear intention of making a criminal profit. In 1623, it was discovered that a ring of workers and laborers had hit upon a method of smuggling saltpeter from the Arsenal storehouses. A shipwright and stores supervisor named Marco di Gasparo reported how the gang made off with the valuable material:

> I . . . heard it said that there was someone who was going four or five times a day out and back from the Arsenal, and . . . saw that it was one Zamaria, who worked as a porter in the saltpeter sheds, and I went directly to him and arriving, I told him to stop. And he wanted to flee . . . [but] I got my hands on him and pulled him to the ground, and [when] I searched him, I found two sacks full of saltpeter tied inside his breeches . . . he put up a great struggle and took back one of the . . . sacks, but seeing so many people around me who doubted for my life, and not being able to recover the other sack, this fellow fled away and went where he usually did . . . to a house not far from the Arsenal, and the following night threw a large amount of saltpeter into the water.[10]

Despite their attempt to destroy the evidence, Zamaria and the *altri compreci* of his gang were soon captured and sentenced by the Patroni to be hanged in the Campo dell'Arsenale—a spot well-suited to impress other potential thieves among the arsenalotti. Bands such as Zamaria's certainly intended to sell their stolen goods to merchants or artisans in the city at large: just the one sack which Marco di Gasparo managed to recover weighed $16\frac{1}{2}$ pounds, with a market value of around a ducat and a half (three days' wages for a master) and well worth the risk in trying to smuggle it out of the Arsenal. Other materials in the shipyards might also catch the eye of organized thieves: an Arsenal appraiser once reported helping to break up a gang that specialized in stealing lead; an oarmaker wrote of uncovering a ring that was carrying off munitions, hawsers, and even small boats from the Arsenal.[11] A favorite target was the varied *ferramente* which the Arsenal produced: nails, spikes, and the variety of metal fittings in common use which were relatively small and therefore easy to smuggle out the gate.

Arsenalotti who stole such useful materials from their workplace did not necessarily expect to sell their booty, however: many either worked in private shipyards or ran their own small shops, where raw materials from the Arsenal's great storehouses would always be welcome. Such a duality of employment marks a significant difference between Venetian shipbuilders and later factory workers, who might well have stolen for profit or maliciousness, but would have had small chance to use such stolen goods themselves; for many arsenalotti the Arsenal could only have seemed a great warehouse available to supply and equip their own private enterprises.

The Patroni were long aware that the dozens of nearby small shipyards could provoke a constant leakage of valuable shipbuilding equipment such as cordage or ship's hardware; as early as the fifteenth century they had ordered the Arsenal's mark stamped on all the products of its forges and conducted periodic raids on private smithies and boatyards to catch those who trafficked in state goods. Yet the great usefulness of these ready-made fittings made the temptation to theft extremely high and insured that the pilfering would continue. A blacksmith like Antonio Trevelin could supply his private shop in the city with the Arsenal's hardware for years, forcing his young apprentices to smuggle out ironwork, and beating them when they failed to do so. After a time, Trevelin also hit upon the plan of bringing his wife Marietta along to his forge as a helper. When leaving, according to his denouncer, Signora Trevelin could hide nails and metalwork inside her clothes and still pass tranquilly out of the shipyards before the eyes of the guards, "because, since she was a woman they did not search her as they do the men."[12]

The unbounded wealth of goods to be found on every side in the Arsenal was thus a prime temptation behind acts of pilfering. Certainly no other workers in Venice were in daily contact with so much valuable material that was neither theirs nor under someone else's constant supervision. Not only were supplies often wastefully misused, but goods in the shipyards also had a way of piling up in storage sheds or in odd corners until they were practically forgotten: such caches of neglected materials, like much of the *beni publici* in the Arsenal, were state property that in the end essentially belonged to no one at all. One enterprising merchant in 1642 was allowed to poke around in the Arsenal's "various attics" and turned up an immense quantity of forgotten old arrows. He subsequently petitioned the Collegio to be allowed to carry off 50,000–60,000 of them, "o più o meno, à prezzo conveniente," refurbish them, and sell them back to the state in usable condition.[13] Clever arsenalotti might notice valuable goods which had been lost and forgotten over the centuries and try to get some reward by calling the Collegio's attention to them, but such proposals could encounter so much bureaucratic resistance that many workers may have decided that it made more sense to let the goods rot or even to steal them. A shipwright named Marin di Antonio had such an experience after overhearing the master in charge of finding lumber *(pescador de legname)* complaining to the foreman shipwright that there was no lumber suitable for the superstructure *(bacalari)* of a galley under construction. Marin, however, thought he could find some:

> I remembered that an old man had told me when I was a boy that behind the wall of the great galleys near the saw pits there was a quantity of timber. . . . I mentioned the wood in a letter [seeking a contract to reclaim it], and because of great obstacles I was constrained to present a new letter and to promise that if it was not true that I would pay the expense [of a search] on my own . . . [but then] they started to dig out lumber of every sort which served for the needs of the [Arsenal] . . . [and] which continues to be dug out.[14]

It has been argued that pilfering and theft in the Arsenal represented the same "indirect forms of resistance" that factory workers would later employ during the industrial era: like work slow-downs, a personal form of opposition to the oppression of workplace discipline.[15] The temptation to view arsenalotti pilfering as taking place in the context of a sort of rudimentary class struggle gains some logic from the conditions of discipline and regimentation under which they worked, conditions that bore some resemblance to those of the later industrial factory. Yet as this discussion of workplace theft demonstrates, the shipbuilders' tendencies toward pilfering should not be overly burdened with notions of class antagonisms, for there were clearly other factors at play in their thieving, both economic and traditional. Even the Patroni's edicts and complaints appear to recognize that the real necessity was simply to keep such claims by arsenalotti within bounds: to prevent masters from helping themselves to good wood as well as useless scraps or from carrying away wine by the tubload from the Arsenal cellars.

Far from indicating worker discontent, much of the pilfering in the Arsenal was only marginally connected with workers at all, but instead arose from the essentially preindustrial nature of the shipyards' administrative structure. With its management pervaded with venality and defined by traditions of hierarchy, network, and clientage, the Arsenal was run by bosses and administrators who were more than willing to bend the shipyards to their own purposes. Indeed, the interests of its administrators could even define what would be considered criminal within its walls: the Patroni themselves admitted that one of the reasons behind the 1613 ban against carrying off firewood was their own desire to maintain the right of patronage over this valuable commodity, giving out scraps on the appropriate ceremonial occasions to those masters whom they decided were especially deserving.[16]

As the legal owners of their offices, Arsenal managers and supervisors certainly pursued their own private interests, and sometimes this led them into plots to rob the shipyards. In their 1613 edict, the Patroni asserted that "with all these provisions [against theft] one can suspect that [only] with the assent and participation of . . . the gatekeepers, timekeepers, overseers, gang bosses, and other officials, are some woodscraps still furtively and secretly being carried home at late and unusual hours."[17] It was ruled that any worker manager caught with *stelle* in his own house faced the loss of his job, while the master who helped him in the theft could be banished for life. Since among all the Arsenal supervisors the four gatekeepers (*portoneri*) had the most discretionary power for deciding who might leave the shipyards without being searched, they were inevitably the officers most frequently accused of complicity and corruption: it became customary when arsenalotti were caught stealing Arsenal property to fine the gatekeepers who had been on duty—often more heavily than the thieves themselves.[18] Gatekeepers not only let workers get out of the Arsenal without searching them, but they also might let outsiders come in without the proper signed permission; they may have been bribed for looking the other way, but it was also true that gatekeepers were not always all at their post, making it much easier for outsiders to sneak in. Thus it happened that once when the Patroni entered the shipyards, they found milling around a large crowd of men and women who had entered the Arsenal *senza licentia*; although they tried to capture the intruders, "of them we only managed to put four in prison, most of the rest having fled and hidden themselves inside the Arsenal."[19]

Laxity and corruption were built into the Arsenal's management system, according to a succession of Patroni and Marine Secretaries, since most supervisory positions in the shipyards were actually exercised by substitutes who rented the post from the few fortunate ones who had bought them or received them from the Senate *per gratia*.[20] A substitute had little if any incentive to perform his duties conscientiously: his only reward for the work was likely to be the bribes he could solicit, and the owner of his post could dismiss him on a whim. Many of these men were of poor quality—perhaps even foreigners, the Patroni darkly hinted—and under their care almost anything might happen in the shipyards:

In the weeks [of service] of said substitutes there have been found
various thieves who were robbing the goods of the Arsenal and carrying them out, being permitted to come and go from the Arsenal at will,
without the necessary care or required inspection. . . . Said substitutes
can be convinced with some bribe to let enter anyone of evil intention
or fiendish spirit, with the worst results.[21]

The Senate refused to heed the Patroni's warnings on the negative effects of venality on Arsenal security, allowing itself to be
swayed by the essentially premodern arguments offered by the
magistrate in charge of selling government posts. These patricians
tended to see Arsenal management positions less as integral to a
manufacturing complex than as part of the state's patrimony of in-
come-generating offices; they pointed out that adhering to a merit
system would of necessity deprive of their legitimate property those
who had previously bought positions, and thus weaken the confi-
dence of potential investors for other offices in the city. The Senate
therefore advised the Patroni to replace or punish any substitute
who failed to carry out the duties of his office, a policy that promised little success when office owners had full freedom to replace a
fired substitute with another one just as bad.[22] Indeed, reports continued throughout the seventeenth century that the state shipyards
were being freely invaded by outsiders: thieves came and went with
apparent impunity; vendors managed to set up illegal taverns (*bettole*) to sell the masters meat, cheese, bread, and wine; even murderers and bandits fleeing the law made the Arsenal their lair and
lived for months at a time in the back corners of the yards.[23]

Smuggling

Arsenalotti did not limit themselves just to stealing from the
shipyards but also specialized in smuggling, a crime with which they
were especially identified during these years. Of the roughly sixty
arsenalotti who petitioned for a reduction or adjustment of a criminal sentence between 1621 and 1670, about a third had been convicted for shipping or holding contraband goods. At first sight,
shipbuilders might appear as unlikely candidates to be Venice's
smugglers, a role that should seemingly have fallen more naturally
to local boatmen, fishermen and sailors, who would have known
the tricky waters of the Lagoon. Yet there were certain factors
that would have accounted for the arsenalotti's predilection as
contrabandieri.

Nearly every Arsenal master had some form of sea experience, plus some familiarity with the medium-sized workboats *(peote)* necessary for a smuggler's trade.[24] Furthermore, the arsenalotti community—self-sufficient, separate, and in that part of Venice most accessible to the Lido and the open sea—was probably an ideal district of the city to plan and carry off smuggling operations. Finally, the Arsenal itself could be said to have helped turn the shipbuilders toward smuggling. Many who worked full time in the Arsenal would not have had the time or the training to compete for extra work in the city's private shipyards; smuggling with its irregular hours would have fit well into their free time. At the same time, arsenalotti were particularly trained to do their work in small, self-led gangs, important for smugglers, who had to carry out their business secretly while avoiding too much compromising contact with others from outside their own community. Less scrupulous shipbuilders would in any event have already been well-versed in the illicit transportation of goods, for many of them were practiced at tying up their boats late at night beneath unbarred holes or windows in the Arsenal walls and then, with the help of accomplices inside, quietly loading up and carrying off stolen state goods across the dark Lagoon.[25]

Their discipline made these squads of arsenalotti especially skilled as rowers, and indeed customs inspector Girolamo Bragadin once asserted that the local traffickers in contraband olive oil were "all of the House of the Arsenal." Rowing a smuggler's boat around the Lagoon has been called work for desperate men, some of the many "disoccupati o . . . miserabili" crowding the city who took the work simply to survive.[26] Many arsenalotti were indeed poor: younger masters especially (those who after all were the best-suited as oarsmen) were often trapped within the Arsenal's rigid scale of low wages until well into their thirties. Yet other smugglers who were arrested turned out to be mature shipbuilders, established men with families; although not exactly well off, they were not the kind of dockyard loungers who would do anything for a few lire.

Simple poverty, then, was not the only factor that pushed the arsenalotti into smuggling; indeed, on one occasion even a gang boss of the shipyards was fined as a trafficker in contraband salt.[27] More likely, in fact, just the opposite was true: smuggling was just too profitable an activity for any enterprising artisan to pass up if, like the arsenalotti, he had the means and skills to get away with it. Especially during wartime, when the custom duties of the city were raised to exceptional levels and extended to cover every conceivable staple, the opportunities were vast both for smugglers themselves and for the gangs of rowers and armed escorts whom they hired as assistants. "The pie was so big that there was a tasty slice for everyone," according to Mattozzi, "and even the crumbs must have been delicious."

Since gangs of arsenalotti busy on various assignments for the shipyards were forever in motion about the roads and canals of the city and *terraferma,* it was easy for those engaged in smuggling to explain their turning up at odd places and times. Ordinary citizens would let Arsenal workers who appeared to be carrying out public work pass by without question; only when masters who were smuggling had the bad luck to accidentally cross paths with the police did they risk discovery. Such was probably the misfortune of the shipwright Zuane Moro (known as "Bisatto," or "the Eel") when he and his companions were surprised by agents of the *Provveditori alla Sanità* while in the act of tying their *peota* up to an officially sequestered ship at Malamocco; or when the shipwright Francesco di Nadalin (called "Zampin," or "Little Feet") was reported seen "in Prassaga and other places . . . taking away wine [that was] smuggled."[28]

Some arsenalotti carried out their trafficking in small, close-knit bands, which relied on family and neighborhood connections to insure security: the caulker Giacomo Porcellotto (known as "Palvello," possibly meaning "Too little too late") did a brisk trade smuggling salt with just his son-in-law and another local master as partners.[29] Other groups were much larger and could involve several families or even an entire neighborhood. Late one winter night in 1661, a boatload of eleven arsenalotti was discovered while rowing contraband glassworks from Murano to a waiting English ship near the Lido.[30] Nine of the accused turned out to be close neighbors, living on San Pietro island in the back neighborhood known as Quintevalle, which consisted of no more than fifty worker households. Two of these *contrabandieri* were father and son, as were the other two of the band, who lived on the adjoining island.[31]

Still other arsenalotti smugglers were residents of the Giudecca (*dalla Zuecca),* like the Quintevalle an especially remote and peripheral worker district. Smuggling in such outlying zones of the city was probably something of a local tradition, nourished by neighborhood poverty, a sense of separateness, and common knowledge of the maze of local channels which spread directly out from the communities into the open Lagoon. Their involvement as *contrabandieri* reflected more than the arsenalottis' sharp eye for profit, however, for smuggling was also an important social element in the tight-knit communities in which the shipbuilders lived. Many arsenalotti were caught in the act of supplying useful contraband goods into their own district, attempting to sell illicit oil, bread, or meats to fellow residents of an area otherwise not well furnished with retail shops.[32]

Magistrates charged with suppressing illicit trafficking waged an endless war against these little enclaves of smugglers, and could be draconian in the penalties they handed out. The caulker Giacomo Porcellotto, caught smuggling salt, was given a choice between six years in the galleys or life in prison, with the confiscation of his goods to the value of 600 lire; his son-in-law Zuanbattista and confederate Bernardo Tampella dalla Zuecca had escaped, but were banned from the Republic for twenty years with an alternative of eight years in the galleys. The Quintevalle gang of glassware smugglers also all managed to flee, but the state pursued them with a vengeance: 3,000 lire were offered for the two suspected ringleaders if they were taken within the Republic, dead or alive, and 6,000 lire if captured outside; for the rest of the gang 2,000 lire were offered; should they be arrested they were to be hanged between the columns in the Piazza San Marco.[33]

Such heavy sentences not only punished the individual offenders themselves but inevitably had wider repercussions. Since most arsenalotti smugglers were concentrated in just a few neighborhoods, the banishment or imprisonment of a gang could have a painful impact on an entire community. Indeed, eight of the eleven Quintevalle smugglers eventually petitioned for an alternative to their sentences of life banishment, claiming to be the sole supporters of no fewer than fifty-four dependents. Without the benefit of their shipbuilding (and smuggling) income, possibly a quarter of the inhabitants in their neighborhood would be in danger of starving.[34] And yet the ferocity of the sentences levied against arsenalotti for these and other crimes may have been more apparent than real; they were often pronounced against criminals who were in any event in hiding or beyond the reach of the Republic. Behind their tough language, such sentences may well have served more as the basis for negotiating an outlaw's eventual return to society than as a message of public justice and retribution.

Lawless and Protected Conduct

That harsh punishments could be negotiable, especially when issued against arsenalotti criminals, was only sensible, for it would

have been of small use to the Venetian state to banish its prize shipbuilders or to throw them in prison until their health and capacity
for work were destroyed. Whatever the satisfaction of letting an especially pernicious arsenalotto criminal rot in prison, it would have
been a waste of valuable human capital, as the Senate was forced to
recognize in the years immediately after the plague of 1630–31,
when good shipbuilders were in critically short supply. Furthermore, exiling as a means of punishment was clearly a two-edged
sword, considering the number of foreign princes that would eagerly bid for a Venetian shipbuilder's services. In their petitions such
arsenalotti, even though condemned by the state, leave no doubt
that they were aware of the leverage which their skills gave them:
mentions of generous offers of employment from *principi alieni* are
not infrequent, even if masters also took pains to stress that all such
temptations were naturally spurned, no matter how lavish they may
have been.[35]

It was thus often considered politic not to risk the complete
loss of even those who had committed significant crimes, but to
offer alternative punishments, usually with the condition that a
criminal give himself up quickly. Typically the sentences offered to
condemned arsenalotti represented a conversion of actual punishment—execution, prison, the galleys, or exile—to a fine which
would be extracted from the master by having him work at reduced
pay for a certain length of time. Sometimes this meant both hardship
and dangers, as when those convicted had to serve as caulkers or
carpenters with the fleet for two or three years at half pay; on other
occasions, however, masters were permitted to do their regular tasks
in the Arsenal itself, evidently able to enjoy all the benefits of Arsenal enrollment except their full pay.[36] Even these fairly soft punishments could be cut still further if the state wanted to strike a deal
with its shipbuilders. The Quintevalle glassworks smugglers, for example, were offered, as an alternative to banishment on pain of
death, a mere year's service with the fleet: working at their usual
crafts at two-thirds their regular pay—as long as they were willing
first to tell all they knew about the case.[37]

Chronically short of both money and workers for its shipbuilding program, the state was often forced to conclude such deals with
arsenalotti to get them out of prison or back from exile. In 1636, the
Senate went so far as to offer especially attractive terms in what
amounted to a general amnesty to all arsenalotti living in exile,
promising them full pay as long as they would work for a few years

at one of the two arsenals which the Republic maintained on the island of Crete (at the cities of Candia and Canea: a reciprocal offer was made to criminal shipbuilders from Crete). The Senators expressed the hope that in this way, "the work of those people will not be lost and that they will have . . . the hope, after rendering service in a place so far away, to come back to the homeland and to their families."[38]

Very likely the Senators convinced themselves that the state was getting the better part of the bargain, since working at half pay under the discipline of the Arsenal bosses or amidst the dangers of the sea were considered hardships. Behind this, however, there may also have been the hope that the state might enjoy a supply of skilled workers who were not only cheaper but also more tractable. Dozens of masters were probably working under such conditions at any given time, and indeed, at one period the Patroni purposefully pursued a policy of procuring cheap sailmakers by recruiting women from the prisons. "So the prisoner will feel the punishment," the Patroni once wrote of the system, "and the Prince [will enjoy] the benefit."[39]

Despite's the state's notion that such sentences still represented a punishment, many arsenalotti nevertheless responded to them as if they were offers of clemency. Between 1621 and 1670, over fifty masters petitioned the Collegio either to propose such a deal or to accept the existing offer to work off their original sentence. The chance to make amends for their crimes simply by doing their normal jobs makes clear the kind of special treatment which Arsenal masters received from the state that employed them. Other criminals among the Venetian *popolani* might well be offered alternative sentences from the magistrate who condemned them, but these represented little more than a choice among evils: twenty years banishment, three years in prison, or two on the galleys as an oarsman were typical options. There were clearly dangers implicit in such leniency, however. Arsenal workers, who already saw themselves as a separate and defined elite among Venetian commoners, could only be expected to exploit the judicial double standard which their special usefullness compelled the state to grant them. Such an attitude would only have been strengthened by the knowledge that the Arsenal administration itself would back shipbuilders up should their cavalier attitudes about the law get them in trouble with other magistrates. When some arsenalotti were put in charge of running a small, state dockyard and warehouse *(tezone)* on the island of Poveglia, they apparently saw no reason not to profit from their position and set about stripping the facility of everything they could sell, including even the stone steps, window frames, and door sills. Finally, the officers of the *Provveditori alle fortezze* complained about them to the Senate, but to no avail, for the Patroni of the Arsenal immediately came to the defense of its workers (and by extension its rights to occupy the site); the ensuing struggle for jurisdiction lasted for months, during which time the fact that the arsenalotti had broken the law by looting the place was evidently forgotten.[40]

From their sense of a privileged position among Venetian workers there naturally developed an arrogance among arsenalotti that could easily lead to violence. When not at work or in their homes, young shipbuilders in particular apparently spent a good deal of time wandering about "their" community in gangs, much like the work squads which masters customarily formed for construction work in the Arsenal. Their discipline and sense of strength in numbers gave them a good excuse to look for trouble, and indeed arsenalotti were forever coming before the magistrates for taking part in brawls (*zuffe* or *brighe*): more often than not, those sentenced for murder or armed violence had committed their crimes while roaming about the district with a gang of fellow shipbuilders.[41]

Violence may well have been a customary prerogative of young arsenalotti much as it was the right of Venetian patricians: after all, the shipbuilders were an aristocracy among the city's artisans.[42] To keep their arrogance from sparking off widening circles of vendetta with neighboring artisans, the Senate had insisted in its 1636 edict that as a precondition for any alternative sentence a convicted shipbuilder had to make a formal reconciliation (*fare la pace*) with the offended party (or with his relatives if murder had been committed). This might also involve the payment of cash damages as well, but the main desire of the Senate was to insure civil peace through mutual forgiveness.[43]

The ritual act of making peace with the offended party was entrusted to an intermediary, and in this the arsenalotti seem to have enjoyed the advantage of their social position, for their connections with high-status individuals in both the shipyards and in the city at large meant that they could bring considerable pressure on the parties they had injured to agree to a reconciliation. When the shipwright Domenico di Zuane and some other arsenalotti killed an artisan named Antonio Martini in a brawl, such influence was brought to bear by his venerable father, Zuane d'Elia, who was personal assistant to the Admiral of the Arsenal. First Zuane went and persuaded Antonio's widow and family to "make a good and sincere peace" with the boy, also paying 100 ducats to them in compensation and a 600 lire fine to the state: such were the preconditions set by the Quarantia Criminal for changing a sentence of capital banishment to one of service with the fleet. But Zuane went still further, presenting the Avogaria di Comun with testimonials from the Admiral, two Arsenal foreman, and several gang bosses on his son's usefulness and his own family's centuries of service in the shipyards. Within the space of six months, Domenico's sentence was reduced again to two year's work in the Arsenal at half pay.[44]

Nowhere is the function of influence and status more evident than in the case of three arsenalotti hauled before the Quarantia Criminal for murder in 1654. On the night of August 20 of that year, three caulkers attacked and murdered a young goldsmith named Santo di Piero dei Preti as he stood about naked with some companions on the Riello bridge, having evidently just finished a swim. Bearing some grudge against Santo or perhaps simply resenting his presence in the heart of arsenalotti territory, the leader of the caulkers, one Zuane di Iseppo Bezzi, had already taken the precaution of arming himself and his companions, Alessandro Pulese and Francesco di Battista dal Zoccolo, before accosting those on the bridge. In the brawl that quickly ensued, Santo was not only stabbed to death with a knife, but Bezzi (according to the Quarantia) "showed the perversity of his heart by also wounding and stabbing another innocent person who happened to be there, and he committed these deeds intentionally, consciously, without legitimate cause, with cruel barbarity, scandal and bad example."[45]

Despite the apparent premeditation of the crime and Bezzi's vicious behavior, the Quarantia still showed some restraint in its sentence, condemning the three to either perpetual banishment, ten years in the galleys, or ten years in prison, rather than outright hanging or mutilation. Since the three were arsenalotti, however, and their victim was an ordinary artisan, the Quarantia treated the murderers as they had Zuane d'Elia's son, offering the option of serving as caulkers at half pay in the fleet for a sentence of five years.[46] Even this much lighter sentence apparently seemed too harsh to the three caulkers: in a joint petition later that year they asserted that

> we would go [to the Fleet] with the greatest speed possible, not only for the longest time possible, but to the very ends of our lives, and in

the most hazardous dangers ... [except that] I, Pulese, have a mother with three nubile sisters; I, Bezzi, a mother with a sister to marry; and I, dal Zoccolo, a father and mother of an age needing help and sustenance.

Furthermore, they pointed out to the doge that since he was already well-supplied with caulkers in the fleet, it would be profitless to risk themselves at sea when they could just as well be at home, working profitably in the Arsenal and caring for their families. Rather than serve five years with the fleet, they offered instead to pay a fine sufficient to outfit forty soldiers (perhaps 200 ducats) and to work in the Arsenal for two years at half pay.[47]

For normal artisans such a petition would have amounted to breathtaking impudence, but these three arsenalotti thugs seem to have possessed a clear recognition of their importance to the Republic and of the special treatment which they could expect as a result. Such an attitude did not endear them to their fellow artisans, who could hardly feel adequately protected by Venice's judicial system in the event of a quarrel with a gang of shipbuilders. The father of Santo, Piero dei Preti, in fact sent the Quarantia an impassioned plea to overrule the various petitions and protestations of the three caulkers who had murdered his son; he urged the magistrate to refuse any reduction of their sentence at all, but rather to remove them from the city as quickly as possible:

> These wicked assassins are seeking such conditions and delays from
> the court not for the purpose of making their case but only with
> the aim to kill me, poor, old and unhappy, or someone of my house-
> hold before they are banished, having made such bold (*brave*) and
> detestable intentions clear to various people, and thus day and night
> ... they are only waiting for the chance to do away with me and my
> relatives.[48]

Before they could expect the Senate to accept their request for reduced sentences, the three arsenalotti first had to secure a reconciliation from the parents of Santo dei Preti, something the angry and frightened couple steadfastly refused, to the point of even refusing to admit to being at home. Nevertheless, the three caulkers persisted in sending a stream of intermediaries on their behalf, who called on the couple at least twenty times: among these were four friars, three priests, two arsenalotti, and the assistant foreman of the caulkers, a *cittadino,* and the nobleman Giovanantonio di Gerolamo Zorzi. Evidently impressed by such support, which effectively testified to the three felons' respectability and local connections, the Quarantia decided to blame the failure to make peace on the stubbornness of Santo's parents. In the end it was decided that the preconditions for the caulkers' reduced sentence had been fulfilled, "as if said condition of peace had been effectively conceded by the father and mother."

As a sort of ritual atonement in cases of violence or murder against social equals, this custom of peacemaking was evidently not unusual in Venice. It could raise special difficulties when arsenalotti were involved, however. As the cases of Zuane d'Elia and Zuane Bezzi make clear, their wide social connections and high status relative to other Venetian artisans could allow even arsenalotti guilty of homicide to virtually dictate a ritual peace, and on far from equal terms. Furthermore, courts may well have been less likely to order arsenalotti to offer satisfaction to victims or their families when they were not clearly the instigators of a brawl or when it appeared to be only a small disturbance: the all too frequent minor *utori, sponte, et altre travagli* which young and aggressive gangs of masters habitually inflicted on bystanders evidently just had to be simply endured.[49]

The *Battagliole sui Ponti*

The arsenalotti also took part in public violence and disorder on a much grander scale than simple street brawls with their artisan neighbors. Almost every year throughout the seventeenth century the Arsenal masters would throw themselves with considerable enthusiasm into the so-called *battagliole sui ponti*, the "little battles of the bridges." These encounters, combinations of violent sport and pre-Carnival festival, were confrontations of enormous proportions in which workers and artisans gathered from every corner of Venice and its surrounding islands to carry on ritualized fist fights on a designated bridge in the city. On such occasions the masters of the Arsenal were especially active, and indeed the *battagliole* provided moments in which all the elements especially characteristic of arsenalotti disorder in Venice were manifested together: the self-led squads of masters, the shipbuilders' special display of group status, and their isolation relative to other Venetian artisans were all important features in how the "little battles" were structured and how they were played out.

The popularity that the *battagliole* enjoyed among all classes of Venetians has resulted in a wealth of contemporary descriptive material on the event. In particular, there survives an exhaustive, virtually year-by-year account of the encounters compiled by an anonymous seventeenth-century observer, who filled over 600 manuscript pages in his record of the *battagliole* between 1632 and 1673. The writer was educated and probably a Venetian; certainly he was an eye-witness to many of the events which he described.[50]

The *battagliole* did have much in common with the local *zuffe*: at least in terms of such ritual activity as challenges, provocations, ambushes, public displays, and vendettas, although on a very much larger scale. But in another sense the *battagliole* were celebrations, civic festivities that brought all classes and groups of the city together in a ceremony of destruction and social renewal, sweeping away in one convulsive outburst the petty tensions and rancors that had grown up in Venice's crowded alleys over the previous year. Such mock battles, often fought with sticks (*canne*) and shields, had once been a characteristic part of popular life throughout northern Italy, reflecting the intense factionalism of the medieval commune. For most Italian princely courts of the seventeenth century, such an explosive mixture of public energies had become too unacceptable and risky, however: only in Republican Venice were the public battles still played out on a regular basis.[51]

The anonymous author of *battagliole sui ponti* (which were also known as the *guerre dei pugni,* or wars of the fists) called the event "the most famous and most sought after recreation of the poor Venetian."[52] Unquestionably they were *popolani* festivities of the first order, even if many of the city's patricians were also passionate fans and supported the contests as both onlookers and organizers. The state's official attitude toward the *battagliole,* on the other hand, was somewhat more ambiguous. As a general rule the fights were considered as illegal as any riot or street brawl, yet there were many nobles who held that the event encouraged martial ardor among the Venetian people: the *battagliole* were in fact considered so representative of Venetian popular culture that the Collegio occasionally ordered the contests staged for distinguished visitors to the city.[53] Since *battagliole* often involved several thousand combatants and tens of thousands of enthusiastic onlookers, there appears to have been little the government of Venice could to control them anyway, except to wait until the popular passions had passed of their own accord. Only then might the agents of the Ten sometimes attempt to arrest the leaders of each faction, evidently concluding that no festivity which had paralyzed normal public activities for days on end should be allowed. More often than not, however, the principal leaders of the teams managed to escape the forces of the law, by hiding themselves with powerful friends or in monasteries; even those who were arrested were soon released through the intervention of patrons among the nobility.[54]

The *battagliole* represented only one (although certainly the most striking) aspect of the ancient rivalries and antagonisms traditionally maintained between the residents of the two great geographical divisions of Venice, known as the Castellani and the Nicolotti.[55] The two rival factions were not established on opposite sides of the Grand Canal, as might be expected, but instead reflected an east-west division of the city, one which was popularly held to date from the original settlement of the Rialtine islands.[56] When battles were held, they generally took place on bridges located near the border zones separating the two factions, either between the *sestieri* of Castello and Cannaregio, or between neighboring parishes within the *sestiere* of Dorsoduro (see map 4.1).

While the two camps drew their partisans from every sort of worker living within its boundaries, each was also dominated by particular artisan groups which contributed special characteristics to their side. For the Nicolotti this was the tightly knit and populous

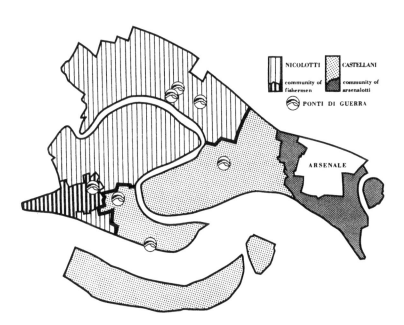

Map 4.1. The *battagliole sui ponti* in Venice in the 1600s

fishing community of the city, centering on the parishes of San Nicolò dei Mendicoli and San Angelo Raffaele; among the Castellani, leadership fell to the arsenalotti, for even though their community was far from the usual scenes of battle, the shipbuilders were the best organized and most enthusiastic participants in their faction.[57]

The Castellani and Nicolotti factions were each captained by a number of squad leaders known as *capi* and *padrini;* these commanders, who wore special cloaks as symbols of their offices, worked the year round organizing and preparing the artisan "soldiers" under their command. The *capi* were drawn from among the most powerful and agressive workers in the city and had the responsibility of leading their squads of fighters into the actual battle on the chosen bridge, while the *padrini,* by contrast, seem to have been older artisans who had proven themselves as champions in earlier *guerre,* and who served as squad leaders and tacticians both before and during the contests.[58] At the same time, each faction was able to boast its own *protettori autorevoli*—that is, noblemen or powerful commoners who patronized and promoted the *battagliole;* not only did these support their squads financially, but they would also defend them against the police of the Ten.

The season for *battagliole* in seventeenth-century Venice was the fall, and one occurred almost every year between the last days of August and the Epiphany. The initial spark for the event usually came from conflicts generated between marginal groups of youths: journeymen or *bravi* who hung about the bridges near the border zones of the two factions. Sometimes quarrels and vendettas enduring from the previous year's engagement also played a part in the initial discord, but in any event there were always enough enthusiasts on both sides who were eager for any excuse to whip up the antagonisms and tension that would set off a *battagliola.*[59] When popular excitement in the city and the public demand for a *battagliola* became insistent enough, the *capi* would decide they could safely afford to ignore the government's official ban on such disturbances and would meet to arrange the date and place for a confrontation. Usually a bridge was chosen that spanned a canal flanked by wide *fondamenta* or with nearby *campi,* so that the contestants could assemble nearby in force; the water running beneath was cleared of poles and other dangerous rubbish and the *fondamenta* might be cushioned as well with bundles of straw.[60]

At least a week was considered necessary for all the preparations for a *battagliola,* and during this time many of the journeymen of the city abandoned their shops, and the younger masters left the Arsenal in anticipation of the event.[61] On the chosen day—generally at about three in the afternoon on a Sunday or holiday—squads supplied by the various neighborhoods in the city and outlying centers or from particular guilds would converge on the designated bridge, playing fifes and drums and accompanied by crowds of their wives, children, and supporters. These "soldiers" and their partisans were decked out in the colors of their faction (red for the Nicolotti and black for the Castellani) and also carried banners and standards to identify their place of origin. When a *battagliola* was well planned and publicized, the crowds in attendance could be varied and vast: nobles and foreign visitors arrived at the scene and competed to pay as much as 10 *scudi* (70 lire) for a well-placed window over the bridge; *popolani* fans packed both the *fondamenta* and the overlooking rooftops on every side. At a contest held in 1639 at the Ponte of the Gesuati, on the Zattere, over 30,000 onlookers were said to have been present, filling the Giudecca Canal with their boats and gondolas until they reached the islands of the Giudecca on the opposite side; the roar of the crowd ("the voices, whistling, and the beating of oars on the boats") was so loud that it was said to have been heard at Fusina, on the Terraferma, and "beyond the Lido for some distance out to sea."[62]

When the two contingents had finished preparing and fortifying themselves with wine at their side's *bastione,* as many as a thousand combatants from each faction assembled on either end of the contested bridge.[63] After a spirited exchange of calls and insults between each group, their *padrini* set in motion the first stage of the *battagliola,* known as the *mostra.* In the *mostra,* individual champions from each side advanced to the wide central *piazza* at the crest of the bridge and presented themselves to the opposite faction, often challenging a specific adversary to come forth and defend his honor. Champions could be rejected by the opposing faction if they were considered unworthy to fight, as happened when the imposing but inexperienced young caulker "Toppo" ("the Stump") offered himself.[64] If the challenge was accepted, the two champions proceeded to exchange blows and punches before the assembled mob of teammates and onlookers until one or the other lost possession of the *piazza* by tumbling off into the canal below. In some *battagliole* over a hundred challenges were issued, often from the older, experienced *padrini* as well, and the *mostra* could last for hours, the more so since a faction that proved unable to find a champion for every challenge would then be scorned and ridiculed by its rival, with partisans among the audience joining enthusiastically into the insults and blows that often resulted.[65]

After the final challenge of the *mostra* had been decided, the *padrini* of each faction then gave the signal to begin the *frotta,* which made up the second and perhaps more characteristic part of the encounter. Here the intention was to gain control of the entire bridge through a mass onslaught of troops: from both sides champions who had already fought and others who had hung back rushed together for the center of the bridge, kicking, swinging, and punching wildly at their opponents until dozens or even hundreds of men had been knocked into the canal (see fig. 4.2).

Those *padrini* who were champions themselves waded into the center of the fighting, while older leaders watched from the wings, ready to call out reserve squads from their faction's headquarters behind the scenes when critical moments in the combat occurred.[66] In the end, sometimes only after several hours of wholesale punching, one side would finally give way and fall back in a rout into the adjoining streets, leaving the victors to plant their standard on the conquered territory.

Such at least were what formal outlines existed for the event. More often than not, however, neither the Castellani nor the Nicolotti were able to triumph permanently in the *frotta,* and with successive counterattacks the possession of the bridge usually changed hands repeatedly until night fell, with the contest starting up again the next day. After dark, regardless of the actual outcome, both factions routinely claimed victory and staged impromptu boat processions on the Grand Canal, displaying satirical placards at strategic border zones, and carrying out raids on each other's territory in the hope of making off with trophies.[67] Many years the *battagliole* continued for a week or more, completely disrupting the economic life of the city for much of that time. In 1632, when the Nicolotti fishermen found that their noble *protettori* would supply them with food and drink for the duration of the *battagliole,* they deserted their work entirely, with the result that for two days no fish was available at either the Rialto or San Marco markets.[68] Moreover, the *frotte* were almost inevitably marred (or enhanced, depending on one's point of view) by fighters who in a moment of anger or desperation pulled out their daggers. *Arme sfoderate* meant a rapid escalation of bloodshed; those of the opposing faction drew weapons of their own, while from the surrounding rooftops outraged and excited onlookers showered down roof tiles *(coppi)* as an expression of their disapproval. In the resulting melee, mass panic sometimes resulted, with an entire faction dissolving in disorder under an onslaught of daggers and roof tiles. In 1639, when a string of *battagliole* went on for fifteen days, over forty participants were killed; during the contest of 1634, it was reported that

> Since for two continuous hours roof tiles and rocks were flying through the air, it is not surprising that more than 100 people were injured and mistreated [and] others died . . . after some days. Nearby houses had their roofs completely stripped of tiles, and also along both *fondamenta* all the paving stones had been dug up with hoes, daggers, and hammers.[69]

The *battagliole sui ponti* may well have regularly spread considerable disorder in the seventeenth century, often paralyzing the city completely, but they also contributed toward a larger form of order, operating as a mechanism through which the Venetian *popolani*

Figure 4.2. Battagliola on the Bridge at S. Barnaba

reestablished an internal equilibrium.[70] Considering the narrow and crowded world to which the Venetian working classes were generally relegated, it is indeed somewhat surprising how rarely serious hostilities did erupt between groups of workers or between the *popolani* and their patrician rulers. Scholars such as Richard Mackenney have given the state credit for the lack of friction that might otherwise have been expected within the Venetian *popolani*: to the Republic's patrician magistrates, that is, who managed to defuse conflict situations by settling guild disputes firmly and with evenhandedness. Edward Muir and others have drawn attention to the state's crowded ceremonial calendar, which regularly served to reunite all the competing and conflicting artisans of the city in the processions and festivals that unfolded under the banner of San Marco.[71]

Some scholars have indeed portrayed the Venetian state as expert in conflict management, with the ability to transform the chaotic instincts of the mass of ordinary citizens into the formal minuets of state-controlled celebrations. But the *battagliole sui ponti* and other popular festivals indicate that Venetian workers could also perpetuate their own ritual public activities, in the form of disorders which the state had to reluctantly tolerate.[72] The author of Cicogna 3161 believed that the *popolani* of the city spontaneously started the *guerre* as a psychologically necessary release, comparing the *battagliole* to "the fevers that when they are goaded and aroused by bad humors suddenly attack a man"; he noted that *capi* and *padrini* feared for the harmony within their factions if working men were denied the outlet (*sfogo*) of a *battagliola* for too long.[73]

The *battagliole* in fact brought about an extraordinary submerging and welding together of the city's artisans: out of hundreds of otherwise powerless guilds and devotional organizations, two enormous and highly agitated factions were formed.[74] In other contexts, such excited mobs rampaging about the city could present a real threat to the established order of the state, but the energies which were released so extravagantly by the *popolani* during the *battagliole* were directed toward a rivalry whose aim was violent sport rather than violent politics.[75] It may be debatable whether the *battagliole* actually developed martial ardor among the *popolani*, but they certainly provided a safe channel for the aggressions and tensions which were regularly generated among workers in the crowded city. More effectively than either staged processions or the more spontaneous carnival celebrations, the *battagliole* provided a sense of temporary unity and violent release for the Venetian laboring classes, while at the same time directing participants' energies and attentions safely away from the Venetian political world and the elite which controlled it.

Besides displaying *popolani* aggressions and discontent away from the city's ruling order, the *battagliole sui ponti* also dissolved many of the antagonisms which flourished within the laboring classes themselves. Conflicts were inevitably generated as workers competed for the limited available wealth and privileges which Venice could bestow, or as elite artisans such as the arsenalotti exercised their dominance over those less privileged; during the *battagliole* these were effectively submerged in the citywide struggle for victory between the two great factions. Even if serious conflicts between groups within the same faction sometimes threatened to break up the teams themselves, in the unrestrained violence of the *frotta* the most persistent grudges arising from in-groups or hierarchies were soon dissolved.[76] From the experience of intense anarchy in the *frotta* there appears to have emerged, in fact, a temporary state of status-free equality and reintegration similar in nature to the "communitas" described by Victor Turner. In the model of social restructuring which Turner, Edmund Leach, and others delineate, a *liminal* period of undifferentiated community can in certain moments replace a society's normal hierarchical structures. In the *battagliole* this *liminal* period emerged with the climax of the *frotta* on the bridge, when the waves of violence dissolved normal ties, hierarchies, and antagonisms that reigned among the Venetian *popolani* throughout the year. Its effects can also be seen in the kind of festive peace that often flowered on both sides during the evenings after the fighting was over.[77]

When the actual combat had finally ended due to darkness, each faction continued to celebrate its community through parades and bonfires into the night. Various artists and craftsmen pooled their talents and creative enthusiasms and worked together to rapidly recreate and relive the events of the day through skits, placards, and satires. Indeed, even the entrenched regional antagonisms between Nicolotti and Castellani might break down as well: men from both factions could be seen in local taverns, drinking together *con somma allegria* until late at night, the victors of the day toasting the losers and teasing them with songs and recollections.[78] In any event, the *battagliola* by the very intensity of its violence made every survivor a victor: more important than winning or losing for participants were the chances it gave them to display individual prowess on a public stage. When the daily routine had finally returned and the normal order of *popolani* society was reestablished, antagonisms would be temporarily dissipated; how effectively could be measured by the number of scars and injuries which artisans proudly bore in the days that followed:

> Both sides would not so easily forget this war on the next occasion, because of the exterior signs: the scratches, bites, ruptures, missing teeth, swollen eyes, medications, and bruises that for a trophy they wore on [their] faces, with [broken] arms at the neck [that] were for some days testimony to their ardor. Their faces were like the masks of the Carnival, and people in the fish markets did not know one from the other for the changes and blackening of their faces.[79]

The arsenalotti were among the most enthusiastic participants in the *guerre dei pugni,* just as they were in both the *forze d'ercole* competitions and in ordinary street brawls. Many of the most renowned *padrini* of the Castellani faction were in fact ordinary shipbuilders during working hours, and arsenalotti usually made up the largest single contingent of participating "soldiers": in 1667, over 400 Arsenal masters joined in to fight with the 1,200-strong Castellani faction for the *battagliola* at the bridge of San Barnaba.[80] Indeed, on some occasions virtually the entire active workforce would take off from the Arsenal for a battle with their traditional rivals: of around 400 masters regularly working in the mid-1630s, fully 300 showed up to fight in the *battagliole* of 1634. So necessary was their presence to a successful encounter, that when the majority of the arsenalotti were summoned away for fleet duty at the beginning of the Candia War, the fights were called off, not to be resumed for six years.[81]

Such whole-hearted involvement by Arsenal masters in the *battagliole* is curious because it required the abandoning of much that helped define them as a particular and high-status group among Venetian workers. Even to get to the site of the encounters in Cannaregio or Dorsoduro, the shipbuilders had to traverse the city, leaving behind their familiar territory around the state shipyards where their superior strength was well recognized by others. Their exclusivity, patronage connections, and legal privileges counted for little in the *mostre:* such contests of honor in fact presupposed that on the field of combat all participants were of equal stature, regardless of their pretensions in daily life; the melees of the *frotte,* further-

more, clearly respected only fists and brute strength.[82] As participants in the *battagliole,* the arsenalotti also abandoned their normal
duties as Venice's worker militia; far from maintaining the orderly
ceremonial and institutional processes in the city as they were
charged to do, shipbuilders instead became a major and most enthusiastic source of urban disorder.

The arsenalotti's abandonment of their normal status and roles
during the *battagliole* often took on aspects of a social inversion, if
not outright parody. Indeed, the *guerre dei pugni* often had something of a pre-Carnival air about them, as many of the normal relationships between individuals and social groups were redefined into
mock-military terms, with wide zones of the city turning into bat-
tlefields and normally solid artisans and their families changed into
soldiers.[83] The arsenalotti themselves may not have always been
aware to what extent they were inverting their own social and ceremonial routines: some of the time the masters would simply have
been adopting the daily procedures they used in the Arsenal to the
special circumstances of the *battagliole.* Some of their actions are
nevertheless striking for their parodic content. Masters came to the
scene of the contest rowing a flotilla of *peote,* or work boats, blowing
on fifes and trumpets; in the prow often rode their own Admiral or
some of the major foremen, all dressed in the formal robes of their
offices. In much the same manner arsenalotti also solemnly rowed
the doge and his councilors to the Marriage of the Sea during the
Festival of the Ascension. Likewise, when a *padrino* or notable
champion of either faction was killed in the course of the contest,
the arsenalotti arrived at his funeral in force, with hundreds carrying candles and serving as an honor guard, even as they did during
ducal funerals.[84]

Although vital to Venice's security, even the Arsenal itself was
not safe from the inversions of the *battagliole.* The shipyards would
be taken over by the masters on the eve of battle, and the *capi* and
padrini of the Castellani faction, both arsenalotti and ordinary artisans, would meet within the secure walls to plot their strategies. In
setting off for the battle site the masters helped themselves to anything in the Arsenal they could carry out that might prove useful for
the encounter: poles, sticks, bells, horns, and rope, as well as sacks
of sawdust to spread on the slippery surface of the bridge; in 1639,
a gang of arsenalotti even made off with an armed sloop, or *barca
armata,* from the shipyards, and sailed their prize past the church of

San Nicolò, playing fifes and castanets ("pifari e gnachere") to taunt their enemies.[85] During the *frotte,* masters often organized themselves into small squads, as they were accustomed to do in carrying out their normal work or civic duties, and made flying attacks on the contested bridge at vital moments. After a victory for the Castellani faction, the arsenalotti—specialized and known for centuries as Venice's firefighting militia—frequently celebrated the event by lighting huge bonfires in the *campi* of their district.[86]

Quite possibly the arsenalotti welcomed the chance offered them by the *battagliole* to temporarily drop their privileged status among Venetian artisans and to more freely play the part of normal *popolani* in the city. Their inversion and parody of many of their civic and ceremonial roles would also seem to indicate a desire among shipbuilders to mock both the Arsenal where they worked and the state which employed them. Their role reversals also could well have formed a part of the carnival structure that underlay the *battagliole,* inversions on a public stage that signaled that the transitional period had begun which would eventually lead to the liminality of the *frotta.*[87]

Whatever may have lain behind the arsenalotti's so enthusiastically joining in the violence of the encounters, it could not have been a simple desire for the pleasure of reinforcing their normal social dominance by thrashing other workers on yet another occasion. Not backed by the authority of the state that they ordinarily enjoyed and armed only with their fists, Arsenal masters in fact turn out to have not been especially formidable opponents. When the season of *battagliole* came to an end each year, the Castellani faction was rather more likely to have been the loser than the victor, driven from the field of combat at least two-thirds of the time. Very likely their poor showing resulted because the most vigorous and best-trained masters were usually absent, serving with the fleet or merchant marine; regardless of their enthusiasm, the veterans and unskilled youths who remained behind would have been no match for the brawn and skillful fighting of the fishermen and weavers of the Nicolotti. The result was yet another inversion: the arsenalotti frequently would receive the thrashing they typically expected to give out to others. Indeed, even the other groups which made up the Castellani faction were perfectly willing to reject the leadership of the arsenalotti squads: men of the Giudecca and from Sant'Agnese parish (the *Gnesotti*) were quite willing to quarrel with the shipbuilders over questions of tactics and the right to lead the Castellani faction into battle or in a victory procession after a successful encounter.[88]

The Castellani's generally poor showing during the *battagliole* gave their Nicolotti opponents ample opportunity to mock them and especially to vent their feelings about the arsenalotti and their arrogant ways. Using satirical placards and songs, the Nicolotti made a point of singling out the Arsenal masters from the rest of the Castellani for special teasing and abuse; the contrast between the masters' normal distinguished status and the special humiliation of their defeats made them too tempting a target to pass up. Popular satirists who celebrated the *battagliole* produced their portraits and squibs with considerable speed, in order to capture the events of the day. The poems on their placards were filled with ribaldry and rude double meanings and lampooned broad targets which could be recognized and appreciated by everyone.[89] The Nicolotti delighted in painting placards which contained the theme of the arsenalotti in chains, as if they were galley slaves with the fleet instead of in their normal roles as ship's petty officers or commanders. Standing over them was a *padrino* of the Nicolotti, wielding a *bastone* that could have been inspired by the red staffs which the arsenalotti swung so freely on the days that they served as Venice's militiamen. An accompanying rhyme in dialect called to passersby:

> Strangers, stay your feet:
> Those bound up here are those that build the fleet,
> Who even though they resisted bowing to the Nicolotti,
> To this pass they've arrived, with Zuecca and Gnesotti;
> When you return home again,
> To everyone make it plain:
> That the Castellani, for all their pains,
> Are slaves of the Nicolotti and stay in chains![90]

The Nicolotti also used their *cartelloni* and satirical poems as a means of denouncing those arsenalotti who blatantly took advantage of their special position. On one occasion they drew up a placard effectively denouncing the shipbuilders' habit of stealing materials for their escapades from the Arsenal; mocking a failed midnight raid against a *campo* in Nicolotti territory, they wrote: "the arsenalotti with these long poles / stolen from the Arsenal (and these aren't trifles) / came to Santa Sofia to steal our Crown."[91]

High managers of the Arsenal such as the Admiral and principal foremen were particular targets of Nicolotti placards, perhaps because they seemed to epitomize all the superiority and social pretensions of the arsenalotti. Certainly they stood to be more thoroughly humiliated by being caught up in a rout, as happened the time the Admiral, dressed in all his finery of office, tried to lead a relief squad of arsenalotti into the battle, only to be met by an angry crowd of Nicolotti women, who chased them off with the taunt, "'Sassini, 'sassini, Castellani infami!"[92] Nevertheless, they came to the contests anyway, although usually more as figureheads than as squad leaders, since in the battles real leadership belonged to the ordinary workers who had won the rank of *padrini*. Using the managers as convenient symbols for all the shipbuilders' arrogance, Nicolotti satirists could better exaggerate the shame of their defeats. In 1667 the Nicolotti constructed a model showing a foreman of the Arsenal coming out of a besieged castle and handing to a *capo* of the Nicolotti the key to all Castello. The pathetic and ineffectual arsenalotti had again proven unable to defend the fortress, as he was forced to admit, with the words: "This is the key / Which opens and closes / Our beautiful castle. / OK, we surrender it to you / Who are the scourge / Of all our band."[93] The image of the castle provided a simple representation for the Castellani faction, but it also could symbolize the walled shipyards themselves and the isolated arsenalotti community associated with them. Capture of the Castellani castle thus indicated the Nicolotti's violation of this protected territory which lay at the faction's very heart, figuratively leaving the humiliated arsenalotti exposed to public amusement and scorn. The Nicolotti thus often chose to portray a fallen or captured castle on their *cartelloni*: in 1632 they celebrated a victory by parading with a model of a castle turned upside-down, waving placards which proclaimed:

> Arsenalotti for the rout which you share,
> Castello has its ass in the air![94]

For the great majority of the Venetian *popolani* the arsenalotti represented a closed and privileged sector of the city's working classes. From the numerous petitions to the Collegio, it is clear that there were many in the city who admired the Arsenal masters and wished to join their ranks; for some the honor appears even to have been worth a cut in income.[95] For many other artisans, however, the arsenalotti often appear to have aroused more negative feelings, despite (or even because of) the pride they displayed in carrying out their public and symbolic roles in the city. Their bullying could clearly inspire fear in some artisans, as with the father of Santo dei Preti. More common, however, were probably sentiments of resentment and envy, caused by the status and honors which the arsenalotti so conspicuously received from the Venetian state and so arrogantly asserted before other workers in the city. It was hardly remarkable that the members of the charcoal dealers guild were heard to grumble in 1624 that the government of Venice really only concerned itself about the well-being of its army and those who worked in the Arsenal.[96]

These resentments and tensions could hardly all be resolved through the legal or ceremonial channels which the Venetian patriciate normally employed to promote civic unity: the Arsenal masters were, after all, a hybrid in the city, coming out of the working classes, but also enjoying some of the prerogatives and powers of a ruling elite. The *battagliole,* by contrast, would appear to have served the purpose admirably. The *guerre dei pugni* represented moments in which the working population of the city could temporarily reclaim the arsenalotti to itself: whether as individual champions in the *mostra* or as the entire Arsenal contingent, the masters who went across town to the battles fought as men like all the others. Rooftop observers could jeer them and throw tiles on their heads if they wished, gangs of women could scold them, and stronger men among the Nicolotti could often manage to toss them into the canal. More than merely instruments for humiliating the arsenalotti in defeat, the satirical placards of the Nicolotti also served as well to make them welcomed among the city's laboring classes: in the teasing which they inflicted, such squibs and burlesques asserted that although the masters of the Arsenal might have been the foremost artisans among the Venetian *popolani,* they were nevertheless fellow workers for all of that.

5

The Civic Role of
the Arsenalotti in
Venetian Society

Although unusual in terms of their workplace and their community, perhaps the most remarkable aspect of the arsenalotti was the special services they performed in the larger society as agents of the state. The shipbuilders were after all only craftsmen like any others, yet the governing elite of Venice singled them out in particular as a part of the apparatus that kept the Republic running smoothly. By the seventeenth century the connection between arsenalotti and the state had evolved to the point that the masters were counted on to carry out a whole range of tasks, from the technically complex to the largely ceremonial: from such specialized duties as salvaging sunken ships to fire fighting and guard duties at Piazza San Marco and the Arsenal. Some shipbuilders, while still on the payroll of the Arsenal, became so involved in these activities that they virtually turned into professional public functionaries. The great majority, however, pursued their outside duties strictly as amateurs, taking on these extra obligations after working hours or on holidays, probably without any clear aim beyond adding to their incomes as shipbuilders. Even if they may have approached their civic duties with a casual attitude, the very fact that Venice had entrusted such tasks to the arsenalotti instead of to a body of profes-

sionals had significant consequences not only for the shipbuilders
themselves but for the state as well. In part the results were practical: using Arsenal masters for civic functions, the seventeenth-century Republic managed to get necessary functions done reasonably
well at a good price. As will be seen, however, the civic work of the
arsenalotti also had the important effect of separating one of the
city's potentially most disruptive and dangerous worker groups from
the mass of artisans in the city and binding it instead with both
economic and social ties to the governing elite of the city. Whether
this detaching of the city's shipbuilders from their fellow craftsmen
was intentional or not, it clearly had real consequences in promoting
the long-term civic peace for which the *Serenissima* was renowned.

Yet, in their civic functions the arsenalotti also helped promote
this "Myth of Venice" in another way. Serving to protect the primary
institutions of the Republic from threats both internal and external,
the masters incarnated the idealized view of the Venetian social contract which saw the strength of the state as deriving from the free
and enduring loyalty of its people; hence they functioned as a highly
visible and potent symbol of the state's ability to sustain itself
through popular devotion, without the need either to coerce its citizenry or to call on the support of the professional soldiery, as did so
many other early modern regimes.[1]

Both the arsenalotti's regular work and their civic duties connected them strongly with the Republic's ruling elite, but significantly, the real source of their prestige and special status among the
city's artisans was less their ties with the Venetian nobility generally
than a close identification with the doge himself. When called upon
to support their prince, the shipbuilders could always be counted
on to respond with alacrity. It was just in this way that they had
entered into the legends of the Republic, when in 1310 they had
quickly armed themselves and came to the defense of Doge Pietro
Gradenigo against the conspirators led by Baiamonte Tiepolo and
Marco Querini. Two centuries later, when Doge Leonardo Loredan
fancied himself in danger from another conspiracy, his surrounding
the Ducal Palace with arsenalotti guards again invoked this legend
of special devotion. Such was their enthusiasm for their prince that
the arsenalotti might even support him against the Republic itself,
as apparently happened when the traitorous Marin Falier plotted to
establish himself as *Signore* of Venice and enrolled a good many
Arsenal masters to carry him to power.[2]

As an expression of this special relationship, arsenalotti were often placed particularly close to the doge's physical person during ceremonies that marked key moments in his rule. Immediately upon his coronation, the shipbuilders bore the doge about the Piazza San Marco on their shoulders; they were also charged with rowing his ornate *Bucintoro* on the yearly voyage that culminated in the ducal Marriage to the Sea on the Day of the Ascension. The doge was also required by the laws of Venice to periodically visit the Arsenal, not only to inspect the state of the Republic's shipyards, but also to review the condition and preparedness of his shipbuilders. Finally, when the prince died, a squad of Arsenal workers carried the ducal bier and stood honor guard at his burial at the church of Santi Giovanni and Paolo.[3] It was this core ceremonial relationship between shipbuilders and their doge that provided the ritual framework in which the arsenalotti carried out their more practical civic duties for the Republic.

The Handymen of the City

Some aspects of their public role were for the arsenalotti little more than extensions of normal work routine, calling for skills they would have acquired in the Arsenal and in particular in the course of their naval service. It was almost universal that shipbuilders passed some time at sea, either by orders of the Senate, for the sake of extra income, or simply as part of family traditions; most young arsenalotti, soon after becoming masters, served at their craft with the merchant marine or the Republic's war fleet. In doing so, they would learn the discipline of naval service, gain training in the use of arms, and often acquire the experience of command, since many rose to positions ranging from petty officer *(compagno)* to bosun *(nochiere)* to ship's captain *(patron da nave)*. Such military training would have been increasingly rare among native Venetians by the seventeenth century: the artisan guilds, *scuole,* townships, and other civic institutions from which a levy for oarsmen had once been raised had by this time generally converted their service obligations into the payment of compensatory taxes. Certainly by the start of the Candia War in 1645, hallowed traditions of direct citizen participation in Venice's war fleet had been largely abandoned. Sailors and masters of the Arsenal remained virtually the only members of the city's *popolani* class who were still expected to serve personally in the Republic's navy, where galleys were no longer crewed by free artisans, but powered instead by masses of convicts, slaves, or hired rowers, while guided by professional sailors, armed by an elite of gunners *(bombardieri)*, and directed by a few noble commanders.[4]

As early as 1487, the Senate had ordered each Venetian war galley to carry two caulkers and three shipwrights on board; a generation later the number of shipwrights was increased to six. Besides performing their own particular crafts while at sea, it was expected that these men would also attend to problems that might arise anywhere in the Empire: they were "reputed the handiest men to have available in any difficulty," and indeed masters were often detached from their galleys by local commanders or passing *capitani-generali* to carry out emergency tasks ashore. Throughout the seventeenth century, shipbuilders could be found everywhere in the Empire: constructing drawbridges in Istria, erecting barracks in Corfù, or repairing harbor fortifications in Candia.[5]

Once they were set on such extraordinary duties abroad, arsenalotti appear to have acted independently of outside command, typically executing their tasks in small squads working under their own leaders. Such a custom was given official sanction during the course of the Candia War, when the state began a regular policy of sending out groups of two dozen or more masters at a time, delegated to tour various detachments of the fleet at their winter anchorages and to carry out needed repairs. A leader was usually chosen from among each contingent, a gang boss who could then see to the details of their journey and to represent them if necessary before the Collegio on their return.[6] Since the refitting needs of the fleet and various imperial cities were complex, their journeys could take several years, as they repeatedly crisscrossed the Empire. Even while they were abroad, it was customary to treat such masters as still attached to the Arsenal, at least in the sense that they continued to collect their daily wages. Their status as arsenalotti was not rigidly defined, however: sometimes masters who happened to show up at an imperial outpost and found that their services were especially needed might strike out on their own, contracting with local authorities to work as independent entrepreneurs.[7]

Once returned to Venice, sometimes after years abroad, the shipbuilders were uniquely suited to serve the city as general handymen and public functionaries.[8] After their service with the fleet, arsenalotti were both more broadly experienced in their craft and more accustomed to working together as independent groups. When the state had need for skilled craftsmen to carry out necessary public works in the city, it could look to its shipbuilders to do any job that custom or law did not assign to another particular individual or guild.[9] Repairing various public warehouses and worksheds was thus a job well suited for Arsenal masters, though perhaps most important was their duty to help at raising sunken or beached ships. Salvaging could be vital when it was a question of refloating and saving a ship that was blocking an essential channel in the Lagoon, but even when they were simply reclaiming the armaments and cargo of a wrecked hulk, the arsenalotti performed an important service. It was a dangerous and highly specialized sort of work, usually involving free-diving under water—a task for which few besides arsenalotti were evidently willing to volunteer.[10]

The arsenalotti also were accustomed to serve as overseers in some public building projects. Whenever construction in the city was undertaken with materials procured from the Arsenal storehouses, the Patroni would also send along a squad of masters, to accompany, protect, and put to proper use the goods of the state. In such circumstances the arsenalotti acted in the name of the Arsenal, but they did not always work as its regular wage employees. Instead, such jobs might also be awarded to the masters by contract, just as they often arranged with the Patroni to build ships by piecework in

Figure 5.1. *Ponte Votivo* to the Redentore in the 1600s

the Arsenal; the rationale in both cases seems to have been that of speed, for when on contract the arsenalotti were known to work much more quickly.[11]

One such contracted public work was the building of the so-called *ponti votivi,* the devotional bridges erected five times a year (six by the end of the century) to connect the center city to the Redentore, Salute, or other shrines of pilgrimage on their festal days (see fig. 5.1).[12]

Bridge contracts were awarded on a competitive, ten-year basis to groups, or *compagnie,* of ship's carpenters; they were expected to begin their building eight days before the actual festival, using materials purchased from the shipyards and as many small, private boats as they felt necessary to requisition. The Senate paid a fairly high price to the contractors for the work, possibly in the hope that it would be quickly and securely done so the processions could come off smoothly: the winning bids ranged around 550 ducats per year for both materials and labor—probably only about two months work annually.[13] The business of building the *ponti votivi* could sometimes bring arsenalotti into conflict with their fellow *popolani,* since the preemptive powers granted by their contracts gave masters wide powers over other artisans in the city: the Patroni noted that when requisitioning private boats to build the bridges, contract holders tended to exempt boats of friends and choose too often those belonging to men whom they disliked.[14]

The Patroni contracted with arsenalotti for a variety of other outside jobs, ranging from building a bridge near Padova to replacing the beams inside the Campanile of San Marco.[15] While the plague raged in the city in 1630 and the Arsenal management and many masters were locked up inside the shipyard walls for their own safety, the Patroni even opened the bidding on who would contract to feed the sequestered shipbuilders. Rather then trust the feeding of such important workers to outsiders, the Patroni decided to limit the bidding just to arsenalotti who had elected to remain on the outside; to make sure they fulfilled their contracts, however, it was also demanded that each supplier put up a *pieggiaria,* or surety, of 200 ducats.[16]

Certain arsenalotti apparently desired outside contract work enough to take the initiative and set up their own agreements with other magistrates besides the Patroni. Thus, two Arsenal masters and a private shipbuilder once entered into a spontaneous competition before the Collegio for the right to fix up a public warehouse (*tezone*) on the island of Poveglia with their own funds and run it privately thereafter as an *appalto,* or monopoly contract, to supply deepwater ships.[17] Likewise, the accounts of the Procurators *di Supra* indicate that they too contracted directly with several *compagnie* of arsenalotti to carry out structural and decorative rebuilding on the peak of the Campanile of San Marco in the 1650s.[18]

In winning contracts, the arsenalotti were at a particular advantage in being accustomed not only to work together in self-organized groups, but also to operate such *compagnie* independently under their own leadership. Gangs contracting for work in the city could be put together from masters who customarily worked together in the Arsenal or at sea; the bosses and contractors that headed up such *compagnie* would quite likely be drawn straight from the Arsenal's management hierarchy.[19] These small and flexible work groups, where masters could pool their various work skills, would have given arsenalotti the edge in competing for contracts with the different magistracies of the state. Able to circulate freely both in the city and the Empire at large, arsenalotti could operate practically as independent agents, negotiating with the authorities for better pay or situations and always on the lookout for the possibilities of profitable jobs to be contracted in *compagnia.*

Watchmen and Ceremonial Guards

As the Republic's handymen, the arsenalotti were state workers who often crossed into the realm of private contractors. As Venice's guards, shipbuilders were more completely public functionaries, yet here too they retained a certain amateur status as worker militiamen. Their guardian responsibilities had probably evolved from ceremonial duties which the arsenalotti had originally performed only occasionally while protecting the doge, but it is not surprising that the masters ended up carrying out such functions on a permanent basis in Venice. Thanks to their contracting work and their service at sea, masters were accustomed to give and take orders, both within their squads and to outsiders. Naval duties also frequently exposed arsenalotti to warfare, giving them combat experience and pike and musket training which assured their superiority as police over the average Venetians whom they would generally be expected to control.

The regular and daily police work in the city was already by the fifteenth century solidly the business of "professionals": that is, squads of *sbirri* under the Dieci, the Signori di Notte, or the Cinque della Pace. Such agents would have numbered around 250 to 300 and were normally led by their own noble captains; they had the responsibility for breaking up brawls, arresting vagrants or beggars, and chasing thieves.[20] The arsenalotti, by contrast, operated in their own squads and patrolled or guarded only certain key areas in the city: principally the Arsenal and its district and the environs of Piazza San Marco. In this civic function, shipbuilders were more an amateur militia than professional guards; unlike police *sbirri* they carried out policing duties only in their spare time, returning to the Arsenal during working hours to do their normal work.

The foremost guard duty of the arsenalotti was at the Arsenal itself, for nothing could be more central to the Republic's safety than the security of the state shipyards. The importance of the Arsenal to Venice makes it all the more striking that the workers themselves were charged with policing their own workplace. One of the Patroni (the *Patron di Guardia*) was in overall command of Arsenal security, but the squads of masters who carried out the actual policing were under the leadership of other shipbuilders, who although appointed by the Patroni, appear to have carried out their duties with considerable independence. Their special training, loyalty, and intimate knowledge of the shipyards did indeed especially qualify the arsenalotti for such sensitive work, but evidently the state had little choice in the matter anyway: the only attempt to place outsiders in charge of Arsenal security caused such an uproar among the workforce that the candidates for the position were hastily withdrawn and the traditional system reinstated.[21]

In all, four distinct companies of shipbuilders guarded the Arsenal during most of the seventeenth century, a total of around 110 men at any one time. The largest of these groups, known as the *guardiani di notte*, numbered eighty masters in the mid-1600s and were men chosen by lot once a year from all arsenalotti between twenty and fifty years of age. At sunset these artisans went to their places as the last of the workforce was filing out, manning the thirteen watchtowers situated around the two-mile perimeter wall enclosing the shipyards. From their vantage points over the darkened yards and docks, these *guardiani* were meant to keep watch for any fires or other unusual disturbances and to respond alertly when called to by their captain in the course of his rounds.[22] This official, appointed from among the masters for a five-year term, was charged with leading six of his guards on a circuit within the shipyards, searching for signs of disorder, fire, or theft, and generally keeping an eye on all the other watchmen under his command. Despite such a formidable collection of regular guards, the Patroni were evidently still concerned about the possibility of fire in the highly flammable docks. In 1638 the Senate gave them permission to chose six masters (specifying that these should be "men experienced also in other public functions") and have them "daily circle all the Arsenal after the workforce has departed, [checking] in both the prows and the sterns of the galleys [and] extinguishing all the fires that they see."[23]

Significantly, the arsenalotti's guardian responsibilities were not only directed inward toward the shipyards, but also outward, toward the surrounding shipbuilding community. Out of the eighty night watchmen, the Inquisitors of the Arsenal selected eight guards with their own leader and ordered them to serve as *guardiani del campo,* responsible for patrolling the Campo dell'Arsenale and surrounding *calli* during the nights.[24] At the Arsenal gates themselves were also stationed six arsenalotti known as *guardiani festivi.* Unlike the night guards, these men held their posts for life; they were charged with watching the main entrance of the Arsenal on the eight or so Sundays and feast days per month when the shipyards were officially closed. In a further security measure provoked by the onset of the Candia War, yet another group of twenty-three masters was organized to *far la ronda* of the surrounding community: patrolling by boat and on land in a circuit outside the Arsenal walls, while on the lookout for potential troublemakers or saboteurs. The squad was not permanent but seems to have been a custom of wartime: it had also been introduced during the period of Spanish tensions from 1618 to 1621, *per sospetti dei moti,* and would be again during the Morean conflict of the 1680s.[25]

As more arsenalotti patrols were sent into the local *campi* and neighborhoods, what had once been guard duty clearly related to the workplace increasingly took on the militia function of patrolling the shipbuilding community around the Arsenal. Logically, the security needs of the Arsenal would not have simply begun or ended at its walls, and Arsenal squads needed wider policing authority if they were to be effective guards. Community police work, as already noted, supposedly was the competence of other magistrates, and indeed the Ten did continue to send night patrols into these neighborhoods. Nevertheless, much of the district evidently came under effective control of the *Patron di Guardia* and his arsenalotti squads, whether for simple convenience or as part of the ministry's perpetual search to expand its authority. In the 1740s, a jurisdictional conflict with a customs patrol finally required the Patroni to spell out what territory they expected their men to patrol: already permitted to send arsenalotti squads into the *campi* and canals adjoining the Arsenal, the Patroni made a wider claim for policing authority, based on the need to protect the forty or so management houses (the *case di ragion*) which the Arsenal owned and maintained in the district.[26] The Patroni thus asserted jurisdiction over all the maze of small *calli* leading up to these houses as well as the *fondamenta* on which they were situated, in effect claiming authority over most of the parish of San Martino, all of San Biasio, and a large part of San Pietro di Castello as well (see map 5.1).

Most masters who were chosen as Arsenal guards apparently saw the duty as supplementary to their regular shipbuilding work, rather than as a full-time job in its own right. The pay for guard duty at any rate would not have been enough to live on, but it did make a useful addition to normal wages at the shipyards. The work certainly must have seemed attractive, for despite the burden which so many extra hours represented and the fact that the night air was popularly considered harmful, the available guard positions were

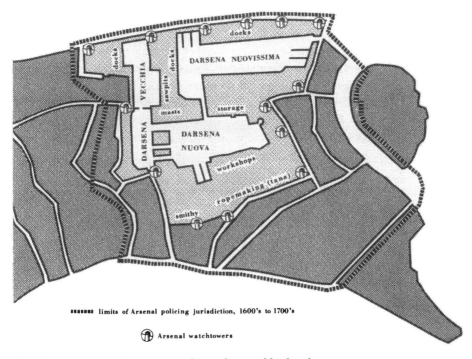

◼◼◼◼◼◼ limits of Arsenal policing jurisdiction, 1600's to 1700's

🏛 Arsenal watchtowers

Map 5.1. Arsenal jurisdiction in nearby worker neighborhoods

always in demand.[27] Night guards could expect half again their daily pay (as much as 20 soldi) for every night they kept watch; those who checked for fires or made the boat patrols around the Arsenal walls received between 8 and 16 soldi for every night's service.[28] The patricians administering the shipyards tended to see guard duty in a paternalistic light, as a chance for deserving masters to augment their rather low state wages; not surprisingly it was therefore felt that the economic advantages of guard duty should be spread as widely as possible, so that "to every one of these workers might come this benefit in turn." This attitude, as much as any growing concern for Arsenal security, would probably best explain the rising number of night guardsmen, which were steadily increased by order of the Senate—from 30 guards in the 1480s to 42 in the mid-1500s, 68 in 1640, 80 in the 1660s, and 115 in the 1730s.[29]

Despite such solicitous treatment, the arsenalotti did not always turn out to make satisfactory guardsmen. The custom of choosing most Arsenal guards by lot every year inevitably produced a number of guardsmen who did not take their policing responsibilities very seriously. So casual were most arsenalotti in showing up for evening duty, that it was not enough simply to take them off the guards' roster; the Patroni instead had to threaten shirkers with docking their daily pay up to 4 soldi.[30] Even when they did come, many watchmen tried to remain together for company in just one or two towers instead of manning all thirteen; when they were separated as required, it was reported that they often lit fires to keep warm and simply fell asleep. The Patroni complained that a system which forced them to form a body of amateur guards from a workforce of artisans resulted in a force of watchmen that were both "poco sufficienti" and of "poco servitio."[31]

In any case, the rounds themselves were enough of a combination of boredom, discomfort, and occasional danger that most masters would have been kept from pursuing their obligations too enthusiastically. Besides risking injuries from fires or stumbling in the dark, the night guards also had to be wary of the murderers and other *banditi* who might be seeking a hiding place in the shipyards. As a guards captain once reported, "I have flushed out many of them from the Arsenal . . . where they hide in the coldest part of the winter . . . for which they have become enraged at me, turning on me and even trying to kill me"; one oarmaker was in fact murdered while making his rounds in the 1630s. To give their guards more incentive to confront such dangers aggressively, the Senate and Patroni occasionally proposed to share the fines levied with those who captured miscreants in the act. Substantial sums were in fact collected, although it is not clear how many arsenalotti were actually tempted by those fines to leave the comfort of their towers.[32]

Indeed, many administrators in the shipyards were evidently convinced that arsenalotti watchmen were less likely to be actively patrolling the Arsenal than spending their duty time thinking up new ways to defraud it. Whenever the Patroni or Inquisitors inspected the more remote reaches of the Arsenal walls—in itself a seemingly rare occurrence—they would turn up mysterious holes which had been bored through in hidden places; the fear was widely expressed that these could only serve as the means by which the guards snuck in and out of the shipyards at night, probably passing stolen goods out to their accomplices. The fact that other arsenalotti were charged with patrolling the waters and alleys all around the Arsenal raised the uncomfortable prospect of collusion between the two groups of guards which could render the shipyards' protective walls completely ineffectual. Night guards were in fact repeatedly accused of conspiring with other masters on the outside in order to pass Arsenal goods through the unbarred windows of their watchtowers to boats which had been quietly moored alongside the shipyard walls.[33] The Patroni also suspected the watchmen of smuggling out woodscraps and other materials when they went off duty, and it was considered necessary to appoint another official in order to search the guards as they left each morning.[34]

The Patroni and Inquisitors were not alone in denouncing the lax discipline among the arsenalotti watchmen, for the guards captains themselves would also petition the Collegio to point out abuses and offer suggestions on how to put the squads on a more professional footing. Many of these captains appear to have made something of a career out of policing the Arsenal, and Battista di Iacomo Piccolo was indeed originally chosen to head the night guards in 1655 because for years beforehand he had showered the Patroni with suggestions on improving shipyard security. Piccolo's successor was Giacomo di Antonio, who also had a long history of police work, serving for some years as one of the *guardiani del campo,* and finally in 1651 being promoted to squad leader; fourteen years later he was named captain of the night guards, a post he held until 1672.[35] Another shipwright, named Zuane di Nicolò Grego, may have kept his place on the Arsenal rosters, but in fact was actually working as a full-time policeman for the *capi* of the Council of Ten, serving as their boat captain and conducting water patrols both in the shipyards and through the city at large.[36]

These guards captains repeatedly warned the Collegio that without experienced and determined leadership, the loose militia of arsenalotti watchmen would never prove effective in their work. The solution which they proposed was to professionalize policing at the Arsenal, starting with their own positions, which they wanted granted for life. Some, such as Giacomo di Antonio, went further, requesting permission to pass his office on to his nephew; Giacomo put his argument in terms of training rather than family ties, stressing that the younger man had gained extensive experience while on the job, serving as assistant (*sottocapo*).[37] Such appeals appear to have had small support from the Patroni, who no doubt feared that like so many other Arsenal offices the posts of guards captain would slip out of their hands and end up as one family's possession or be sold to the highest bidder. Fearing corruption and cronyism more than inefficiency, they convinced the Collegio that captains should receive no more than one extension of their five-year terms. The Arsenal thus retained its fully amateur militia of guardsmen, with both its popularity and its disadvantages: indeed, the discipline problems with the night guards that Piccolo claimed to have resolved in 1658 were the same ones that Giacomo di Antonio would find it necessary to confront eight years later.

In Piazza San Marco, where they were highly visible to both Venetians and visiting foreigners, several other groups of arsenalotti acted as public guardsmen. One such squad consisted of thirty-two masters who patrolled the Piazza at night, keeping an eye on the Ducal Palace, the offices of the Procurators, and the *Zecca,* or public mint. The custom of posting arsenalotti in the Piazza at night is of uncertain origin, but it may well have been a continuation of that guard of one hundred armed masters that Leonardo Loredan had initiated during the popular unrest of the 1510s; besides the Piazza, masters were also posted in the San Marco clocktower and on the Rialto. By the mid-seventeenth century such political turmoil was much reduced, and arsenalotti watchmen seem to have taken on a more ceremonial function, except during the last weeks of Carnival, when thousands of revellers were certain to pass the nights in the Piazza. As compensation for their services they were to be paid $3\frac{1}{3}$ ducats each per month, but since this money came from the Office of the *Ragion Nuove* and not the Patroni, it was evidently often long overdue, sometimes more than a year late.[38] Nevertheless, the duty was considered a desirable one; requests by arsenalotti for a post were frequent and a waiting list seems to have been kept for the next available place.[39]

A separate contingent of eighty arsenalotti was selected by the Patroni in three months' rotation to serve as an honor guard for the Sunday meetings of the Maggior Consiglio. These workers, with halberds, muskets, and distinctive jackets, were to draw themselves up in review as the members of the Council were gathering and then disperse to mount guard: some within the *Loggietta* of Sansovino, at the base of the Campanile, where they guarded the Procurators of San Marco (see figs. 5.2 and 5.3); and others in the various entryways to the Ducal Palace, where they made sure that no one attempted to come within while carrying a weapon or that no noble member of the Council tried to sneak away during the proceedings.[40]

These eighty *guardiani* were more clearly intended for ceremonial purposes than the other arsenalotti patrolling the Piazza. Although armed, it is doubtful that they could be counted on to provide much actual defense of the Palace, even though this may have been the Senate's original intention in the sixteenth century when it had ordered the Patroni to provide a fully armed force of the strongest masters under the command of their Admiral for every Sunday meeting. Decades of civic tranquillity would seem to have changed the original role of the Palace guards to one more purely symbolic, as a public reminder that the ruling order enjoyed sufficient popular support in the city to protect itself simply with a militia of workers. By the 1600s, many of the arsenalotti serving as Sunday guards were little more than elderly place-holders: when in 1618 it was discovered that sixty of the eighty masters were too old to carry the usual halberd, it was decided that they should instead be allowed to arm themselves with only short swords (*meze spade*). To a certain extent, the Patroni singled out such elderly masters, giving them the duty with its extra morning's pay as a reward for past services; on the other hand, younger arsenalotti do not seem to have much favored working on Sundays and avoided it whenever possible.[41]

Under such conditions, the arsenalotti guarding the Maggior Consiglio had become a somewhat shabby crew by the 1600s: a good number were said to lack adequate training in loading and firing a harquebus, or indeed failed to even possess one, perhaps

Figure 5.2. Arsenalotti standing guard at the *Loggietta* for a Sunday
meeting of the Maggior Consiglio

because for years they had never been assigned a captain to lead
them. In any event, many seemed to think that they were only required to put in an appearance during the short review while the
nobles arrived to take their places in the Maggior Consiglio, so they
simply borrowed the necessary weapons from a friend and then afterwards wandered off, rather than mounting guard at the Palace
doors.[42] The Patroni evidently did not take the task of guarding the
Maggior Consiglio nearly as seriously as they did that of the Arsenal,
for the tightening of security which took place at the shipyards on
the outbreak of the Candia War was not reflected by any similar
reform at the Palace. Only in 1655 did the Patroni order a more
careful accounting of who was actually serving on the Sunday
squads, and as late as 1661 the honor guard still had no captain,
according to one shipbuilder who aspired to the post.[43]

A third and much more robust group of arsenalotti guards was
employed in Piazza San Marco for the celebrations that marked the
selection and coronation of a new doge. These festal events demanded much more aggressive squads than those that sufficed to
guard the Maggior Consiglio, and it is likely that the Patroni made
their selection from among the strongest arsenalotti rather than
from the most deserving. The occasion of his coronation was one of
the most public moments in any doge's reign, and it began with his

presentation to all the populace of Venice from the altar of the
Church of San Marco. Thereupon, the newly designated prince
mounted a kind of portable pulpit known as the *pozzetto* and was
carried, along with a few close relatives and the Admiral of the Arsenal, on the shoulders of about forty arsenalotti through the crowd
which thronged the Piazza. This *giro della Piazza,* as it was known,
thus demonstrated to the world with clear symbolism that the doge,
representing the Republic in its continuity, derived his pre-emi-
nence from the support of the Arsenal.[44] From the point of view of
ordinary Venetians, who had no role at all in choosing their new
ruler, it also might well have seemed a moment of long-awaited
compensation for their normal political powerlessness: as he made
his way among the people, displaying the *bolletino* which conferred
his office, the doge and his retinue showered the crowd with gold
and silver coins specially minted for the occasion.[45]

By all accounts, most commoners saw this rain of wealth as the
high point of the whole ceremony, and it inevitably resulted in con-

Figure 5.3. Arsenalotto guard
with jacket and halberd

siderable disorder, as waves of poor Venetians, onlookers, and tourists attempted to get at the rolling and flying coins. Although the doge was not meant to need armed troops for his daily protection—he could supposedly entrust his safety to the loyalty of his subjects—the moment of the *giro della Piazza* was generally one of such frenzy that he often risked being overturned and spilled from the *pozzetto*. To keep events under control, a squad of forty or so arsenalotti, each armed with a long red staff, was therefore stationed along the doge's route through the Piazza, with the understanding that they could use whatever force was necessary to keep the populace away from their ruler.[46] The many paintings and drawings of the seventeenth and eighteenth centuries which depict the *giro della Piazza* leave no doubt how eagerly these masters would carry out their duties, showing little reluctance to put their staffs to use or indeed to wade directly into the masses of their fellow *popolani*, swinging their red *bastoni* about them quite freely (see figs. 5.4 and 5.5).

A curious situation thus would arise during the *giro*, where doge and ruling elite flung treasure with abandon toward the people but forced them to undergo a beating if they hoped to get their hands on any of it. It was in this moment of the *giro* that the masters of the Arsenal seem to have most completely abandoned any normal affinities they may have had with the laboring classes of the city. Instead they stoutly set themselves to defending their personal patron the doge and to pushing their own group honor, as select militiamen who defended the majesty of the state while asserting the power and superiority of their own ranks.[47] Other ducal ceremonies may have also stressed the special status of the arsenalotti among Venetian artisans: the 100 masters who rowed the *Bucintoro* to the Marriage with the Sea on the Feste della Sensa, for example, were honored afterwards with a sumptuous banquet at the Ducal Palace.[48] Yet no other occasion in Venice's festal calendar could quite so graphically reveal the superiority and separateness of the shipbuilders as did the *giro*, nor allow them to so aggressively demonstrate their dominance over ordinary citizens, as they strode through the crowds who groveled on the paving stones of the Piazza San Marco, beating their fellow commoners back from Venice's primary public stage, the center of which they shared only with their admiral and the doge himself.

Not counting the various contingents formed for such special ducal ceremonies as coronations or burials, around 220 arsenalotti

Figure 5.4. The *Giro della Piazza* seen by Giovanni Franco

at any given time would have been engaged in Venice as guardsmen:
at least a quarter of all masters actively working in the Arsenal. They
were almost as numerous as the total regular police forces of the city
and much more visible to the public. In fact, as many as 80–90
percent of all arsenalotti would have had at least some experience
during their lives with these kinds of militia duties, thanks to the
system of yearly and trimonthly rotation which prevailed in the se-

lection of most guards, not to mention the tendency of many masters with lifetime positions to hire themselves substitutes from among other shipbuilders.

From the point of view of the Senate, there would certainly have been sound social and economic reasons for maintaining this worker militia of arsenalotti guardsmen, whatever its practical inadequacies may have been. As amateur guards who maintained their status as artisans when off duty, shipbuilders probably could expect to receive more respect from fellow *popolani* than would the professional *sbirri* of the policing magistrates. Likewise, in a state which, despite a rigid aristocracy, still prized its free and republican traditions, using garrison troops for such functions would certainly have been politically unwise. In seventeenth-century Venice professional soldiers would rarely have been locals, but were overwhelmingly recruited from the peoples of Albania or Dalmatia; native-born Arsenal workers were bound to be more acceptable to Venetians as guards than even a few companies of such foreign soldiers.[49] In any event, the price of forming a militia out of Arsenal workers would

Figure 5.5. Arsenalotti controlling the crowd during the *Giro della Piazza* in S. Marco

by itself have made a good case in its favor to the patricians who ran the city. The state had no need to pay the price for nobles or outside mercenaries to command their militia guards, since the arsenalotti led themselves. Nor was it necessary to invest in barracks to accommodate them, because when their duties were finished, the masters simply returned home. Venice could thus enlist the services of more than 200 men in what were considered vital civic services for just over 8,000 ducats per year, or 40 ducats per worker.[50] Still more attractive, these arsenalotti would be bringing home extra pay which represented a vital economic contribution to one of the city's largest and most important worker communities.

Firefighting Brigades

As a worker militia, the arsenalotti were also expected to control the fires that regularly broke out in the city. Originally firefighting in Venice appears to have been taken care of by the popular militia, or *duodena,* of each parish, the members of which were chosen from all adult males by the Council of Ten.[51] By the beginning of the sixteenth century, however, the role of the parish *duodena* had clearly diminished as citywide organizations began to replace local civic groups generally. It would appear that the arsenalotti took over the job of firefighting by degrees, coming to perform a public service in much the same way that artisans from building guilds did in other Italian communes.[52] Very likely in Venice's case the Arsenal workers would have naturally emerged to fill the gap left by the *duodena* due to their own experience with fires in the shipyards, where runaway blazes in highly flammable materials such as pitch, dry timbers, sailcloth, and gunpowder were common occurrences. In addition, the fleet's biscuit ovens on the Riva of San Biagio practically adjoined the Arsenal and were also especially prone to outbreaks of fire. Constantly having to cope with such emergencies in and around their own workplace, the arsenalotti must have learned at an early stage the organizational means to deal efficiently with fires. Since the primary virtues for coping with blazes were team effort and personal bravery, the arsenalotti would have been in any event well qualified for the work.

Yet by the early sixteenth century there was also a general conviction in Venice that the city should have the services of real firefighting professionals. Perhaps the sentiment caught on after a particularly bad series of blazes around 1536, when certain problems associated with using the arsenalotti in the role of firemen became evident. As an essentially volunteer militia, the Arsenal masters appear to have been quite willing to deal with blazes that broke out in their workplace, but they tended to consider showing up at a fire outside the shipyards as more a matter of choice than as a firm obligation; in the mid-seventeenth century their guild leaders were still pointedly reminding the Collegio that "these workers . . . are not really obliged [to go] to any fire in the city."[53]

Fearing that the number of arsenalotti who might turn out for a fire was too variable and uncertain, the Senate therefore decided to rationalize and expand the city's firefighting force, voting to establish a permanent squad of men that would always be available. The first such team was set up in 1536, and although it was not composed of arsenalotti, one was chosen as its captain: a shipwright named Zorzi Libana. Eventually two squads of full-time firefighters were formed, one of thirty men to deal with fires in the city and another of fifteen for outbreaks in and around the shipyards themselves. Each group was placed under an Arsenal master (traditionally drawn only from the ranks of the shipwrights), who was assigned a large converted warehouse behind the Church of San Biagio as his headquarters. Here each commander lived with his family and the fifteen or thirty firemen, who were all required to spend each night under his roof.[54]

The Senate's plans for establishing a permanent firefighting brigade in the city may have been well-intentioned, but they did not prove too successful in practice. Even when both squads of firemen were used together, they could prove inadequate for the kind of blazes which broke out in some of Venice's larger structures, which were especially prone to fires: besides the particularly flammable sites around the Arsenal, fires repeatedly started in churches and convents, patrician palaces, and many other public buildings.[55] More important, in its efforts to keep down expenses, the Senate had decided to form this permanent fire brigade out of porters and longshoremen—the *fachini* and *bastasi* who worked Venice's docks and warehouses. Every month forty-five of these men were chosen from a pool of such laborers who were unable or unwilling to pay an exemption tax that would have otherwise freed them from such low-paid services demanded of all *fachini* by the state. The result was a collection of men who were not only continuously changing and poorly trained, but also basically unwilling to serve. One of the contractors who had agreed to supply them contemptuously called these porters "people completely incapable of reason," by which he evidently meant that they showed scant willingness to accept a system that made them leave their homes and spend an entire month locked up every night in the house of their squad captain.[56]

As a result of the regular city fire brigades' inadequacies, the arsenalotti were kept on as firefighters, continuing to work at least through the seventeenth century in tandem with the forty-five porters: when there was a smaller fire in the city, one or both the squads of *facchini* would have been able to handle it on their own, but at large conflagrations or at fires at the shipyards themselves, the arsenalotti were called out as well. Working under their own leadership in small, disciplined groups, Arsenal masters would not only have exhibited more flexibility than the reluctant longshoremen in coping with emergencies, but they could also have commanded more respect and exercised greater authority over their fellow Venetians than any mere dockyard porters raised up to act as the city's firemen.

When fire broke out in the Arsenal or the city, the masters were summoned from their workplace or homes (an easier task once they had begun to move closer to the shipyards) by an alarm bell in one of the towers flanking the water entrance to the shipyards. When enough workers had arrived to deal with the fire, they were drawn up in ranks in the Campo dell'Arsenale by the Patron di Guardia and dispatched in squads by him and the captain of the *guardiani del campo*.[57] Once arrived at the site of a blaze, squads of masters under their own leaders separated off to carry out a number of necessary militia functions. When fire broke out near the offices of the Procurators in Piazza San Marco, where vital public records were at risk, shipbuilders were sent to the more important buildings to protect them from flying sparks and to drive away the curious or potential looters. Guards also had to be posted when fires broke out at the Arsenal: at a fire in the shipyards in 1645, a shipwright named Gasparo di Constantin and a squad of masters armed with muskets were put in charge of controlling the main *fondamenta* leading from the city to the Arsenal. Gasparo was given the authority, as he put it, "to let pass those who I knew could be of use and to exclude those [who were] either foreigners or others that could only serve [to increase] the confusion."[58]

Major fires in the city provided intense public spectacles, drawing large crowds to witness the blend of chaos, excitement, and danger. Although firefighting was certainly a dangerous activity, fires also provided arsenalotti with the occasion for demonstrative acts of heroism on a dramatic public stage. Arsenal masters who described their firefighting exploits in petitions seem to have considered the duty almost as a privilege: just as with their guardian activities, firefighting gave them an opportunity to dominate and excel before their fellow Venetians. Especially intrepid acts of bravery could turn a master or a squad of arsenalotti into overnight heroes in their community, and certainly the deeds of particular firefighters would remain in the collective memories of some arsenalotti lineages for generations. In 1633, the shipwright Giovanni di Pietro Mezzavolta recalled his great-grandfather's heroism in fighting the fire that had raged in the Arsenal on the night of San Biagio over a hundred years earlier; he even included such details as the extent of the blaze and the conditions of the wind. In 1624, an elderly caulker told the Collegio how nearly fifty years earlier, during the fire which had gutted the Ducal Palace in 1577, his squad of masters from the Giudecca had entered the courtyard of the building, even though leads from the burning roof were showering down. In the ensuing turmoil, two *facchini* were killed.[59]

The greater the danger, it seems, the better the shipbuilders' chance to show off their bravery. When a group of arsenalotti arrived at a fire which had broken out at the smithy in the shipyards, they discovered that someone had stored a number of loaded muskets in the attic of the building. Nevertheless, "without any regard for their own lives, they entered headlong into the . . . workshop, although there was a great quantity of muskets loaded with shot which were discharging on every side, with the clearest danger [that they might] end up dead there."[60]

Public demonstrations of courage only took on meaning if they were played out against a background of real danger, and although arsenalotti may have found firefighting gave them an attractive chance to demonstrate their bravery, it could also cause them serious injuries. When Zorzi di Zorzi was awakened by the Arsenal fire that was the "universal terror and fear of all Castello," he quickly thought to organize a supply of water for the other masters: locating a forgotten well nearby, he jumped in and spent the next five hours passing up buckets of water, but after working all night in the middle of winter, he would later come down with a "long and deadly illness."[61] While helping at a shipyard fire, Francesco Scagnelli, coadjutor of the Arsenal's *Scrivan Grande,* was painfully wounded when a burning beam fell on his leg. Despite his injury, he reminded the Collegio, Scagnelli came to assist at two later Arsenal fires as well.[62]

There were of course practical factors which could spur masters to run the risks of firefighting. Among the crowds that inevitably turned up at the scene of a blaze, various senators and patricians would also be found, just as the Patroni and other administrators could be counted on to arrive as observers when fires broke out at the shipyards themselves. An Arsenal master who had especially distinguished himself before the eyes of such powerful men could hope for their support later on, especially when he petitioned the Collegio for a pension or raise based on such services. A sailor named Antonio di Vicenzo, who worked in the shipyards, noted in his supplica that he had fought a recent fire "with all my spirit," and that "the Signore Admiral with the other Foremen will be [among] those that corroborate and authenticate the fruit produced by my labors." Even the Admiral himself, Zuane di Domenigo Luganegher, was well aware of the impression his conduct at a fire could make on noble observers: "at the recent fire in the blacksmiths' shed," he wrote with pride, "I exerted myself in a manner well-noted to a great many noble *signori* who happened to be present." When they wrote in support of Luganegher's petition, the Patroni of the Arsenal picked up the theme as well, saying: "Your Serenity personally and a great many very important Senators have had occasion to know in action the accomplishments and the quality of this minister."[63]

For sailors and other artisans aspiring to a place among the Arsenal shipbuilders, fires could provide a golden opportunity to prove that a petitioner possessed the character and skills appropriate to an arsenalotto. Zorzi di Zorzi, the sailor mentioned above, reminded the doge after fighting the fire in 1645, that one "who with zeal, vigilance, and faithfulness serves You, especially in occasions so important [as fires]," was worthy to be admitted as a master in the Arsenal.[64] An apprentice at the shipyards would go along to fires in the hope that his obedience and bravery during the emergency might help gain him a reduction in the time required before he could take his master's exam. Even some of the clerking and bookkeeping staff of the Arsenal became active firefighters on occasion, either expecting a raise in their salary or hoping to join the ranks of the shipbuilding masters. The coadjutor Scagnelli petitioned the Collegio to assert that he deserved some kind of further *gratioso assignamento,* considering "the efforts and labors undertaken by me in putting out the three fires . . . in the Arsenal and the ovens . . . [and that] so many most worthy noble signori saw me working . . . [and] in continuous motion over the course of an entire night and half the following day, as is notorious to anyone."[65]

Besides a potential for support in guiding a petition through the channels of the Senate or an enhanced place in the city's web of patronage networks, there were also material rewards to be won from the dangers of firefighting. All masters who took part in putting out a blaze could generally count on a share of the cash award, or *donativo,* which a grateful Senate would vote for their services. The size of these grants varied widely: from 60 ducats to be divided among the masters who put out the fire at the convent of the Carità in 1630, to 800 ducats for those who fought a blaze at the Arsenal in 1602. The Senators who approved the amount of each particular *donativo* appear to have based their decision on the importance of the blaze, the number of men involved, and their alacrity in carrying out their work. After especially spectacular fires, masters who had particularly distinguished themselves might also hope for a permanent recognition. This usually took the form of a lifetime raise of 4 soldi to their regular Arsenal wages (about $8\frac{1}{2}$ ducats per year), an award that the Senate was only willing to make rarely, realizing that many would still be collecting their rewards decades later.[66]

The Loyal Worker Militia

Besides their guardian and firefighting duties, arsenalotti also carried out a range of lesser public services in Venice and the *dogado.* Masters would sometimes be delegated to work in the *Zecca,* evidently combining the roles of guard and worker; some of them also had the task of inspecting the ships of the fleet. During the intensely cold weather so typical of the 1600s, arsenalotti could be called out to provide services that ranged from sweeping snow to breaking the ice on the Brenta canal.[67]

The masters carried out these extra duties in their usual working mode of small, independent squads working under their own leaders. By the end of the seventeenth century Venetians would come to depend on the shipbuilders to keep their society operating in a variety of ways, small and large, expecting that in times of emergency these specially designated fellow citizens would be able to respond with the initiative and skill demanded by any difficulty.

Such an active group of public functionaries drawn from the working classes provided all Venetians with a convenient and visible symbol of the traditional greatness of the Republic. At a time when most Venetian citizens had begun to limit themselves to more modest horizons, the arsenalotti could still evoke strong images of both imperial and communal glories. Masters of the Arsenal served with the fleet and in outposts of the Empire to an extent equalled only by Venice's professional sailors and the militarily active nobility. They brought back to the city a range of skills and experiences gathered from all parts of the Mediterranean, and remained relatively cosmopolitan citizens of the Republic at a time when Venice was declining to the status of a regional port center.[68] Even if they sometimes placed their own profits or amusements before the full pursuit of their duties, in their pronounced loyalty to the state the masters of the Arsenal at least recalled the citizens' spontaneous public service which had once been the bulwark of the communal Republic. In them the Venetian state possessed an idealized *popolani* militia, perhaps not always efficient but certainly effective as a unifying symbol for the Republic. In leaving their workbenches at the Arsenal and mustering as a volunteer militia, the arsenalotti were workers actively displaying the kind of *virtù* which had been held since the Renaissance as productive of a good citizenry in a free Republic. If by the seventeenth century such *virtù* was more frequently praised than actually exhibited by most Venetians, the masters of the Arsenal were all the more important for their moral reminder that civic rectitude could still be attained by a special few.[69]

How were the arsenalotti themselves affected by their civic role in Venice? Certainly a large number of masters would have appreciated extra tasks such as firefighting and guard duties simply for the chance they gave to earn extra income; these civic roles can indeed be seen as an enormous source of overtime work for the masters, helping to keep their shipbuilding community, if not exactly prosperous, at least above the level of subsistence. Yet public duties, by their very nature, cannot be considered solely from an economic perspective, for they brought with them a degree of public honor that could give a sense of superiority to even the humblest among the arsenalotti. Honor is not as quantifiable as wages, but unquestionably arsenalotti experienced as valuable the status which they derived from duties that gave them a dominant position over other Venetian workers and artisans. Their civic functions in this sense paid the shipbuilders a considerable dividend, adding extra worth to their positions as arsenalotti and no doubt dissuading many from rebelling against the daily discipline and routine which the ongoing rationalization of the Arsenal workplace would have implied. Rank and standing in the larger Venetian *popolani* society thus in effect compensated rank-and-file masters for the factory conditions under which they labored in the shipyards.

It might be argued that any group of workers as compact and self-conscious as the arsenalotti should have served as more of a progressive or even revolutionary force in a rigidly hierarchical city like Venice. Maurice Aymard concluded his recent survey on shipbuilding in Republican Venice with the proposal that the giant factory complex of the Arsenal was in fact anything but a tranquil workplace, and instead offered clear signs of the formative stages of worker consciousness and class struggle in an *ancien regime* state. For Aymard, who saw covert rebellion in the arsenalotti's persistent pilfering, an even clearer testimony of the masters' resistance to the state's repressive work regime was in the handful of wage riots which shipbuilders mounted in the sixteenth century: a sign, in short, that the great majority of arsenalotti were laboring "in a climate often tense with worker struggles."[70]

Yet expectations of class consciousness among arsenalotti are undercut by their actual collective behavior during the seventeenth century, when little indeed of such "worker struggles" was in evidence. The wage riots of the 1500s were a part of the process whereby independent Venetian shipbuilders were made into state employees: these eventually ceased, even though pay and working conditions in the Arsenal certainly did not improve. Despite a workplace that was increasingly regimented during the seventeenth century and despite the ever larger demands which the state made upon their time and independence, arsenalotti nevertheless remained unprovoked and peaceful, evidently having little interest in organizing to challenge the state which employed them. True, by the 1660s their bosses in the workplace had been given permission to arm themselves while carrying out their duties, "to repress the audacity and pride of these workers," but such a thin stratum of managers (recruited, after all, from the shipbuilders themselves) would never have stood up to a serious worker challenge, should one have ever been mounted.

Aymard has blamed the absense of any substantial echoes from the labor and management clash that should have taken place in the shipyards not on the state's efficient repression or even on the arsenalotti's refusal to fight back, but on the one-sidedness of available archival sources: any testimony of class conflict would have been

"deformed or minimized by a documentation [which is] partial, because official."[71] But was this the case? It should not be forgotten
that during the seventeenth century a whole succession of special
Inquisitors were sent by the Senate to the shipyards precisely to
discover and root out whatever traces they could of the slightest
worker unrest. Despite their best efforts (and they had every reason
to make the most in their reports of whatever they came across), the
Inquisitors, and indeed the Secretaries of the Marine and the Patroni
themselves, were only able to come up with the occasional cases of
pilfering or personal corruption. Of united action or plots of the sort
that had connected the shipbuilders with the traitor Marin Falier in
the fourteenth century, there was never a clue.[72]

That the arsenalotti among all Venice's workers should be so
peaceful is all the more remarkable since, as Robert Finlay has
noted, these were "men used to united action, accustomed to weapons, directly employed by the government, [and] conscious of the
need for their services." Without any garrison normally in the city,
the state would, in fact, have had little force to oppose the arsenalotti, should they ever have decided to make this implicit power felt
through open rebellion.[73] But despite their low pay and often difficult working situation, the masters of the Arsenal never really did
rebel. Their unwillingness or inability to provide any real focus for
the discontent which would inevitably have surfaced among the
city's thousands of artisans and laborers was indeed perhaps the real
Marvel of the Arsenal, for the institution that might have been a
source of constant unrest in the city was instead a factor in its stability. By refusing to provide any rallying point for revolt, the shipbuilders helped to insure the social harmony which was one of the
foundation stones of the Republic.

If the Arsenal's relative peacefulness in the seventeenth century
confounds expectations of class conflict in an industrialized setting,
it is still remarkable enough to require some sort of explanation. An
opposite tack from Aymard's has been taken by those who have suggested that the political tranquillity of the Arsenal workplace and
community was the result of the Venetian patriciate's manipulative
skills: their genius for social control that kept the state from ever
being too completely cut off from the arsenalotti or unable to antici-
pate and confront worker grievances before they became crises.
Such a model of worker-state relations would assume such solici-
tude and paternalism on the part of the ruling elite as a natural
expression of the state's recognized dependence on these valuable

workers. The paternalist system, moreover, was closed and reciprocal, for the arsenalotti would have responded in their turn with an exemplary loyalty and self-discipline. The result was a unique labor-management relationship that has been described in the most idyllic of terms:

> To the shipbuilding craftsmen the magistracy of the Arsenal was not only their employer but their government; the turreted enclosure was not a mere workshop, they called it their home. The managers of the Arsenal did not regard the craftsmen as factory hands but as a valuable arm of the state which it was their duty to strengthen.[74]

Yet if a class-conflict interpretation of the Arsenal workplace suffers from a lack of any substantial evidence, so too does this paternalistic model of worker tranquillity seem inadequate, if only because (as Marxist scholars have pointed out) such an explanation would have unrealistically reduced the shipbuilders to a status of childlike trust and dependency on an all-wise patriciate.[75] Such portrayal of passive loyalty would hardly appear to be borne out by the arsenalotti's alacrity at squeezing out the maximum personal profit possible from that work which they did for the state, nor by the evident need for their overseers and supervisors in the shipyards to carry arms to protect themselves while on the job.

It has thus been useful to follow these masters not only in their workplace, but in the course of their various civic duties as well, as they acted the role of the Republic's worker militia. In this way it has become clearer that the Venetian state secured the loyalty of the arsenalotti less by repression or paternalism than by cooption, managing to integrate this key and otherwise potentially disruptive group of artisans into the social fabric of the city by supplying them with a personal stake in its well-being.[76] Determined to extract as much production out of its Arsenal while paying the least possible in wages (in a manner certainly consistent with the "modern" economic world view of later factory owners), the Venetian government evidently realized that securing the loyalty of its shipbuilders under such circumstances would depend on finding an honorable place for them in the Venetian social hierarchy.

In part, this was accomplished through the establishment of worker self-management and supervision in so much of the Arsenal industrial process. By tacitly turning the day-to-day running of the shipyards over to the workforce, the state created an entire hierar-

chy of worker management positions open only to shipbuilders—
themselves an already highly exclusive group of workers. Such a
management structure provided the most aggressive and enterprising among the arsenalotti with a focus for their ambitions, offering
opportunities for personal advancement that could lead to recognized status and power both within the shipyards and in the surrounding community. It also gave many workers a stake in the continued smooth running of the Arsenal production system.

But their civic duties in the larger Venetian society operated as
an even stronger force for integrating the arsenalotti with the ruling
elite of the state. Work as the Republic's handyman contractors gave
many masters a chance for personal enrichment, again giving them
a stake in the stability of a regime which they helped keep running.
Even more important, their service as the doge's special worker militia gave the shipbuilders (and indeed their entire community) an
honor and status among the city's artisans that could have only
bound them more firmly to the elite from which such distinctions
flowed.[77] Not easily converted to simple economic worth, such
honor was nevertheless accompanied by material rewards, in the
form of extra pay, *donativi,* and occasional gold medals—all of
which not only gave arsenalotti the possibility to better themselves
financially but also fulfilled important functions at a considerable
savings to the Republic: a classic example of the kinds of compro-
mises between social estates that made the Myth of Venice work.

Yet the model of cooption was two-sided: equally important as
the profits that the arsenalotti reaped from their workplace and public roles were the losses that their status and notoriety brought
them. Certainly their serving as part of the ruling circles of the city
made it all the more difficult for them to act in concerted opposition
to that government when it functioned as their employer in the shipyards. Still more significant, however, was the way in which their
civic functions served to redefine the shipbuilders' social position
relative to the rest of the city's artisan population. Allowed to more
or less exercise their militia duties at their own discretion, the Arsenal masters were not shy about lording it up over other workers,
giving commands to other *popolani* or even thrashing them inso-
lently with their red *bastoni* during public festivals and celebrations.
While certainly respected and tolerated more than the detested
sbirri of the Ten, the arsenalotti, in their compact and coordinated
groups, were thus often at odds with the rest of their fellow *popo-*
lani, and paid for their pleasures of dominance by ending up effec-

tively cut off from the mass of Venice's artisans. As a result, this largest and most compact worker community in the city found itself in the rather uncomfortable position of straddling the line which separated rulers from ruled in the city—simultaneously artisans and minions of the state, belonging to both, but not completely members of either side. Any possibility that the skills and discipline of the arsenalotti might be put at the service of a general class conflict in Venice was by the seventeenth century negated by their very services as the Republic's worker militia—duties which enhanced their own corporate myth, but which also resulted in their isolation from the mass of the city's working population.

Frederic Lane, who probably first introduced the Venetian Arsenal to the English-speaking public, warned his readers against treating this manufacturing center as if it were an industrial factory on the nineteenth-century model. Convinced that the Arsenal was instead a massive agglomeration of semi-independent workshops, Lane went on to caution those who might seek in the arsenalotti themselves a kind of "proto-proletariat," specifying that the shipbuilders who worked in these yards were by no means "'factory hands' . . . [but] differed in spirit and in discipline, for they were master craftsmen and naval reservists."[78] Certainly his warnings were salutary, especially for scholars tempted to find an "industrial proletariat" involved in every manufacturing process from medieval Florentine woolshops to the royal manufactures of the *ancien régime.* Yet the terms "craftsman" and "factory hand" clearly go beyond normative descriptions of work processes: they imply differing models of social organization, relationships to political power, and indeed of individual workers' entire self-awareness. When Lane assigned the arsenalotti to a world of craftsmen (albeit one conditioned by military service), he placed them not only in the artisan's *bottega,* but equally in the realm of craft standards, guild sodality, and corporate government. But was this in fact the social reality of Venetian state shipbuilders?

The first part of this study has attempted to demonstrate that the arsenalotti in fact shared little in the values of urban guildsmen, especially when these shipbuilders are followed into the relatively uncharted historical waters of the seventeenth century. Systematically disciplined to the needs of an integrated production system, the majority of the city's independent shipbuilders were in time turned into a mass of relatively undifferentiated arsenalotti, laboring under the direction of a steadily more remote management hierarchy. The very conditions under which these workers were trained and labored effectively separated them from the traditional guild experience, giving them a set of skills and workplace attitudes that were indeed more appropriate for factory laborers than for the independent craftsman in his own workshop. Even if state shipbuilding in Venice remained organized into the same guild structure that provided other Venetian workers with their corporate identity, the arsenalotti craft guilds were, as Lane himself admitted, little more than traditionalist window-dressing—a shell of self-regulation designed to cover up the state's nearly complete takeover of every substantive guild concern, from apprenticeship training, to master's examinations, to the setting of wages and benefits. By the seventeenth century even the business of petitioning was no longer a corporate affair among the arsenalotti, but had passed instead to the individual guildsmen.

It has also been an underlying assumption of this study that the arsenalotti defined themselves by more than simply their tools, their pay, and the hierarchy on the factory floor, and that to arrive at an understanding of the self-perception of these (or indeed any other) workers it would be necessary to deal as much with their larger community as with the specific context of their institutional workplace. For it was precisely in Venetian society as a whole that the shipbuilders showed their lack of this "master craftsmen's spirit" with which Lane has credited them. Certainly the arsenalotti's self-consciousness as a worker group was both well-developed and intense, but their awareness was more a pride in their place of work, their own community, and their special duties and privileges than a sense of identification with other Venetian workers. The shipbuilders showed little or no awareness of nor acted upon any "shared cultural identity" with other Venetian artisans—none of the sense of common moral standards or recognized mutual interests that have been observed among a variety of European guildsmen, from German home towns to cities like Dijon and Marseilles.[79] In spite of their poor wages and often oppressive discipline, the arsenalotti stubbornly continued to identify with the state that employed them rather than with the concerns they seemingly shared with fellow artisans. It was an attitude that would outlive the Republic itself: in 1848 the arsenalotti spearheaded the only significant worker rebellion which the city would ever see, not as an industrial confrontation but in patriotic alliance with the city's bourgeoisie—to end

Austrian dominion and recreate the old regime that had once given shipbuilders their special role.[80]

Were the Venetian shipbuilders' roles and status so particular as to make them unlike any other worker community in the early-modern age—simply another quirky manifestation of what was already perhaps the most anomalous state of *ancien régime* Europe? Until more study is undertaken on the worker communities of mines, shipyards, foundries, or other large-scale, state-run manufactories elsewhere on the continent, it will be impossible to say. Certainly research carried out to date on shipyards alone has underscored the considerable variations with which labor in such enterprises was organized: from loosely organized and largely self-regulating guildsmen entrepreneurs in Holland to a system of virtual forced labor in England; whether other large worker communities of this era managed to secure rights and civic responsibilities as extensive as those won by the arsenalotti, thereby to be "tamed" in the process, still remains to be seen.[81]

Appendix 1

Suppliche in Venice

The petitions, or *suppliche,* submitted to the Venetian Collegio represent a comparatively late archival source in the history of the Republic. This may be one reason for their relative neglect by scholars, although the vast and chaotic jumble of subjects with which such petitions deal is very likely another: everything from pleas for pensions and requests for citizenship to anonymous denunciations and offers of inventions are mixed together in the series. Although some material has survived from as early as the year 1511, the series begins as a continuous collection only in 1563, then running until the fall of the Republic in 1797. In the first decades of the collection there are not many petitions preserved for each year, but despite this somewhat slow beginning, the suppliche process certainly did come into its own by the following century: just between 1621 and 1670, the Collegio series titled *risposte di dentro* amounts to an estimated 25,000 petitions from Venice, its *dogado,* and other nearby areas of the *terraferma.* A number nearly as great was also submitted from the Veneto and around the Empire, gathered together in the series *risposte di fuori.*

The practice of petition writing was by no means uncommon in early modern Europe, but it was in Republican Venice where petitioning took on such a central social role that it could fairly be termed an institution in its own right.[1] The custom of Venetian citizens' petitioning their government certainly dates back to at least the thirteenth century, when the first collection of *gratie* issued by the Maggior Consiglio indicates that subjects were already active in seeking favors. By the sixteenth century, much of the actual business of reviewing suppliche had shifted from the Maggior Consiglio to the Pien Collegio. The Collegio was originally designed in 1442 as a kind of legislative clearing house for the Senate and Maggior Consiglio, but it also made good administrative sense to have it take on the task of hearing petitions. Much smaller than either of the Republic's rather unwieldy legislative bodies, the Collegio, consisting of the doge and his three ranks of advising secretaries *(savi)*, was well-placed to deal with any sort of problem that petitioners might present. Both highly competent and at the center of power, the Collegio was especially useful in dealing with petitions generated as a result of the Republic's growing bureaucracy.[2] Able not only to override the decisions of lesser magistrates but also to demand that they provide a written explanation of their actions, the board could offer a high-level review for petitioners; in a sense it made possible a certain amount of bureaucratic accountability in the Republic (see fig. A.1).

It was indeed with bureaucratic complaints that a substantial percentage (if not a majority) of suppliche to the Collegio were concerned. Venetians were forever finding themselves unhappily caught up in the processes of a government where magistrates could prove unwilling or unable to take on responsibility for vital decisions or where unclear jurisdictional boundaries resulted in one council revoking what another had just bestowed. As a result, suppliche to the Collegio turn out to have been overwhelmingly from the social groups most likely to have gotten caught up in problems of taxes or magistrates: propertied elites of the Republic such as Venetian nobles and *cittadini*, foreign merchant communities, religious corporations, *scuole*, and governing bodies from dependent townships. Petitions to the Collegio from the artisans and *popolani* who made up the great majority of Venetians were correspondingly rare, probably not more than 5 percent of the total. Instead of coming before the Collegio, most Venetian workers with grievances submitted their petitions to those lower-level magistrates especially designated to handle their affairs.[3] Moreover, on the relatively infrequent occasions when they felt it necessary to go beyond such boards and

to bring a case before the Collegio, workers almost never did
so as individuals, but instead petitioned collectively. Usually only their guild chiefs *(gastaldi)* and a lawyer spoke on their behalf, appearing before the board to argue the petitions drawn up by them collectively.[4]

A few categories of Venetian artisans did habitually petition the Collegio, however, and did so as individuals rather than collectively, thanks largely to the particular situations in which they worked. Some, such as the fifty or so master gold and silversmiths who worked in the state mint *(Zecca)* apparently did so because they were considered government employees. The Republic's professional sailors and some categories of porters evidently had to petition individually before the Collegio because they had no guild of their own.[5] The Senate's own laws required many independent shipbuilders to come before the Collegio with a formal request every time they needed more of the Republic's scarce oak to finish their construction work.

But the most numerous of all such artisan petitioners were cer-

Figure A.1. The Pien Collegio in the seventeenth century

tainly Arsenal workers, who indeed submitted more suppliche to the Collegio than all other Venetian craftsmen together. Officially, supervision of the arsenalotti was the responsibility of the three Patroni of the Arsenal (to whom the shipbuilders also occasionally addressed some petitions), but the real power over their lives rested with the Collegio: in particular with the five Secretaries of the Marine, who paid close attention to the shipbuilders as part of a larger responsibility for reviewing all matters concerning the state shipyards. Considering the importance of the arsenalotti as government workers, no administrative board other than the Collegio would in any event have had the power or the competence to deal with the great variety of their needs. Despite the supposed authority of the Patroni over the state shipyards, the Collegio kept for itself all decisions concerning admission to the workforce, wage adjustments, reimbursements, and the award of offices: the very subjects that were most likely to prompt the shipbuilders to petition. Even though the board was designated to carry out the highest business of the state, the nobles on the Collegio evidently felt that listening to the complaints and requests of these ordinary shipbuilders was very much part of their duties.

The Petitioners

Unlike other Venetian guildsmen, the arsenalotti only rarely petitioned the Collegio collectively; this failure to resort to corporate action is hardly surprising, since already by the Middle Ages, the state had rendered shipbuilding guilds largely powerless.[6] Of the over 975 arsenalotti suppliche presented to the Collegio during the years 1621–70, only 30 were submitted by one or more of the Arsenal's three principal guilds. Petitions by these guilds tended to be defensive in nature, often attempting to repeal or postpone new tax assessments or unpopular changes in work regulations. In this the Arsenal guilds had some success, at least in putting off if not actually repealing such rulings; indeed, the corporate appeal was probably workers' most successful means for reminding the Collegio of the traditional privileges and exemptions which they had come to regard as their due.

Arsenal guilds were less successful in petitioning for general pay raises in the shipyards. Four times in the decade after the plague of 1630–31, the *gastaldi* petitioned to increase their members' pay maximum to a level closer to that of other Venetian artisans, but on each occasion they were turned down: none of their lawyers' figures and arguments managed to convince the board to abandon the Arsenal's fifty-year-old wage ceiling.[7] On the other hand, corporate suppliche that simply asked the Collegio to call the Arsenal pay board (*Colleggietto*) were generally successful. Without such prodding, the Senate might easily let six or seven years go by before getting around to initiating the pay reviews that were by law meant to be held every two years.

By contrast, individual arsenalotti were altogether more enterprising in their petitioning. By the Collegio's own orders, the Patroni and the Colleggietto had only limited powers to promote the interests or ambitions of individual workers, and for any kind of pay increase beyond the rigidly held 40-soldi daily maximum, a master had to come before the board. As the seventeenth century progressed, masters apparently became more adroit in using the suppliche process, asking not just for raises or promotions but indeed for anything the Collegio might conceivably bestow, including monopolies, wage parity with other masters, newly conceived offices, and privileges for their descendants. In the hands of many Arsenal masters the suppliche process became a means of self-advancement; unlike the defensive petitions submitted by their guilds, those presented by individual workers made a virtue out of boldness and creativity.

Petitions to the Collegio concerning the Arsenal were submitted by four general groups of artisans and *popolani*. Of 936 such petitions from around 750 individuals submitted during the years 1621–70, the great majority fell into one of three roughly equal-sized categories: outsiders who wished for enrollment in the Arsenal, ordinary rank-and-file shipbuilders (*operai* or *maestri*), and the shipyards' worker managers, called *ministeri*. A fourth, much smaller group consisted of female relatives of arsenalotti who made up their own suppliche to the Collegio.

About half the 297 outsiders who petitioned for a place in the Arsenal during these years were sailors. By the time these men asked for enrollment on the shipyards' rosters, they were usually well beyond middle age, having served some years with the fleet or merchant marine. Generally they hoped to be rewarded for past services, given a place with the other elderly workers (the so-called *vecchi à riva*) doing light work making chests, benches, or cabins, in a sort of working retirement ashore. Using the Arsenal as a reward and a repository for elderly sailors had become a kind of state policy by the seventeenth century, for as the Patroni themselves pointed out

in 1636, when sailors were in extremely short supply such inducements were useful in attracting more of them.[8]

Another 54 of these outsider supplicants had followed a life
similar to sailors but had as younger men actually been arsenalotti.
Many had stayed away from the regular work of the shipyards too
long and had missed one of the sporadic pay reviews held by the
Colleggietto, causing them to be stricken from the Arsenal rosters.
Like sailors, many of these ex-arsenalotti were also older men, seeking some light work and steady pay in the Arsenal when they found
themselves too elderly and feeble to secure profitable work at sea or
in the city's private shipyards.[9]

The remaining 97 of this group of petitioners were active artisans: shipbuilders in the private yards of the city or craftsmen in
such trades as turner, cooper, or gun carriage maker, all of which
had potential use in the state shipyards. Most of these applicants
were men in the prime of their lives and many ran their own shops
in the city; their petitions gave every indication that they intended
to continue working privately as well as in the Arsenal should they
be accepted. Although working for the state often paid a craftsman
far less than he could expect from his own shop, membership
among the arsenalotti conferred honor, security, and important tax
breaks. Sometimes entire groups of such artisans petitioned the Collegio to enroll in the Arsenal, evidently in the hope of avoiding their
military and financial obligations as guildsmen.[10]

The number of women from the arsenalotti community who petitioned the Collegio was quite small compared to other outsiders: a
mere 27 over the years 1621–70. Generally, they were widows or
mothers of deceased arsenalotti hoping to win a pension based on
the services which their men had once rendered the state. Women
may have been reluctant to ask for such assistance simply for their
own sake, but would willingly present themselves as agents for their
orphaned children: seeking a dowry for a daughter or a pension
until their young sons were old enough to support the family.[11]
Their petitioning appears to have been a temporary activity, a role
to be relinquished as soon their sons reached majority; some even
appeared in their turn as aged dependents in the petitions of the
next generation.[12]

Despite casting themselves in the secondary role of family agent
when petitioning, arsenalotti women could still make their cases
quite forcefully with a direct and aggressive spirit. Some wives proposed a scheme to buy the freedom of their imprisoned husbands in

a way that would profit both the state and themselves; a widow was
not too modest to point out to the Collegio that the shipbuilding
talents of her young sons derived as much from her own lineage as
from her husband's.[13] Nor might a woman be above trying to shame
the Collegio into generosity, complaining perhaps of the low wages
her husband had received while alive, or even threatening that her
daughters might be forced to dishonor themselves (and, presumably, the shipyards as well) if the state did not come through with a
pension.[14]

The remainder of the collection of suppliche used in this study
were written by shipbuilders actually working in the state Arsenal.
Of these, 319 were submitted by "rank-and-file" workers in the shipyards; with the number of enrolled arsenalotti averaging around
1,500 during these years, these petitioners could be said to represent
around 6–7 percent of all the individual master artisans and apprentices attached to the Arsenal.[15] As a sample, these petitioners tend
to overrepresent both the youngest and the oldest of the shipbuilding workforce, a reflection of the general exodus of masters in their
prime to find better paying work in the free labor market.[16]

The final 293 arsenalotti suppliche were submitted by the foremen, supervisors, and bosses who ran the shipyards: the eighty or
so workers whose offices gave them authority and command over
other masters. Clearly a much more prolific group of petition writers, these worker managers are thus the arsenalotti most accessible
through the series of suppliche; indeed, an estimated 50–60 percent
of these men petitioned the Collegio at least once, and some of them
did so half a dozen times or more.[17]

Overall, around 40 percent of all Arsenal petitioners actually saw
their suppliche granted by an award (*gratia*) of the Senate during
the years of this study.[18] Different sorts of petitioners had different
expectations of success, however, ranging from only around 30 percent for petitions awarded to rank-and-file arsenalotti, to 40 percent
for outsiders seeking to enroll, to nearly 50 percent for worker managers of all types, to an almost 80 percent success rate for the suppliche of the Admiral and four principal foremen.

Even though most ordinary arsenalotti could not have been particularly sanguine on their chances of success, the number of suppliche from the shipyards was clearly on the increase during these
years, spurred on perhaps by the knowledge that *gratie* were mul-
tiplying just about as fast as the petitions themselves. The mid-

seventeenth century was indeed the time in which Arsenal workers discovered and learned to use the suppliche process: from relatively small numbers in the first decades of the century, petitions from arsenalotti and those who wished to enroll with them showed a nearly fivefold increase by 1670. Their enthusiasm for petitioning grew to such an extent that at times it threatened to swamp the state in the paperwork it generated (see graph A.1).[19]

The steady increase of arsenalotti petitions to the Collegio reversed only twice in these years, both times when the workforce itself was sharply diminished: in the aftermath of the 1630–31 plague and during the heavy conscription marking the opening years of the War of Candia.[20] As the number of petitions grew, the profile of the supplicants began to shift downwards in social and economic terms; the original preponderance of work managers was replaced, first by ordinary masters, and then by increasing numbers

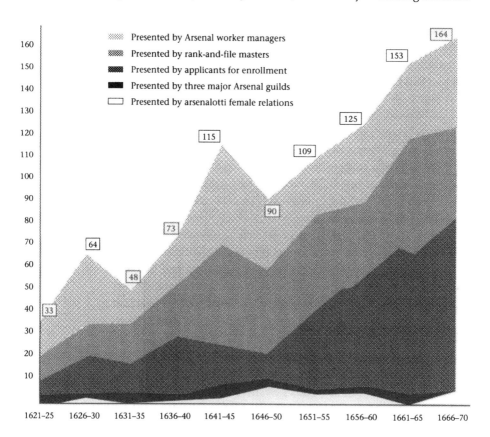

Graph A.1. Arsenalotti suppliche to the Collegio, 1621-1670 (consecutive five-year totals)

of outsiders seeking to enroll. The state was aware of such trends and apparently did not approve of them: masters who won raises through petitioning were forbidden further wage increases by their Colleggietto, and one of the first cost-cutting suggestions that the Patroni made to the Senate in 1669, at the end of the Candia War, was to refuse outsiders admission into the Arsenal by petition.[21] Such moves apparently did little to discourage petitioners, however, especially among outsiders; so widespread was the desire to join the arsenalotti that despite such edicts the number of suppliche for enrollment was just as high in 1680 as it had been in the 1660s.[22]

The Petitioning Process

Like all who wished to make a plea to the Collegio, arsenalotti had to begin by drawing up a petition. Since many shipbuilders were illiterate, this meant finding a scribe to assist them in making their request. Scribes were not only for the unlettered, however: the worker managers of the shipyards were also willing to pay for such services, even though they themselves routinely knew how to read and write. Besides providing superior penmanship, scribes were aware of the grammar and usages expected for such formal writings: they could be counted on to avoid dialect expressions or the kinds of spellings based on Venetian pronunciations to which even literate masters were prone; indeed, even patricians might employ a scribe if the petition were important enough.[23] For those who wished a still more cultivated petition, it was also possible to hire a scribe who would indulge in a few Latin phrases or baroque flourishes.[24] For their work, scribes might demand between 20 and 40 soldi, according to the length and nature of the document—as much as a day's wages for an ordinary Arsenal master.[25] Quality of script might well have made a difference in price as well: few arsenalotti petitions are found in the fancier hands preferred by the Venetian elite, probably since masters judged the results as not worth the price. Instead, shipbuilders' petitions are generally in a few simple but neat hands, very likely indicating that they habitually patronized the same small circle of local, less expensive scribes.[26]

Petitioners could also probably reduce the cost of a suppliche by having it composed of largely stock phrases. Although a personal and evocative story was an essential part of most petitions, there was also certainly much that could be left up to the scribe to fill in. Suppliche routinely began with a formal salute to the *Serenissimo Principe,* and concluded with words both contrite and flourishing ("humbly kneeling I appeal to You and the Public Majesty, imploring that help which Your Serenity would be pleased to grant me"): lines that were probably charged out to the customer at a fixed rate. The formulaic phrasings were not unique to suppliche prepared by scribes, but also appear in those obviously written by shipbuilders themselves: an interesting indication as to how far down the social scale such polite usages could penetrate. Certain petitions were evidently entirely prewritten, with only the name and occupation of the customer waiting to be filled in. Two 1643 requests made by different masters for a sailor's pension known as the *poveri al pevere* were identical in every word but their names, yet written in different hands: likely evidence that form petitions for common sorts of requests circulated about from scribe to scribe.[27]

The cost of a scribe does not in any event seem to have been a major factor in discouraging arsenalotti who wished a hearing before the Collegio. Nearly fifty masters in fact presented two or more suppliche between 1621 and 1670; some did so twice in the same year. An especially enterprising shipwright named Marin di Antonio paid for no fewer than twelve petitions between the years 1627 and 1664, many of them to offer his inventions to the Collegio. These included a fireproof method of baking ship's biscuit, a means of ousting rats from the sailcloth storeroom, a design for a type of armored ship, and a fountain for dispensing the Arsenal's wine.[28]

To better support their narratives, many Arsenal workers who petitioned the Collegio also submitted a collection of personal testimonials, known as *fedi* or *attestationi*. The term *fede* derived from the documents' opening phrase: *faccio fede,* or "I bear witness." Although no more than scraps of paper on which someone of authority had written a few lines to attest to the petitioner's good character, accomplishments, or service, fedi were the essential means through which a worker established his reputation. Fedi were also the state's way of keeping itself informed about its subjects: written by Venice's nobility, clergy, or accredited officers, they could be demanded by other authorities as an *attestazioni di buona fama* (or at least of the absence of past misconduct) from any worker who was seeking a position or promotion. When reviewing a master's petition for the Collegio, one of the Patroni's main chores was indeed to check the reliability of his fedi.[29] It was best if the fedi were written by men of high status: testimonials by officials from below a certain level in the state bureaucracy could well prove unacceptable in higher government circles, to the extent that a petitioner might have to produce a second fede to attest to the trustworthiness of the writer of the first.[30]

When sailors petitioned the Collegio, they were required to produce fedi in order to present a full account of their past; in particular the board seems to have been concerned that those wishing to enroll in the Arsenal had no gaps or ambiguities that might indicate a spell spent with a foreign navy. Sailors picked up their fedi from each commander at the time their vessel completed its voyage; sometimes in a lifetime at sea they managed to collect as many as fifteen or twenty such testimonials. Most appear to have handed over their actual fedi with their petitions; some, such as Andrea da Cherso, had so many that they decided to provide a *sommario* instead, indicating the precise dates of each voyage and the position held.[31] The Collegio's need to know all about a sailor's past was not always easily satisfied, however: if a ship sank and lost its records or its commander, survivors were without a fede to explain their whereabouts for the entire period of the voyage.[32] Despite the risk of losing them, most sailors apparently still persisted in carrying their fedi while at sea, evidently on the chance that they might take a new berth while away from Venice.[33] For a Venetian sailor, a collection of fedi provided legitimization, and their loss threatened him with complete personal disaster, as Zuane di Antonio lamented after some of his *diversi attestati* had disappeared during a shipwreck.[34] Those without their fedi might be forced to take extreme steps to satisfy the Collegio's curiosity. After the sailor Iseppo di Antonio Tesser lost his fedi during a sixteen-year spell of enslavement in Tunis, he was forced to hire a notary and scour his neighborhood in Venice in order to find six old companions who could vouch for him and provide statements on his past.[35]

Arsenalotti also presented fedi to the Collegio to back up the personal narratives contained in their suppliche. Since most of them had served at sea at some time in their lives, they usually offered testimonials from naval commanders, just as sailors did. In addition, many arsenalotti also offered fedi as supporting evidence about the quality and extent of their work at the shipyards. Many shipbuilders would therefore include an appropriate fede from their superiors or the Patroni. Higher managers such as the four major guild foremen and the timekeepers seem to have been constantly writing fedi, stating their judgment on workers' obedience, their technical skills, past service, and even their literacy.[36] At least some managers realized considerable profit as fedi writers: the Arsenal timekeepers once even attempted to establish a *tariffa* for each type of fede that they supplied from their rosters, an indication that charging for fedi was an ordinary reward of office. The timekeepers' fedi typically ranged in price at around half a masters' daily pay each.[37]

By the seventeenth century an entire network of fedi writing had grown up within the state shipyards, reaffirming and codifying the power and prestige of those administrators who possessed the authority to supply testimonials for their underlings.[38] Yet even if fedi could work as instruments of repression or exploitation in the hands of state authorities, they also had a more benevolent place in the suppliche process. Fedi traced the networks of patronage and reciprocity that flourished in the Arsenal, cementing ties as on such occasions when an elderly gang boss testified on behalf of his apprentice who aspired to his same position.[39] They also made an acceptable excuse for long or irregular absences when secured from doctors or government authorities.[40] Simple fedi of baptism, issued by the parish priest or curate, were put to use to demonstrate the burdensome size of the family which a master had to maintain; one shipwright produced a fede to prove he could not have been responsible for a certain debt, simply because he had only been five years old when it had been contracted.[41] Sometimes local priests might turn the baptismal fede into a virtual character reference for a master they considered especially worthy, as when a curate of San Pietro di Castello wrote on behalf of the pulleymaker Salvador Negrini, "[he is] an elderly man of around 90 years old, fearful of the Lord God, faithful to his Prince, but unlucky in life and worthy for his good and honest qualities of being helped by any charitable support."[42]

Born into the system of fedi, many arsenalotti turned out to be especially adept at manipulating them to their own advantage. To assert a claim for wage parity, a clever foreman would go to the Arsenal bookkeeper not only for a fede recording his own salary, but also those of his better-paid colleagues holding similar positions.[43] One shipwright contended in his supplica that he could legitimately hold an outside office while still on the Arsenal pay rosters and submitted a fede with the names of several arsenalotti past and present who had done just that.[44] Masters collected the scraps of paper for years in anticipation of the moment when they could best be put to convincing use. Whenever they were called upon to do extraordinary or risky work, arsenalotti evidently made a point of requesting a fede from whatever authority might be at hand, to prove that they

had been ready to face such dangers as a salvaging job which no one
else would accept, or that they had demonstrated special bravery
during such emergencies as fires.[45]

Arsenalotti customarily presented their suppliche and fedi personally to the Collegio; those who were too sick to do so seem to have considered the circumstances unusual enough to mention in their petitions.[46] Since many were illiterate, their suppliche were presumably read aloud to the doge and the sixteen *savi:* very likely the petitioner would then be questioned by the nobles of the board. Some supplicants claimed that the whole procedure was quite embarrassing for a worker cadre as proud as Venetian shipbuilders, asserting that they "desired more to merit rather than request rewards"; they prefaced their petitions by insisting on not being in the habit of making such requests, out of a desire not to cause irritation to their prince.[47] Yet arsenalotti were seemingly not at all intimidated being cross-examined by the elite of Venice's aristocracy, and indeed some were prepared to take advantage of all the opportunities which such an encounter offered. Masters might bring in models of ships they had designed or inventions they were proposing and then demonstrate them before the council.[48] One sailor seeking enrollment in the Arsenal addressed himself personally to the presiding doge Francesco Erizzo, recalling how years earlier, when *Provveditore General da Mar,* Erizzo had been his commanding officer and had written fedi on his behalf.[49] Personal appearances in the meeting room of the Collegio certainly offered arsenalotti the chance to dramatize their suppliche. Asking to be deferred from service with the fleet, the young oarmaker Iseppo di Bernardin opened his request to the council with the words:

> Whether I am able and capable of such service, my few years and my illnesses clearly show . . . and each of Your Excellencies can visually see me [and decide] whether I am in a state equal to what the law requires, since I have a continual flow of blood from my nostrils and mouth and a perpetual stomach problem.[50]

Once handed over to the Collegio, suppliche followed a long and sometimes perilous path through the bureaucratic channels of seventeenth-century Venice, as can be seen from a 1627 petition by the sailor Luca di Vicenzo Luppi da Cattaro. Two years earlier, Luca wrote, he had petitioned the Collegio for a place in the Arsenal as a pulleymaker. After his appearance in the chambers, his supplica had been accepted by the members of the council, dated, copied, and committed to the Patroni of the Arsenal. Not only did this magistrate review petitioners' fedi, it was also responsible for verifying wages and clarifying for the Collegio those cases that might have any special or complex features.[51] The judgment of the Patroni was then returned to the Collegio, which consigned it together with the rest of a petitioner's file to the *signori savij:* that is, the five Marine Secretaries. This subcommittee, having considered the report of the Arsenal magistrate, then voted on the supplica, and if they passed it, sent the entire file to the full Collegio, which voted on it in turn and fixed any special conditions that might limit the final award. At this point, it was necessary to enter the decision of the Collegio on the Senate's calendar for a final vote, generally the stage of the process in which the longest delays occurred.[52] Not until the Senate's vote was officially inscribed could a petitioner expect his reward. So Luca found out to his regret after having waited two years for the Senate to act, only to discover that, although passed by the Collegio, the entire file of his petition ("tutte le scritture") had subsequently been lost, and it would be necessary for him to start all over again.[53]

If losing Luca Luppi's first petition caused the Collegio any embarrassment, the board did not make amends by speeding up his second: fully twenty-eight months went by from the time this petition was received until the Senate voted to approve it and grant Luca his admittance to the Arsenal. Considering the complexity of the suppliche process, it is not surprising to find that the procedure could be quite slow. In the 1620s around two to four years typically elapsed between the Collegio's first dating a petition and the Senate's final vote on it; for some unlucky petitioners, six or more years might go by.[54] In time, however, the procedure was sped up, probably in response to the shortage of masters brought on by the plague of 1630–31 and by the demands of the Cretan War. By the 1650s many petitions were received and approved within the space of only six months, although long delays still sometimes occurred.

Yet even after the Senate had voted and inscribed an award, there was still no guarantee that a master would necessarily enjoy what he had requested. Acting on the Patroni's advice, the Senate often decided that while a supplicant might be worthy of a *gratia,* his request had been either too large or inappropriate.[55] On such occasions the worker was granted something less than what he had asked. In addition, the award itself might prove hard to collect, as some petitioners discovered when they came to the Palazzo Ducale and found their claim disputed by ministers and bureaucrats who raised expensive technicalities or other difficulties. So the caulker Christofolo di Zordan bitterly complained: while trying to receive a *gratia* awarded to him earlier, he had been forced to "argue with great and authoritative people," and had spent "hundreds of ducats," but still failed to obtain what the Senate had granted him.[56]

Appendix 2

Organization of the Arsenal Workforce in the Mid-1600s

I. Patrician administrators (Banca)
- A. Overseeing magistrates
   1. 3 Provveditori all'Arsenale
   2. 2–3 Inquisitori all'Arsenale (after 1633)
- B. Operating magistrates
   1. 3 Patroni all'Arsenale with separate authorities:
      - a. Patron di cassa (Accounts Lord)
      - b. Patron di guardia (Security Lord)
      - c. Patron delle maestranze (Workforce Lord)

II. Under the authority of the Patron delle maestranze
- A. Ammiraglio all'Arsenale (Admiral of the Arsenal) plus 2 Aiutanti all'Ammiraglio (assistants) *who together commanded:*
   1. 3 Capi manoali (heads of launching squads)
      - a. 3 squads of 10 laborers and sailors
   2. 4 Soprastanti di Casa (warehouse supervisors)
      - a. Soprastante di legno vecchio (for old lumber)
   3. Soprastante dei respetti (for reserves)
   4. Soprastante dei 7 magazeni (for gunpowder)
   5. Capo dei 30 facchini (head of 30 laborers)
      - a. 30 laborers trained for fires in city

     6. Sottocapo dei 15 facchini (deputy head)
       a. 15 laborers trained for fires in Arsenal
     7. Proto dei favri (foreman smith)
       a. ca. 7 blacksmiths
     8. Proto dei mureri (plant foreman)
       a. ca. 5 wallers
     9. Mistra delle vellere (mistress of the sailroom)
       a. 25–40 seamstresses for sails
   10. Custode alle tele (guard for sailcloth stores)
   11. Proto carreri (foreman of the guncarriage makers)
       a. 2–5 carreri (guncarriage carpenters)
   12. Netta galie (cleaner of the galleys)
   13. Deputato al Bucintoro (attended the *Bucintoro*)
   14. Governar li piatoni (attended ceremonial barges)

B. Proto dei marangoni (foreman shipwright) and Sottoproto
  dei marangoni (assistant foreman) and his helper *who together commanded:*
     1. 2–4 Stimadori (appraisers)
     2. 10 Capi d'opera (gang bosses) plus 1–10 Capi d'opera
       soprannumerari (in emergency)
       a. ca. 10 sottocapi (assistant bosses)
       b. ca. 400 active marangoni (master shipwrights)
          i. 75–120 fanti minuti (regular apprentices)
         ii. 10–60 fanti grossi (special apprentices)
     3. Proto dei tagieri (subforeman pulleymaker) and his
       Sottoproto
       a. 15–30 active tagieri (pulleymakers)
          i. 10–15 garzoni (regular apprentices)
     4. Proto delle sieghe (subforeman sawyer) and his Sottoproto
       a. ca. 10 regular sawyers
       b. ca. 20 piecework sawyers
     5. Proto alle carieghe (subforeman of deck works)
       a. 2 assistants
     6. Proto ai banchi (subforeman of galley benches)
       a. 4–5 elderly assistants
     7. 2 Deputati al legno dolce (deputies for softwood)
       a. assistant
     8. Pescar legnami (deputy for retrieving lumber)
     9. Appontador (overseer for foreman shipwright: super-
       vised woodcarvers and gilders)

    D. Ammiraglio and Proto dei marangoni together *also had some authority over*

        1. Proto dei alboranti (foreman of the mastmakers) and his Sottoproto

            a. 20–50 active alboranti (mastmakers)

                i. ca. 10 garzoni (regular apprentices)

        2. Proto dei remeri (foreman of the oarmakers) and his Sottoproto

            a. 40–70 active remeri (oarmakers)

                i. ca. 25 garzoni (apprentices)

            b. ficcar cavalletti (sawhorse maker)

            c. 10–15 facchini (laborers)

    C. Proto dei calafati (foreman of the caulkers) Sottoproto dei calafati (assistant foreman) *who together commanded:*

        1. Sottoproto, calafati da maggio (subforeman)

            a. soprastante pegola (supervisor for pitch)

                i. 6–10 laborers for cooking pitch

            b. soprastante stoppe (supervisor for oakum)

        2. Sottoproto, calafati da fizer (subforeman)

            a. soprastante ferramenti grossi (for hardware)

            b. soprastante ferramenti minuti (for nails)

        3. 8 Capi d'opera (gang bosses)

            a. ca. 400 calafati da maggio and da fizer (oakum and planking caulkers)

                i. 100–120 fanti minuti (regular apprentices)

                ii. ca. 10 fanti grossi (special apprentices)

        4. Sunar ferramento vecchio (collected scrap metals)

  III. Under authority of the Patron di guardia

    A. In conjunction with the Proti of marangoni, calafati, and remeri and their Sottoproti

        1. Appontador della prima polizza (first timekeeper) and viceappontador (assistant) supervised half the shipwrights

        2. Appontador della seconda polizza (second timekeeper) supervised remaining shipwrights, plus pulleymakers and mastmakers

        3. Appontador dei calafati (caulker's timekeeper) supervised caulkers

        4. Appontador dei remeri supervised oarmakers, sailmakers, laborers, wallers, and blacksmiths

5. Despontador dei marangoni (shipwrights' overseer) oversaw all shipwrights, pulley, and mastmakers
6. Despontador dei calafati (caulkers' overseer) oversaw all caulkers
7. Despontador dei remeri oversaw oarmakers and all unenrolled craftsmen, laborers, and apprentices
8. Revisor alle maestranze (workforce overseer)

B. Under direct command of the Patron di guardia
   1. Capitanio del Arsenale (captain and jailer)
   2. Capo dei guardiani notturni (head of night guard)
      a. 80 guardiani (night guards)
   3. Appontador dei guardiani (timekeeper of the night guards)
   4. Capo del campo (head of outside patrol)
      a. 8 guardiani (patrolmen)
   5. 6 Guardiani festivi (gatekeepers for holidays)
   6. Stuar li fuochi (fire inspector and extinguisher)
   7. Deputato al Restello (guard for main watergate)
   8. Deputato ai 2 ponti (guard for 2 drawbridges)
   9. Deputato ai 2 stendardi (displayed Arsenal flags)
   10. Tener orologio (set Arsenal clock)
   11. Sonar campanella (Arsenal bellringer) [1]

Source: ASV:Collegio V (Segreta), bu. 57, Relazione of Andrea Marcello (1645), and of Francesco Cornero (1696); ASV:CRD suppliche and SM (filze), passim, and MC:Ms Gradenigo, bu. 193 II, ff. 80r–82v (1688) and 118r–119v (1708).

Notes

Key to Abbreviations

ASV   Archivio di Stato, Venice
CRD   Collegio, *risposte di dentro*
DSD   Dieci Savi sopra le Decime in Rialto
MC   Museo Correr, Venice
PS   Provveditori alla Sanità
SM   Senato Mar
SUP   Sant'Uffizio, *processi*
TA   Provveditori e Patroni all'Arsenale, *terminazione*

f.   folio
filze   file
m.v.   Most Venetian documents of the seventeenth century were dated in *modo veneziano,* that is, with the year beginning on March 1. This system has been followed in this book: thus, 25 Feb 1645 m.v. is actually 25 Feb 1646 by the modern calendar.

Introduction

1. In fact, far from being rooted in Latin, the word *arsenale* probably came to Venice from Arabic sources. Nani Mocenigo, *L'Arsenale di Venezia,* 18; Sansovino, *Venetia, città nobilissima,* 366.

2. ASV:Collegio V (Segreta), Relazione of Zuane Bernardo (1676), f. 1r; also ASV:Collegio V (Segreta), bu. 57, Relazione of Bertucci Trivisan (1669), f. 1v; Relazione of Sebastian Foscarini (1670s), f. 1r.

3. Coryat, *Coryat's Crudities*, 1:358. According to Coryat, Guasto "said, that put to his choice to be lord either of foure of the strongest cities of Italy or of the Arsenall, he would preferre the Arsenall before them." Also Lassels, "Description of Italy," 226–27; Lassels attributed this story to the French King Henry III. Peter Mundy, *The Travels of Peter Mundy*, 1:96–97.

4. "A True Description," 5:3. For estimates of the size of the Arsenal: Moryson, *Itinerary*, 1:191; Evelyn, *Diary and Correspondence*, 1:208; Lane, *Venice, A Maritime Republic*, 362.

5. Skippon, *An Account of a Journey*, 6:509; Evelyn, *Diary*, 208.

6. Coryat was especially taken with the arms depots: "There I saw abundance of helmets, shields, breastplates, swords, &c. Their swordes were prettily placed upon some dores opposite to each other, where some were set compasse-wise, some athwart and a cross, some one way and some another, with such witty and pretty invention, that a man could not but commend the devisor thereof": Coryat, *Crudities*, 360–61.

7. According to Lane, this Venetian tour de force probably consisted of only launching and outfitting an existing ship. It was still an impressive feat, and considering how it seems to have grown with the retelling, an even more impressive piece of Venetian propaganda: Skippon, *A Journey thro' Italy*, 509; Lane, *Venetian Ships and Shipbuilders*, 144; Mundy, *Travels*, 96; Reresby, *Memoirs and Travels*, 60.

8. This 250,000 ducats a year, like much else about the arsenal, appears exaggerated: Lassels, "Description of Italy," 227; Moryson, *Itinerary*, 191; Coryat, *Crudities*, 358; Skippon, *A Journey thro' Italy*, 509; "A true Description," 1–3.

9. Evelyn, *Diary*, 208.

10. Studies of the Venetian Arsenal, to which this work is particularly indebted, include the following: Casoni, "Breve storia," 1:84–165; Marchesi, "L'Arsenale di Venezia," vol. 2; Veludo, *Cenni storici*; Nani Mocenigo, *L'Arsenale di Venezia*; Luzzatto, "Per la storia delle costruzioni navali a Venezia"; Forsellini, "L'Organizzazione economica," 7:54–117; Lane, *Venetian Ships and Shipbuilders*; Romano, "Economic Aspects of the Construction of Warships in Venice," 59–87; Aymard, "L'Arsenale e le conoscenze tecnico-marinaresche," 3/2, 289–315; Chirivi et al., *L'Arsenale dei veneziani*; Pizzarello and Fontana, *Pietre e legni dell'Arsenale di Venezia*; Bellavitis, *L'Arsenale di Venezia*; Concina, *L'Arsenale della Repubblica di Venezia*, and "Venezia: arsenale, spazio urbano, spazio marittimo," in Concina, ed., *Arsenali e città nell'Occidente europeo*; Gennaro and Testi, eds., *Progetto Arsenale*.

11. See esp. Sella, "The Rise and Fall of the Venetian Wool Industry"; Tucci, "The Psychology of the Venetian Merchant in the Sixteenth Century"; Lane, *Venice, A Maritime Republic*, 377–427; Krantz and Hohenberg, eds., *Failed Transitions to Modern Industrial Society*; Rapp, *Industry and Economic Decline*; Dooley, "Crisis and Survival in Eighteenth-Century Italy."

12. On declining Venetian shipbuilding after 1600, see Lane, *Venetian Ships and Shipbuilders*, 213–33, and "Venetian Shipping during the Commercial Revolution" and "The Mediterranean Spice Trade: Further Evidence of its Revival in the Sixteenth Century," both in Pullan, ed., *Crisis and Change*, 22–58; also Tenenti, *Piracy and the Decline of Venice*; the resilience

of Venetian shipbuilding is still more significant in the light of urban "de-industrialization" generally during these years: Van der Wee, ed., *The Rise and Decline of Urban Industries.*

13. Three noble Inquisitors were assigned by the Senate to carry out major investigations of the Arsenal in 1640–41, 1660, and 1679. Beginning in the 1590s, one of the Collegio's five Marine Secretaries was supposed to report on the state of the Arsenal every two years, although before 1624 and during the Candia War entire decades elapsed between reports.

14. The protoindustrialization debate is best summed up in Kriedte, Medick, and Schlumbohm, *Industrialization before Industrialization;* and Clarkson, *Proto-Industrialization.* For the best case study of rural manufacturing in Italy, see Sella, *Crisis and Continuity,* 24–46, 105–34.

15. Coad, "L'architettura storica della marina reale inglese," in Concina, ed., *Arsenali e città,* 189. Studies on state shipyards that have been essential for this work include the following: Coleman, "Naval Dockyards under the Later Stuarts"; Davis, *The Rise of English Shipping,* 1–80; Bamford, *Fighting Ships and Prisons,* 52–94; Symcox, *The Crisis of French Sea Power,* 12–55; Unger, *Dutch Shipbuilding before 1800;* Formicola and Romano, "Vascelli napolentani."

16. Pollard, *The Genesis of Modern Management,* 84; also Cipolla, *Before the Industrial Revolution.*

17. With special regards to Venice: Muir, *Civic Ritual in Renaissance Venice;* Romano, *Patricians and Popolani;* Mackenney, "Arti e stato," and *Tradesmen and Traders;* Zago, *I Nicolotti.* For studies on the contrasting social and economic world of workers elsewhere in Italy: Sella, *Salari e lavoro;* Goldthwaite, *The Building of Renaissance Florence;* and Cohn, *The Laboring Classes in Renaissance Florence.*

18. Compare with Pollard, "The Factory Village in the Industrial Revolution." The literature on Italian urban communities is vast; particularly important in shaping this study have been the following: Herlihy, *Medieval and Renaissance Pistoia;* Kent and Kent, *Neighbors and Neighborhood in Renaissance Florence;* Brown, *In the Shadow of Florence.*

19. Especially the works of anthropologists Turner, *The Ritual Process;* Pitt-Rivers, "Honour and Social Status"; and Geertz, "Thick Description." Especially helpful for showing the possibilities of this methodology have been Muir, *Civic Ritual;* Weissman, *Ritual Brotherhood;* Peter Burke, *The Historical Anthropology of Early Modern Italy* (Cambridge, 1987); and Davis, *Society and Culture in Early Modern France.*

Chapter 1. Formation and Nature of the Arsenal Workforce

1. Forsellini, "L'Organizzazione economica," 55–56. On the production of rope in the Arsenal department known as the *Tana,* see Lane, "The Rope Factory and Hemp Trade in the Fifteenth and Sixteenth Centuries."

2. On the *facchini,* see Forsellini, "L'Organizzazione economica," 91–95; on *segadori,* see Gallo, "Segadori trentine nell'Arsenale di Venezia."

3. ASV:SM, filza 572, 1 Feb 1669 m.v.

4. The former were known as *calafati da fizer* and the latter as *calafati da maggio;* for the sake of simplicity, however, it will be convenient to refer

to both branches of the guild merely as caulkers: Lane, *Venetian Ships and Shipbuilders,* 98 and n.

5. The mastmakers, as will be seen, were considered the most important of all these minor craftsmen, and had their own *proto,* or foreman, who was treated as the equal of the foreman of the oarmakers: Lane, *Venetian Ships and Shipbuilders,* 88–99. Compare this fragmentation of shipbuilding crafts with Holland, where not only pulley and mast makers but caulkers as well were inscribed in the shipwrights' guild: Unger, "Regulations of Dutch Ship-carpenters in the Fifteenth and Sixteenth Centuries," 515.

6. ASV:CRD suppliche, filza 93, 3 Dec 1680; ASV:SM, filza 315, 20 Nov 1637.

7. Aymard, "L'Arsenale e le conoscenze tecnico-marinaresche," 301–2; Lane, *Venetian Ships and Shipbuilders,* 140–45, 213–16, and *Venice, A Maritime Republic,* 384–89; Nani Mocenigo, *L'Arsenale di Venezia,* 36–42; Beltrami, *Storia della popolazione di Venezia,* 212.

8. Lane, *Venetian Ships and Shipbuilders,* 142–43.

9. The privilege of guaranteed wages was first noted in 1422, although it was not firmly established until 1447: for the progress of the three major guilds in obtaining this right, see Lane, *Venetian Ships and Shipbuilders,* 18, 135–36, 176–83.

10. Especially serious disturbances took place in 1569, when 300 arsenalotti invaded the Collegio and refused to leave until the doge promised to investigate their grievances, and in 1581, when a number of masters broke into the grain warehouses near San Marco and made off with 120 bushels of flour: Finlay, *Politics in Renaissance Venice,* 48–49; also Lane, *Venetian Ships and Shipbuilders,* 192–93.

11. Lane, *Venetian Ships and Shipbuilders,* 18.

12. Romano, "The Construction of Warships," 71–75; Forsellini, "L'Organizzazione economica," 54; ASV:Collegio V (Segreta), bu. 57, relazione of Mattio Zorzi (1624), f. 2v.

13. The total booty at Lepanto amounted to 117 galleys and many smaller vessels; Venice received the lion's share: Lane, *Venice, A Maritime Republic,* 372–73, 384–85.

14. On the effects of Lepanto on Venetian ship production, see Romano, "The Construction of Warships," 73, notes 1 and 4, and 78; ASV:SM, reg. 67, 28 June 1605.

15. In all, 331 caulkers, 183 shipwrights, and 48 oarmakers died in the city during the decade 1605 to 1615: ASV:SM, reg. 75, 19 Aug 1617. On the Arsenal Patroni, see below pp. 48–50.

16. ASV:SM, filza 235, 16 Apr 1622.

17. Lane: *Venice, A Maritime Republic,* 384; *Venetian Ships and Shipbuilders,* 232–33; and "Venetian Shipping during the Commercial Revolution," 20–22. Also Tenenti, *Piracy and the Decline of Venice,* 92–99.

18. ASV:SM, reg. 74, 18 Mar 1616.

19. Perhaps because better-paid work was again available in private shipyards. The number of enrolled caulkers declined from 825 in 1609 to 594 in 1624, forcing the Senate to revert to earlier practices of worker conscription: ASV:SM, reg. 74, 21 Jan 1616 m.v.; reg. 75, 23 June 1617; reg.

76, 4 Jan 1618 m.v.; reg. 78, 24 Mar 1620; and filza 342, 9 Nov 1641.

20. ASV:SM, reg. 72, 7 Feb 1614 m.v.; reg. 74 18 Mar 1616; reg. 75, 19 Aug 1617.

21. ASV:SM, reg 76, 12 Jan 1618 m.v.; reg. 83, 28 Feb 1625 m.v.; reg. 85, 14 Aug 1627.

22. Despite the Senate's assertion that the register "will be also to comfort these workers so that they will remain inspired in the public service and so that they will increase in number and quality," there is no indication that the masters actually requested it. ASV:SM, reg. 87, 14 Nov 1629.

23. Rapp, *Industry and Economic Decline*, 21, 42–48. Earlier, Greeks had been especially important in the Arsenal: Lane, *Venetian Ships and Shipbuilders*, 56–59.

24. Aymard, "L'Arsenale e le conoscenze tecnico-marinaresche," 311; also Forsellini, "L'Organizzazione economica," 77–78.

25. ASV:Collegio V (segreta), bu. 57, Relazione of Alvise Molin (1633), f. 10v; ASV:CRD suppliche, filza 23, 28 Oct 1632.

26. ASV:SM, reg. 110, 15 June 1650.

27. ASV:SM, reg. 89, 27 May 1631; and reg. 93, 23 Feb 1635 m.v. These provisions also allowed the inscription of nephews as apprentices.

28. ASV:TA, reg. 139, 1 Oct 1633.

29. ASV:SM, reg. 110, 15 June 1650: in 1629 the Senate had written: "figlioli legitimi . . . gionti . . . all'età di dieci anni, possino immediate esser descritti per fanti in essa Casa." In 1650, however, the "possino" was changed to the more imperative "siano." Forsellini, "L'Organizzazione economica," 78, stressed the voluntary nature of the 1629 edict, although he was evidently not aware that the register was recreated in 1650.

30. Thus, it was necessary for the Senate to open their rosters to outside enrollments on several occasions. ASV:SM, reg. 124, 2 June 1660; reg. 125, 9 Apr 1661; reg. 127, 7 Apr 1663.

31. ASV:Collegio V (Segreta), bu. 57, Relazione of Francesco Cornero (1696): the Senate's successive closures and reopenings of the baptismal register from 1671 to 1685 are listed on f. 3r.

32. Lane, *Venetian Ships and Shipbuilders*, 189–90.

33. ASV:Collegio V (Segreta), bu. 57, Relazione of Piero Mocenigo (1660), f. 24v. On the fluidity of construction workforces and their organization in medieval Florence: Goldthwaite, *The Building of Renaissance Florence*, 287–301.

34. Such disciplinary problems would also plague factory managers in the early Industrial Revolution: Pollard, "Factory Discipline in the Industrial Revolution," 254–56; and Thompson, "Time, Work-Discipline, and Industrial Capitalism," 81–83.

35. A confusion encouraged by those who claimed that there was little to distinguish between the two sets of figures: Romano, "The Construction of Warships," 86–87.

36. Martin, "In God's Image," 133–34; Romano, "The Construction of Warships," 75–76. For a discussion of other sources that have tended to produce exaggerated estimates of Arsenal workforce size, see Lane, *Venetian Ships and Shipbuilders*, 253.

37. Lane, *Navires et Constructeurs,* 231. A Marine Secretary suggested that much of the disparity between the actual and the nominally enrolled workforce may have been due to slowness of the bookkeeping staff in removing the names of ineligible masters from the work rosters: "it could be that many live on inscribed in the rolls who are [actually] dead, or banned, or in service with the fleet": ASV:Collegio V (Segreta), bu. 57, Relazione of Polo Baldi (1645), f. 29r.

38. "Then become adults, in the time that your excellencies should see flowing the fruits of your expenditures, they run to where the greater inducement of money calls them, and every memory of the Arsenal vanished, they use up on the outside the prime of their lives, until having lost every trace of vigor, useless for any fatigue, they return idle to receive the public charity": ASV:Collegio V (Segreta), bu. 57, Relazione of Bertucci Trivisan (1669), f. 9r, and of Francesco Sanudo (1670), f. 4v. On the attitude of other preindustrial workers toward free time: Goldthwaite, *The Building of Renaissance Florence,* 300.

39. ASV:Collegio V (Segreta), bu. 57, Relazione of Francesco Sanudo (1670), f. 4v; and of Vettor Grimani (1683), f. 2r. Also ASV:SM, reg. 85, 14 Aug 1627; and reg. 87, 14 Nov 1629, where it was noted that 130 out of 430 shipwrights and 52 of 290 caulkers were "vecchi et impotenti."

40. Lane, *Venetian Ships and Shipbuilders,* 184–85; ASV:SM, reg. 137, 14 Mar 1671.

41. Guild leaders complained, "Before the recent plague, being many workers . . . we had the opportunity to serve one week within [the Arsenal] and the next outside in private yards and ships, whence we had 4, 5, or 6 lire per day, such that the good earnings of the one made up for the little of the other . . . but now [after the plague] we have to remain at nearly continuous service in the Arsenal, and we can no longer maintain ourselves as before": ASV:CRD suppliche, filza 23, 28 Oct 1632; also ASV:SM, reg. 92, 12 Aug 1634.

42. ASV:SM, reg. 91, 13 May 1633. After a protest by the Arsenal guilds, the Senate decided to allow masters to count the half day if they could provide a legitimate excuse, such as government service, for their absence: reg. 92, 26 May and 9 Dec 1634.

43. Roughly 180 days per year: ASV:TA, reg. 140, 30 Aug 1651. An example of this requirement appears in ASV:SM, filza 502, 15 Feb 1658 m.v. For petitions to waive the requirement: ASV:CRD suppliche, filza 32, 26 Aug 1641; filza 39, 16 Sept 1648; ASV:SM, reg. 92, 26 May 1634. For an example of a master punished by the 6 soldi reduction, see ASV:CRD suppliche, filza 40, 24 Mar 1649.

44. On the Colleggietto in the sixteenth century: Lane, *Venetian Ships and Shipbuilders,* 177–82. ASV:SM, filza 342, 9 Nov 1641, gives the impression that the Colleggietto of the caulkers had been meeting with no fixed schedule at all until after 16 May 1609, when the Senate ordered that it be made biannual; this command, however, seems to have had no effect whatsoever. Later the two Colleggietti were also given control over the pay of the guild's timekeepers and gang bosses: ASV:SM, reg. 87, 7 Sept, 1629; reg. 90, 10 Apr 1632; reg. 93, 23 Feb 1635 m.v.

45. ASV:SM, filza 223, 19 Sept 1619; filza 309, 31 Jan 1636 m.v.; ASV:CRD suppliche, filza 18, 17 Aug 1627; filza 70, 24 May 1668.

46. As when the Senate ordered a Colleggietto to form in 1626, but some of the Secretaries appointed claimed to have other obligations; in the end the Senate decided to recall Secretaries from the previous board: ASV:SM reg. 84, 4 Mar 1626. The Senate also once ordered a sitting Colleggietto to continue meeting, despite the fact the some of its members had already left it: reg. 90, 28 Sept 1632.

47. ASV:Collegio V (Segreta), bu 57, Relazione of Polo Contarini (1643), f. 11v. Considering the size of the workforce in the seventeenth century and the number of masters who were eligible, each review would probably have amounted to around 2,500 ducats per year in raises.

48. According to the Patroni, the board gave masters raises based on "assiduous service in this Arsenal and the testimonials of their foremen, if they have with merit deserved them": ASV:SM, filza 499, 20 July 1658; Lane, *Venetian Ships and Shipbuilders*, 179; Forsellini, "L'Organizzazione economica," 86.

49. Already by 1600, it was decided that masters who failed to come to the shipyards for two complete years (the theoretical span between two sittings of his Colleggietto) would be expelled from the work roster; in 1618 the requirement was extended to apprentices as well: ASV:SM, reg. 76, 12 Jan 1618 m.v.

50. The caulker Antonio di Paolo da Venetia had been "fuori della città, non essendo stato alcuno de'miei consapevole della riduttione di queli Eccelentissimi Signori, restai senza poter portar le miei ragioni." ASV:CRD suppliche, filza 62, 30 July 1664. For the Colleggietto's use of the time-keepers' records: ASV:SM, filza 502, 15 Feb 1658 m.v.

51. ASV:SM, reg. 71, 16 Nov 1613 readmitted the caulkers thrown out by the Colleggietto of 1609; reg. 80, 16 Dec 1622, and filza 235, 16 Apr 1622, for the reinstatement of 32 caulkers who had been expelled by the Colleggietto of 1620.

52. ASV:TA, reg. 140, 3 Aug 1648; ASV:SM, filza 505, 10 Sept 1659.

53. Work on Sundays or holidays at the shipyards was rarely mentioned: ASV:SM, reg. 113, 6 July 1652; ASV:CRD suppliche, filza 34, 2 June 1643; evidently it was not popular with the masters: Forsellini, "L'Organizzazione economica," 85.

54. Lambert, "Drink and Work-Discipline in Industrial South Wales," 289–93.

55. *Vino puro* is specified since the *bevanda ordinaria* of the Arsenal was watered down 2:1; see ASV:TA, reg. 140, 30 July 1646.

56. ASV:TA, reg. 139, 21 Mar 1630. On the tenacity of such popular festivals as wakes in the face of attempts to discipline workers, see Thompson, "Time, Work-Discipline, and Industrial Capitalism," 76. ASV:SM, reg. 75, 19 Aug 1617; and reg. 87, 14 Nov 1629, for death rates among masters. The plague would soon make a mockery of the Patroni's worries about workers wasting time in funeral processions.

57. It required a similar degree of workplace integration (usually with the advent of steam power) before factory owners of industrial Britain be-

gan to actively oppose their workers' Saint Monday: Reid, "The Decline of Saint Monday," 95–98; Thompson, "Time, Work-Discipline, and Industrial Capitalism," 73–76.

58. ASV:SM, 3 July 1546.

59. According to the caulkers guild, the Senate was already allowing shipwrights to come to work any day they chose, for in the 1622 edict the caulkers were told they could come to work in the Arsenal "every week of the month and all the workdays, like the shipwrights do": ASV:SM, filza 235, 16 Apr 1622; ASV:CRD suppliche, filza 32, 26 Aug 1641.

60. The Inquisitors noted that "The good progress of the shipwrights' product consists in having the work of the caulkers *da fizer* ready [on time], it being necessary that the timbers worked and put in place by the shipwrights quickly receive the required fitting, otherwise they will twist, departing, so to speak, from their pattern": ASV:SM, filza 342, 9 Nov 1641.

61. ASV:SM, reg. 103, 24 Aug 1645.

62. ASV:SM, filza 402, 2 Apr 1648; for petitions from guilds see: ASV:CRD suppliche, filza 36, 6 July 1645; filza 39, 23 Jan 1647 m.v.; filza 53, 10 Nov 1659; filza 62, 22 Apr 1664.

63. Not unlike punishments used by British factory owners a century later: Pollard, "Factory Discipline," 260–62.

64. Aymard, "L'Arsenale e le conoscenze tecnico-marinaresche," 191. ASV:SM, filza 286, 20 Sept 1633. Colombin may appear an extreme example (he eventually returned to Venice and contented himself with a mere half scudo per day and a small house near the Arsenal), but see also filza 307, 28 Nov 1636.

65. ASV:SM, filza 505, 10 Sept 1659.

66. The exemption covered rents of up to 20 ducats per year, which probably accounted for around 75 percent of all arsenalotti. Those who were a few days short at the end of the year were given the chance to make up the time or present an excuse: ASV:SM, filza 304, 14 Apr 1636; see filza 348, 13 Oct 1642; and filza 390, 13 Mar 1647 for extensions of the exemption.

67. See, e.g., ASV:SM, filza 347, 9 July 1642, where the Patroni praised the "longo continuato impiego in servitio di Vostra Serenità" of the aged pulleymaker Salvador di Bernardin; also filza 356, 30 Oct 1643: the oarmaker Marco di Luca was praised because "è stato fatto maestro sin l'anno Agosto 1628 [e] dal quel tempo sin'hora . . . ha sempre frequentato come frequenta pure l'introdursi nell'Arsenale."

68. Forsellini, "L'Organizzazione economica," 114–17; Rapp, *Industry and Economic Decline,* 150, n. 26. On artisans seeking a "natural" level of subsistence, see Thomas, "Work and Leisure in Pre-industrial Society," 58–62; Coleman, "Labour in the English Economy of the Seventeenth Century"; Reid, "The Decline of Saint Monday," 78.

69. Lane, *Venetian Ships and Shipbuilders,* 178–79. Twenty soldi were equal to 1 lira; throughout the seventeenth century the Venetian ducat was fixed at 124 soldi.

70. Caulkers were still paid 30 soldi in winter and 42 soldi in summer for another forty years: ASV:SM, reg. 78, 5 Dec 1620.

71. In 1407 shipwrights were paid 6 *grossi* a day, equal to 24 soldi after

the ducat was stabilized a century later at 124 soldi. The six *grossi* of 1407 had been equal to about 23 percent of a gold ducat. The 24-soldi wage maximum of 150 years later was worth 19 percent of an inflated ducat of account, but only 15 percent of an actual gold one; after the raise of the pay ceiling to 40 soldi, a master's wage was again worth just over 23 percent of a gold ducat: Lane, *Venetian Ships and Shipbuilders,* 177, n. 6; 251–52.

72. Pullan, "Wage-Earners and the Venetian Economy," 173; Lane, *Venetian Ships and Shipbuilders,* 162–63, 244. During these same years, the assigned pay of master builders also roughly doubled in Florence, Paris, and south England: Goldthwaite, *The Building of Renaissance Florence,* 438; Phelps Brown and Hopkins, "Seven Centuries of Building Wages"; Baulant, "Le salaire des ouvriers du bâtiment à Paris," fig. 4.

73. One turner claimed that at private work he made "il gudagio al meno de lire 6 al giorno," while another asserted that with his shop he was earning "more than a scudo [9 lire] per day," CRD, suppliche, filza 29, 13 Nov 1638; and filza 30, 11 Apr 1639. Rent (averaging 90 lire a year) and other expenses would of course have considerably lowered this gross figure. On builders' wages: ASV:S. Gerolamo, bu. 8, filza 4, 1642; S. Maria Celestia, bu. 6, 1645; S. Nicolò della Latucha, bu 15, filza 15.

74. The caulkers claimed that the cost of services had nearly doubled since the plague; and asserted that, "tutti gli altri giubilano de loro guadagni . . . gli operari della città hanno trovato rimedio al suo male col farsi pagare ingordamente le mercedi": ASV:CRD suppliche, filza 23, 23 Apr and 28 Oct 1632.

75. The caulker Zuane di Dionise, before he had been named gang boss and supervisor in the Arsenal (at 64 soldi per day), had been able to do much better in the city: "because there was assigned to me for my pay 7 or 8 lire (140–60 soldi) per day": ASV:CRD suppliche, filza 23, 28 Oct 1632; also filza 62, 29 July 1664. Only after a campaign of 17 years did the *squera-rioli* manage to gain recognition in 1606 as a separate guild of shipbuilders: Lane, *Venetian Ships and Shipbuilders,* 84–85.

76. ASV:CRD suppliche, filza 19, 10 Oct and 16 Oct 1628; filza 26, 31 July 1635; filza 58, 27 Jun 1662; filza 62, 28 Apr 1664; filza 93, 18 Nov 1680.

77. For both fifteenth-century Florence and seventeenth-century Milan, 200 workdays a year has been considered a maximum for construction masters, with 180 days more typical for rural laborers: Goldthwaite, *The Building of Renaissance Florence,* 300; Sella, *Salari e lavoro,* 20–21.

78. ASV:Senato Terra, 20 Mar 1717, exempted the following merchants from Sunday closing: pharmacists, butchers, barbers, and dealers in bread, oil, food, coffee, *acquavita,* and firewood. The list is considerable, especially when compared with the services available on Sundays in Italian cities today. See also ASV:Compilazione leggi, bu. 206, filza 5/117, for seventeenth-century closings.

79. Mackenney, *Tradesmen and Traders,* 141–49, 180–81.

80. Lane, *Venice: A Maritime Republic,* 163–64.

81. ASV:Collegio V (Segreta), bu. 57, Relazione of Giovanni Priuli (1591), quoted in Concina, *L'Arsenale della Repubblica di Venezia,* 175.

82. ASV:Collegio V (Segreta), bu. 57, Relazione of Vettor Grimani

(1683), f. 2v. On the responsibilities of the five Marine Secretaries, see Lane, *Venetian Ships and Shipbuilders,* 148, and Finlay, *Politics in Renaissance Venice,* 40.

83. ASV:Collegio V (Segreta), bu. 57, Relazioni of Bertucci Trevisan (1669), f. 8v; Sebastian Foscarini (1670s), f. 3r; and Polo Contarini (1643), f. 11v.

84. ASV:Collegio V (Segreta), bu. 57, Relazione of Matteo Zorzi (1624), f. 5r; Polo Contarini (1643), f. 12r; Piero Mocenigo (1660), f. 23r; Francesco Sanudo (1670), f. 4v.

85. ASV:Collegio V (Segreta), bu. 57, Relazione of Piero Mocenigo (1660), f. 26r. The problem of apprentices without tools had already troubled the Senate for some time: see ASV:SM, reg. 75, 3 Oct 1617.

86. ASV:Collegio V (Segreta), bu. 57, Relazione of Polo Contarini (1643), f. 11r–v.

87. ASV:TA, reg. 139, 8 Jan 1620 m.v., and 22 Aug 1625; ASV:SM, reg. 77, 5 July 1619.

88. The Patroni and Inquisitors of the Arsenal, as well as the Senate, issued edicts against both masters and outsiders who clandestinely operated *bettole* (little taverns) in the shipyards, selling *robbe commestibili* like "bread, cheese, wine [*romanie*], and other edible things": ASV:TA, reg. 140, 15 May 1645; ASV:SM, reg. 111, 21 Jan 1650; ASV:SM, filza 511, 4 Sept 1660.

89. ASV:TA, reg. 137, 14 Nov 1607; ASV:Arsenale, bu. 557, Inquisitors, 1640, f. 10v.

90. The misuse of these semiprivate *camarelle* and *fogoni serati* (locked kitchens?) between the vaults of neighboring shipyards became such a problem that the Patroni had to order masters to dismantle them or face a wage reduction of 4 soldi: ASV:TA, reg. 140, 23 Sept 1644.

91. ASV:CRD suppliche, filza 34, 9 Oct 1643; also ASV:TA, reg. 137, 23 Mar 1601; and reg. 141, 6 May 1664.

92. ASV:SM, reg. 116, 10 Jan 1653 m.v. The Arsenal purchased strong wine from Zante, Greece, or southern Italy and watered it down at 2:1 to make the *bevanda delle maestranze,* which served not only to nourish and stimulate workers ("restore the forces and increase the spirits"), but also supposedly to make their drinking water safer: ASV:SM, reg. 73, 15 Sept 1615; and filza 335, 7 Dec 1640. Spirits and ale would be distributed to industrial workers in the Scottish lowlands for both these reasons: Donnachie, "Drink and Society," 9–10.

93. Taking the Inquisitors' calculations, this averaged out to one bottle (.72 liters) of strong *vino puro* per worker per day (three bottles of the diluted *bevanda*): ASV:SM, filza 335, 7 Dec 1640. This meant that arsenalotti typically drank well over 150 liters of strong wine per year just while on the job, far more than the quantities Braudel considered a threshold of drunkenness in the early modern era: Braudel, *Capitalism and Material Life,* 165–67.

94. ASV:TA, reg. 140, 30 Mar and 11 Jan 1651 m.v.

95. Outsiders who were found to have come into the shipyards for the purpose of drinking were to be strictly punished, according to an order of

the Council of Ten of 26 Aug 1579. Since *nobili e cittadini* were excused from this order, however, considerable abuse was still possible: ASV:TA, reg. 140, 30 Mar 1651; and reg. 141, 7 Dec 1658.

96. ASV:Collegio V (Segreta) bu. 57, Relazione of Vettor Grimani (1683), f. 3r.

97. Forsellini, "L'Organizzazione economica," 87; ASV:Collegio V (Segreta), bu. 57, Relazione of Zuane Bernardo (1676), f. 6v. Butchers *(luganegheri)* in the communal slaughterhouse were also paid a wine ration: ASV:CRD suppliche, filza 28, 16 Mar 1637.

98. As when the Senate made 300 ducats available for "many good and sufficient tools for the good of the workers that have the most need of them": ASV:SM, reg. 75, 3 Oct 1617. Such loans were evidently not usually offered by craft guilds to their masters, perhaps because they lacked the funds: Lane, *Venetian Ships and Shipbuilders,* 72–83; Goldthwaite, *The Building of Renaissance Florence,* 256–72. Caulkers received a supplementary 2 soldi a day: ASV:CRD suppliche, filza 23, 28 Oct 1632.

99. MC:Gradenigo, bu. 193 II, f. 78r, 23 Apr 1681.

100. Overtime strictly meant extra wages proportionate to extra hours worked; it had been customary in the construction industry, at least as far back as fifteenth-century Florence: see the *Libri di Ricordi* of stonecutter Maso di Bartolommeo, in a forthcoming edition by Harriet Caplow. For Arsenal work hours: Crovato, "Arsenale e arsenalotti," 51, and ASV:SM, reg. 96, 17 Sept 1638 (for a *quarto*); reg. 102, 4 Feb 1644 m.v. (a *terzo*); and reg. 97, 14 July 1639 (for a *giornata e meza*).

101. In 1696, 13,407 ducats, or nearly a tenth of the total wage labor budget, were paid out in overtime that year, probably a fair indication of how much masters worked extra in the shipyards: ASV:Collegio V (Segreta), bu. 57, Relazione of Francesco Cornero (1696), ff. 11r-12r.

102. During much of the War of Candia, special large work gangs of shipwrights and caulkers were organized to finish and outfit large frigates and warships used for transport; masters in these gangs were paid an extra half pay for every long day's work, with the requirement to stay in the shipyards during lunch. For the series of overtime shifts to *conciar* various large ships, see ASV:TA, reg. 141: 11 Jan 1651 m.v., 28 Dec 1653, 19 Dec 1656, 7 Feb 1658 m.v., 16 Feb 1659 m.v., 22 Jan 1660 m.v., and so on, nearly every winter for the rest of the war.

103. On the *tansa,* see Rapp, *Industry and Economic Decline,* 52–54. For guild petitions to review levies ranging from 1 to over 20 ducats per master, see ASV:CRD suppliche, filza 60, 8 May 1663; filza 64, 17 May 1665; filza 69, 3 Nov 1667; filza 70, 9 May 1668.

104. ASV:SM, reg. 66, 28 Nov 1602.

105. The Senate gave the exemption to all masters who worked at least 150 days per year and paid 20 ducats (124 lire) or less per year for rent. The magistrate responsible for levying the *Quarto* calculated that the exemption would cost the state about 1,200 ducats per year, around a soldo per workday for the 405 masters eligible at the time. ASV:SM, filza 304, 14 Apr 1636. Rents were in any event falling in the post-plague period: ASV:CRD suppliche, filza 25, 5 Apr 1634.

106. ASV:CRD suppliche, filza 23, 21 Dec 1632; filza 34, 13 Jan 1643 m.v.; filza 64, 19 Aug 1665.

107. Of 105 apprentice caulkers inscribed in 1613, only 11 had enrolled as caulkers *da fizer*: ASV:SM, reg. 72, 7 Feb 1614 m.v.

108. ASV:SM, filza 342, 9 Nov 1641. This despite the fact that caulkers who refused to take the examination of the other branch risked losing their right to sign on new apprentices: ASV:SM, reg. 70, 16 May 1609; reg. 71, 28 May 1613.

109. From 262 enrolled in 1606 to only 149 in 1622, according to a note of their timekeeper included in ASV:SM, filza 235, 16 Apr 1622; filza 342, 9 Nov 1641.

110. "Con tutto ciò, che mi fu dato calafati moderni, che havevano fatto la prova de due arti, che non sapevano dar principio nel forar un buso, et io con mio valor ho fatto ogni cosa, che sono stato bonissimo": ASV:CRD suppliche, filza 17, 25 Nov 1624.

111. ASV:SM, reg. 83, 20 Sept 1625; reg. 89, 27 May 1631; and filza 396, 24 Sept 1647.

112. As long as they were at least fifteen years of age: ASV:SM, filza 94, 30 May 1636.

113. Lane, *Venetian Ships and Shipbuilders,* 186.

114. ASV:CRD suppliche, filza 67, 7 Feb 1666 m.v.; also filza 42, 17 Sept 1652; and filza 56, 30 Mar 1661.

115. "Tanto più, che la Casa de detti maestri ne tiene molto bisogno et molti di migliori da pochi anni passati alla miglior vita": ASV:CRD suppliche, filza 73, 30 Dec 1669. A similar argument was offered by the apprentice oarmaker Zuanbattista di Zuanbattista: filza 43, 22 Jan 1652 m.v.

116. ASV:Collegio V (Segreta), bu. 57, Relazioni of Bertucci Trevisan (1669), f. 9r; of Francesco Cornero (1696), f. 3v; ASV:SM, reg. 74, 18 Mar 1616.

117. The Senate observed that: "many apprentices of both shipwrights and caulkers have had to stop coming to be listed (*appontare*) in the Arsenal, some for two years some for three years at a stretch . . . because to them it was not allowed to be listed when their master did not come." The *parte* concluded that "it is hoped that . . . by being the actual sons or grandsons [of masters . . . the apprentices] will be well disciplined and will learn their craft": ASV:SM, reg. 87, 14 Nov 1629.

118. ASV:Collegio V (Segreta), bu. 57, Relazione of Francesco Sanudo (1670), f. 4v.

119. In the fifteenth century, fourteen years old was apparently considered a maximum: Lane, *Venetian Ships and Shipbuilders,* 83–84; when the Senate voted to enroll a block of apprentice caulkers in 1614, the Patroni were ordered to "far descrivere due cento fanti di calafati di età di anni dieci," ASV:SM, reg. 72, 7 Feb 1614 m.v.

120. ASV:SM, filza 328, 3 Dec 1639; filza 371, 9 Jan 1644.

121. Rapp, *Industry and Economic Decline,* 42–44.

122. ASV:SM, filza 362, 6 July 1644; ASV:Collegio V (Segreta), bu. 57, Relazione of Domenico Lion (1636), f. 2r; Forsellini, "L'Organizzazione economica," 78–79.

123. The use of *fanti grossi* apparently originated only in the late six-teenth century: see the *Capitolare* of the Arsenal of 10 May 1580 governing how *fanti grossi* were to be selected and paid, cited by Forsellini, in "L'Organizzazione economica," 78.

124. ASV:SM, reg. 74, 18 Mar 1616; reg. 76, 12 Jan 1618 m.v.; reg. 79, 29 May 1621.

125. ASV:SM, reg. 90, 15 July 1632; filza 93, 23 Feb 1635 m.v.; filza 308, 31 Dec 1636; filza 309, 31 Jan 1636 m.v.; filza 312, 18 July 1637.

126. ASV:SM, filza 272, 8 June 1630; filza 326, 4 Aug 1639.

127. ASV:CRD suppliche, filza 37, 8 May 1646; also the similar petition of ship captain Antonio Cadena: filza 43, 9 July 1652.

128. ASV:CRD suppliche, filza 20, 27 Mar 1629: filza 93, 20 Aug 1680.

129. ASV: Collegio V (Segreta), bu. 57, Relazione of Bertucci Trivisan (1669), f. 8v. Another Marine Secretary suggested that the state give aged sailors a cash pension but keep them out of the state shipyards: Relazione of Polo Contarini (1643), f. 12r.

130. Since shipbuilding guilds required that new masters pay an en-trance fee, the Patroni suspected that the *gastaldi* were too eager to inscribe new members and had become lax with the examinations: Lane, *Venetian Ships and Shipbuilders,* 179–80.

131. Ibid., 83–84. When the sailor Lorenzo Cabiato gave his master's examination, there were thirteen *gastaldi* present, as well as the foreman shipwright and the Patron Antonio Molin: ASV:SM, filza 298, 13 Oct 1635.

132. ASV:SM, filza 287, 28 Nov 1633; filza 294, 10 Feb 1634 m.v.

133. Two possibly atypical examinations were described in *fedi* of this period. In 1633, the aspiring gang boss Giacomo Colombin was required to make and fit into place on a galley a "piece of wood called a *sfogio*": ASV:SM, filza 286, 20 Sept 1633. Four years later a shipwright and guncar-riage maker named Francesco Furlan made a "letto da artegliaria da cam-pagna da falcon da tre sforzato" as his examination. Francesco seems to have had no time limit for the task and was apparently even able to call on two fellow workers for assistance. The results were passed by two Arsenal ap-praisers and a *capo dei bombardieri*: ASV:SM, filza 313, 2 Sept 1637.

134. ASV:SM, reg. 71, 28 May 1613.

135. Annibal di Andrea Ricciadei successfully claimed to have learned to "lavorar e fabricar diversi vascelli e fuste" while a slave in Tunisia; the Patroni did order that he take his master's examination before they would support his petition before the Collegio: ASV:SM, filza 274, 16 Jan 1630 m.v. The story of Bortolo di Battista Querego was similar: "et fatto schiavo, non tralasciando di apprendere tutta quella peritia, che si conviene à buon marangon, acconciando nelli bisogni li vasselli dove mi ritrovavo": ASV:CRD suppliche, filza 23, 13 Jan 1632 m.v. See also: filza 20, 23 Feb 1629 m.v.; and filza 21, 1 Oct 1631.

136. ASV:CRD suppliche, filza 19, 14 Mar and 19 Dec 1628; and filza 64, 2 Mar 1665; filza 64, 10 Apr 1665; filza 69, 4 Jan 1667 m.v.; filza 43, 17 Feb 1652 m.v.

137. "Tutto lo dedico . . . nella profettione di marangon, della quale mi sono sempre dilettato, e n'ho in tutti gli anni di mia vita fatto particolar

studio, havendo massime in essa Casa molti miei parenti, tra quali un mio cugnato et un nipote . . . col documento de quali ho potuto apprendere quello che alla profettione di marangon s'aspetta": ASV:CRD suppliche, filza 27, 28 Apr 1636.

138. Lane, *Venetian Ships and Shipbuilders*, 215–16; Concina, *L'Arsenale di Venezia*, 174–75 and 205–6; see also Gugliemo Zanelli, "L'Arsenale: Storia di industria e di città," in Chirivi et al., *L'Arsenale dei veneziani*, 64–68.

139. Thus, the gang boss Steffano di Zuane di Michiel, after helping a Dutch master build a ship "of a quality not seen here for 35 years," petitioned the Collegio, saying he still possessed the plans and a model: "so if anyone wishes to build a similar ship in the Arsenal, I offer myself as very ready for the job." There is no record of the project; evidently Steffano's proposal was turned down: ASV:CRD suppliche, filza 64, 6 Mar 1665. For other innovations offered and seemingly ignored: ASV:CRD suppliche, filza 44, 31 July 1653 (on preventing shipworm damage); filza 38, 12 June 1647 (building an armored ship "all'usanza di Spagna"); Concina, *L'Arsenale di Venezia*, 174.

140. Romano, "The Construction of Warships," 81–83.

141. The normal eight-year Arsenal apprenticeships were indeed about 30 percent longer than those of other seventeenth-century Venetian guilds: Rapp, *Industry and Economic Decline*, 45; Dutch shipbuilders served apprenticeships of only three years, presumably because a stretch of journeyman's service then followed: Unger, "Regulations of Dutch Shipcarpenters," 512.

142. Aymard, "L'Arsenale e le conoscenze tecnico-marinaresche," 296–97.

143. ASV:Collegio V (Segreta) bu. 57, Relazione of Alvise Molin (1633), f. 12r; Relazione of Piero Mocenigo (1660), f. 22r.

144. ASV:SM, filza 351, 4 Feb 1642 m.v.; filza 367, 24 Jan 1644 m.v.; and filza 371, 27 Sept 1645.

145. Thus, the Arsenal aimed at a workforce much more like those of factories of the following century than like the usual independent master craftsmen of the 1600s: Pollard, "Factory Discipline," 258–60; and Thompson, "Time, Work-Discipline and Industrial Capitalism," 86–90.

146. "Interrogazioni" (no date, but evidently from the 1680s or 1690s): "da farsi dall'Eccelentissimo Colleggietto, all'Ammiraglio e protti sopra le maestranze, che verranno nominate": MC:Mss Gradenigo, bu. 193 II, f. 85r.

Chapter 2. The Arsenal Worker Managers

1. Lane, *Venetian Ships and Shipbuilders*, 145–75; Forsellini, "L'Organizzazione economica," 58–65; Crovato, "L'Arsenale e Arsenalotti," 50–59.

2. ASV:Collegio V (Segreta), bu. 57, Relazione of Francesco Cornero (1696), ff. 7r-15v. Cornero also listed 17 officers of the *Tana*, or state ropeworks. Minor "offices" came and went in the Arsenal: a master elected to "vasi spiumazzi et argane delle galie" (build the winches and cradles for launching galleys), another charged with inspecting the satin covers on the doge's three ceremonial barges *(piatti)*, yet another to supply oarmakers with sawhorses *(cavalletti)*. Although their duties were humble, such minor

supervisors should still be distinguished from ordinary workers, if not for higher wages, at least for their greater independence and personal control over their work: ASV:TA, reg. 139, 29 Apr and 14 May 1624, and 20 Sept 1625.

3. Lane, *Venice, A Maritime Republic,* 14–15, 48; Concina, *L'Arsenale di Venezia,* 9; Forsellini, "L'Organizzazione economica," 57.

4. The Senate noted the offices of Admiral and foreman shipwright as early as 1301: Lane, *Venetian Ships and Shipbuilders,* 55–56 n., 130–33, 165; Concina, *L'Arsenale di Venezia,* 9–21, 40, finds reference to the two *protomaestri* in guild *capitolari* dating from the 1270s; also Nani Mocenigo, *L'Arsenale di Venezia,* 24.

5. A distinction that would be typical of factories in the industrial age: Spencer, "Between Capital and Labor," 184. On appraisers, see Lane, *Venetian Ships and Shipbuilders,* 157.

6. The Admiral and the foreman shipwright were forbidden from working on the outside as early as 1301, the foreman of the caulkers by the 1450s, and the foreman mastmaker not until after 1500: Lane, *Venetian Ships and Shipbuilders,* 165.

7. Di Grassi eventually managed to talk his way out of the fine: ASV:TA, reg. 140, 16 Dec 1652.

8. Concina, *L'Arsenale di Venezia,* 51, 74–94; Lane, *Venetian Ships and Shipbuilders,* 137–40.

9. Lane, *Venetian Ships and Shipbuilders,* 129, n. 5, and 130–36.

10. Lane, *Venice: A Maritime Republic,* 160–65, 363.

11. Lane, *Venetian Ships and Shipbuilders,* 161–62.

12. There were, e.g., subforemen of the caulkers appointed in 1501, 1531, and 1556: ASV:TA, reg. 137, 7 Mar 1602. For attempts to control the unauthorized delegation of power in the Arsenal, see ASV:SM, reg. 85, 22 Sept 1627; and ASV:Collegio V (Segreta), bu. 57, Relazione of Polo Baldi (1645), f. 27r. ASV:CRD suppliche, filza 35, 13 Oct 1644; filza 38, 17 June 1647. New duties were doled out in especially great numbers by the Inquisitors: ASV:Arsenale, bu. 557 (1640), ff. 26v–27r.

13. Zorzi di Pierantonio Grandi passed 9 of his first 25 years as foreman mastmaker working in the forests; his colleague the foreman oarmaker spent over 2 years out of 8 away map making and directing logging operations: ASV:CRD suppliche, filza 34, 16 Feb 1643; and ASV:SM, filza 336, 9 Feb 1640 m.v., *fede* dated 11 Oct 1639. On life-tenure for salaried positions, see ASV:TA, reg. 138, 19 June 1619; reg. 139, 25 Sept 1623; reg. 139, 20 July 1635; ASV:SM, filza 512, 23 Oct 1660; ASV:CRD suppliche, filza 35, 13 Oct 1644; filza 60, 5 July 1663. When quite old, Grandi petitioned for an assistant so that he could stop working but still continue "to enjoy for the little time that is left to me the salary, house, and benefits belonging to my position": ASV:CRD suppliche, filza 54, 13 Apr 1660.

14. On the duties of the assistant: ASV:CRD suppliche, filza 67, 28 Sept 1666. See also filza 34, 17 Sept 1643; filza 35, 13 Oct 1644; filza 44, 22 Jan 1653 m.v.

15. ASV:TA, reg. 137, 2 June 1612; also reg. 139, 18 Mar 1633. Besides his regular helper, the foreman shipwright Zorzi di Zuanfrancesco Lazari

also had his own "appontador" to direct the work of Arsenal sawyers and gilders (*battadori* and *pianadori*) : ASV:CRD suppliche, filza 64, 8 July 1665. The carpenter Domenico di Michiel claimed some years service as helper to the foreman shipwright's assistant: ASV:CRD suppliche, filza 65, 29 Dec 1665.

16. The position was probably established in the late fifteenth century, deriving from the word *appuntar,* to take note of. Forsellini, "L'Organizzazione economica," 63; ASV:Collegio V (Segreta), bu. 57, Relazione of Francesco Sanudo, 1670, f. 4v; and Relazione of Francesco Cornero, 1696, f. 12r. Lane, *Venetian Ships and Shipbuilders,* 189–90.

17. Lane, *Venetian Ships and Shipbuilders,* 191; ASV:CRD suppliche, filza 39, 22 June 1648.

18. Andrea di Micali, elected *despontador* of the oarmakers in 1623, said that his responsibilities included, "non solo de' remeri, ma fabri [blacksmiths], fanti [pages], mureri [wallers], galieri [galeoti?], spaderi [swordmakers], manoali [laborers] all' Ammiraglio, manoali all'remeri, manoali alla pegola, [e] donne alle velle [sail seamstresses]": ASV:CRD suppliche, filza 22, 10 Sept 1631.

19. Forsellini, "Organizzazione economica," 63–64: *despontar* meant to cross out; also ASV:CRD suppliche, filza 20, 31 Mar 1629.

20. ASV:Arsenale, bu. 557, Inquisitors (1640), f. 10r. Referring either to the threats he received or to the informing he had to do, the overseer Picolo termed his position "unbearably infamous" (*troppo grave oborioso*) : ASV:CRD suppliche, filza 20, 31 Mar 1629.

21. ASV:TA, reg. 140, 15 May 1645; ASV:SM, reg. 110, 21 Jan 1651 m.v.

22. ASV:TA, reg. 138, 17 Apr 1619. There also appears to have been a small prison on the premises at the shipyards, to lock up those condemned by the Inquisitors or the Patroni: ASV:CRD suppliche, filza 33, 7 Aug 1642.

23. The right of masters to choose where they wished to work in the Arsenal was especially disruptive: ASV:Collegio V (Segreta), bu. 57, Relazione of Mattio Zorzi (1624), f. 5r; also Lane, *Venetian Ships and Shipbuilders,* 146.

24. Ibid., 60–61.

25. The state contracted for shipbuilding within the Arsenal as early as 1422 and in private yards at least from the eleventh century: ibid., 113, 124–27, 200–205; and Lane, *Venice, A Maritime Republic,* 48.

26. Contractors were specifically forbidden from employing any masters who were also collecting a daily wage from the Arsenal: ASV:SM, reg. 71, 18 Apr 1613; reg. 73, 19 Feb 1615 m.v.; reg. 75, 7 June 1617.

27. Since his contract gave him a specific amount of time to carry out his construction, a *fabricante* also had to be experienced and willing in driving his men to work hard, lest he fail to fulfill his contract on time and have to finish the work at his own expense: Lane, *Venetian Ships and Shipbuilders,* 54–71, 200–202. Masters who worked for them could expect double or better the Arsenal's wage maximum: ASV:CRD suppliche, filza 16, 5 Oct 1623.

28. "A qualche galera osserviamo applicato un capo d'opera con un marangon, et noi lo assimigliamo ad un capitano che stimasse haver una

compagnia fatta con un fante solo": ASV: Collegio V (Segreta), bu. 57, Relazione of Polo Baldi (1645), f. 30v; Lane, *Venetian Ships and Shipbuilders*, 162, 198–99, 204–5.

29. As the Patroni would later write, "all the building that is done depends on them [the gang bosses], and all the rest of the workers carry out their designs and construction": ASV:SM, filza 266, 13 Feb 1628.

30. Lane, *Venetian Ships and Shipbuilders*, 202–5. ASV:SM, reg. 62, 31 Jan 1601 m.v. Gang bosses continued to evade such requirements until finally the Patroni threatened to deprive them of their positions both as boss and as master if they failed to come in regularly; the Patroni also forbade local ship captains to sign them on for voyages unless they could show a written permission from the Arsenal: ASV:TA, reg. 141, 8 July 1665; also reg. 140, 22 Nov 1646, 7 Apr 1647, 4 July 1651, and 4 Mar 1653.

31. Lane, *Venetian Ships and Shipbuilders*, 207–9. Assistants were evidently to help with the paperwork: ASV:CRD suppliche, filza 65, 1 Sept 1665; filza 93, 12 Dec 1680.

32. As with the di Grassi family, whose members moved freely between Arsenal management and private shipbuilding; a father and one son were foreman and gang boss of the caulkers and other sons owned several shipyards; their contracts for private construction just in the year 1665 amounted to four ships totaling 2,500 *botte* (around 1,750 freight tons): ASV:CRD suppliche, filza 64 and 65, 23 May, 15 June, 9 Sept, and 10 Feb 1665 m.v.

33. On wages of work bosses and supervisors: ASV:TA, reg. 139, 24 Jan 1624 m.v.; Lane, *Venetian Ships and Shipbuilders*, 191. On the rigidity of *salariati* pay: ASV:CRD suppliche, filza 26, 4 Sept 1635; filza 27, 13 May 1636; filza 35, 12 Mar 1644; and ASV:Collegio V (Segreta), bu. 57, Relazione of Francesco Cornero (1696), ff. 7v-8r. For a gang boss losing income upon election as foreman shipwright: ASV:TA, reg. 140, 12 Apr 1651.

34. In 1639 contracts were awarded for supplying oars; converting galleys to sail; building *barche armate* (cutters of about fifty feet); and other small vessels. The conversion of *galee alla vella* ("come al presente s'usa") seems to have paid contractors especially well, perhaps because of the hurry or for the special skills involved: ASV:SM, reg. 97, 10 Mar, 27 May, 4 July, 12 Aug, 1 Feb 1639 m.v.

35. ASV:CRD suppliche, filza 37, 18 Sept 1646.

36. ASV:CRD suppliche, filza 30, 17 May 1639; filza 33, 1 Dec 1642: from the gang boss Dorigo di Antonio, who asked for a *fante grosso*, "as they have always been given to so many [other] work bosses"; also 12 Jan 1642 m.v.

37. ASV:SM, filza 387, 30 Oct 1646; ASV:TA, reg. 137, 20 June 1603.

38. ASV:TA, reg. 137, 12 Nov 1603; reg. 139, 9 Mar 1620 and 26 Oct 1632.

39. ASV:TA reg. 141, 30 Apr 1675.

40. The houses of the Patroni actually formed part of the Arsenal wall, on either side of the Great Gate, and were called, for no apparent reason, "Paradiso," "Purgatorio," and "Inferno": Lane, *Venetian Ships and Shipbuilders*, 129. By 1789 the number of Arsenal houses had grown to 52, although

the share given to worker managers had only increased to 26: Archive of the parish church of S. Martino (E/1, f. 10r–v).

41. ASV:CRD suppliche, filza 15, 12 July 1623; ASV:SM, reg. 109, 8 Oct 1469; ASV:TA, reg. 141, 21 Mar 1671. Since certain houses were not identified with particular positions, some masters hoped to receive an unattached one from the Patroni, whose job it was to assign them: ASV:TA, reg 138, 29 May 1619; and reg. 139, 4 Sept 1634. Eventually, the Inquisitors ordered that each house have an office assigned to it, and that the title of the position be chiseled over the doorway; four of these still survive: ASV:SM, filza 336, 22 Jan 1640 m.v. For a descriptive *catasto* of the houses: filza 336, 19 Feb 1640 m.v.

42. The four principal foremen each had two *anfore* (1,202 liters) of pure wine delivered to their houses yearly (the Admiral received three *anfore*): Forsellini, "L'Organizzazione economica," 59–61. Managers received varying amounts of sailcloth according to their relative importance in the shipyards; rag dealers would pay around 6 ducats for the roughly 40 yards (60 *bracchie*) that were a top foreman's yearly share: ASV:SM, filza 301, 23 Feb 1635 m.v., and filza 338, 4 May 1641.

43. These benefits further broke down as follows: 4 percent from the income from his two *fanti grossi*, 10 percent from his cut of the city's anchorage tax, 3 percent from the tax-exempt value of his free wine, 10 percent from the compensatory value of his house; Bisson was Admiral between 1723 and 1746: MC:ms Gradenigo, bu. 193 I, f. 103r.

44. Lane, *Venice: A Maritime Republic,* 333–34. Compare with the Patroni themselves, who were paid only 316 ducats per year, and that subject to taxes: ASV:SM, filza 509, 17 Apr 1660.

45. ASV:SM, filza 235, 30 Mar 1622; filza 256, 22 Apr 1627; filza 344, 4 Apr 1642; filza 384, 9 June 1646; filza 534, 22 Apr 1664.

46. Lane, *Venetian Ships and Shipbuilders,* 54–71.

47. Thus, the foreman shipwright Vicenzo Vice warned than his salary was not enough to buy the robes of his office or "to maintain myself in public dignity": ASV:CRD suppliche, filza 35, 12 Mar 1644. On the Venetians' high esteem for title and position: Burke, *The Historical Anthropology of Early Modern Italy,* 150–67; Logan, *Culture and Society in Venice,* 269–76.

48. ASV:CRD suppliche, filza 32, 11 Mar and 7 Sept 1641; filza 33, 12 May and 3 Sept 1642.

49. An honor enjoyed by the three gang bosses of the early 1660s who supervised the Arsenal's first two full-rigged men-of-war, the *Giove Fulminante* and the *Costanza Guerriera*: ASV:SM, reg.134, 21 Apr 1668; and ASV:CRD suppliche, filza 71, 6 Feb 1668 m.v. By the eighteenth century the procedure had become formalized, with bosses receiving a 50-ducat medal (about two ounces of pure gold) if they had directed work on a first-class ship, a 40-ducat medal for a second-class ship, and a 30-ducat for third-class: MC:Mss Gradenigo, bu. 193 II, f. 120r.

50. In the end, the subforemen were given the right to dress themselves in the same *habito longo* as the Admiral and major foremen, but only in black (the color inside their sleeves was left to their discretion): ASV:TA,

reg. 139, 17 May 1621; also ASV:CRD suppliche, filza 22, 12 Sept 1631; also filza 24, 6 Dec 1633; and filza 30, 17 Oct 1639.

51. The Admiral and principal foremen protested that the gift should serve as a reward for those particularly linked to the Arsenal and had been cheapened when the original thirty-four recipients was increased to over eighty in the course of the early 1600s. Part of the honor of the *fustagne vecchie* seemingly lay in its also being granted to the doge and his retinue: ASV:S,. filza 301, 23 Feb 1635 m.v.; and filza 338, 4 May 1641.

52. The Patroni decided to award precedence to whichever one had held his post longer: ASV:TA, reg. 141, 13 May 1667.

53. ASV:CRD suppliche, filza 16, 4 Sept 1623; and filza 32, 2 Mar 1641; also filza 56, 3 Aug 1661.

54. ASV:CRD suppliche, filza 47, 17 Mar 1656.

55. For a list of the Arsenal's more exalted visitors between 1649 and 1719, see MC:ms Gradenigo, bu. 193 II, ff. 87r–88r.

56. ASV:TA, reg. 138, 25 Dec 1615. Richard Lassels noted, "we tooke Gondola, and went to the Arsenal . . . leaving our Swords at the doore with the porter, as a pledge rather for his fee, than for any other reason," Chaney, *The Grand Tour,* 226. Every sort of worker also apparently dogged the steps of visitors, trying to make themselves useful in the expectation of receiving a tip; a seventeenth-century tour book writer called such tips "Drink-money" and suggested that they be given nine times in the course of a tour: "A True Description," 2–3.

57. Sometimes, however, the selection was made by the Colleggietto: ASV:TA, reg. 140, 14 Feb 1638 m.v.

58. For aspects of the boss's examination: Lane, *Venetian Ships and Shipbuilders,* 88–99; ASV:TA, reg. 137, 6 Nov 1606; ASV:SM, filza 228, 29 Sept 1620; filza 286, 20 Sept 1633 (*fede* dated 28 July 1633); and filza 419, 29 Sept 1649.

59. As the shipwright Zuane di Antonio enlisted the support of the Admiral when he petitioned for a vacant position as gang boss: ASV:TA, reg. 140, 21 May 1638; also ASV:CRD suppliche, filza 65, 16 Nov and 29 Dec 1665.

60. ASV:TA, reg. 137, 2 Aug 1603; and reg. 138, 9 Mar 1616; ASV:CRD suppliche, filza 58, 27 Apr 1652; and filza 71, 12 Dec 1668.

61. The Venetian Republic indeed did not establish a training course for shipbuilding engineers until 1759 at Verona, and not until 1777 at the Arsenal itself. France, a chief galley-building rival, had already set up such a school in Marseilles during the ministry of Colbert: Concina, *L'Arsenale di Venezia,* 221–22; Bamford, *Fighting Ships and Prisons,* 74–75. For the belief in native shipbuilding genius: ASV:SM, filza 256, 22 Apr 1627; filza 348, 5 Sept 1642; filza 358, 30 Jan 1643 m.v; also Aymard, "L'Arsenale e le conoscenze tecnico-marinaresche," 302–4; Finlay, *Politics in Renaissance Venice,* 81–96.

62. ASV:CRD suppliche, filza 45, 9 Apr 1654.

63. "Da Antonio di Marco . . . capo d'opera dei marangoni, [sono stato] instrutto et allevato nell'arte de marangon; m'imparò anche il modo di fabricar galere di mio sesto et altri sorti di legni, che ordinariamente si fabrica

in detta Casa." ASV:SM, filza 511, 1 Sept 1660; also filza 482, 2 Dec 1655; and filza 482, 30 Jan 1653 m.v. For a work boss of the caulkers trained by his uncle who was *proto alle stoppe,* see ASV:SM, filza 426, 29 June 1650.

64. As the Patroni wrote about Zuane Luganegher, the son of a foreman who was later both foreman shipwright and Admiral: "under the discipline of his father so well did he turn out, that hardly had he taken his [master's] examination than he was made gang boss": ASV:SM, filza 234, 31 Dec 1621; also ASV:CRD suppliche, filza 35, 13 Oct 1644; and filza 36, 2 June and 4 Dec 1645. Twenty-six out of sixty-two work bosses (42 percent) petitioning the Collegio between 1621 and 1670 noted that they had been apprenticed to another gang boss; only five (8 percent) specifically stated that they had not had such training, while the remainder offered no such details.

65. ASV:Collegio V (Segreta), bu. 57, Relazione of Andrea Marcello (1645), ff. 135–37; and Relazione of Francesco Cornero (1696), ff. 11–12v; MC:Mss Gradenigo, bu. 193 I, ff. 285r–288r (1660). The role of families in Venetian shipbuilding thus lay somewhere between that in Marseilles, where state galley building was dominated by just two great lineages, and that in England, where few shipbuilding families lasted even beyond two generations: Bamford, *Fighting Ships and Prisons,* 73–74; and Davis, *The Rise of the English Shipbuilding Industry,* 54–55.

66. The shipwright Alessandro di Michiel successfully completed four or five such contracts on his own in the 1630s and had been chosen as work boss by 1645: ASV:SM, filza 499, 16 July 1658.

67. Usually, it is true, the task fell to the Patroni and Provveditori, but if they could not agree, the decision might by taken elsewhere: ASV:TA, reg. 141, 18 Feb 1661 m.v.; Lane, *Venetian Ships and Shipbuilders,* 164.

68. ASV:TA, reg. 137, 3 Jan 1612 m.v. and 1 June 1613; the chief stores officer of the Arsenal *(masser)* could also suggest candidates for supervisory posts: ASV:TA, reg. 139, 1 June 1630.

69. ASV:CRD suppliche, filza 34, 17 Sept 1643. For the firing of a supervisor by the Patroni, on the advise of the Admiral, foremen, and *masser,* see ASV:TA, reg. 139, 14 May 1624.

70. ASV:TA, reg. 139, 8 Jan 1620 m.v; also reg. 139, 30 Aug 1633, 6 Apr 1634; and ASV:CRD suppliche, filza 19, 6 Apr 1628. Lane, *Venetian Ships and Shipbuilders,* 170.

71. As in the 1663 election for foreman of the oarmakers, which ran on for five ballotings: ASV:TA, reg. 141, 4 Feb 1663 m.v; also reg. 137, 21 May 1601; reg. 139, 25 Sept 1623; reg. 141, 12 Dec 1658; ASV:SM, filza 510, 2 June 1660; and ASV:Collegio V (Segreta), bu. 57, Relazione of Polo Contarini (1643), f. 11v.

72. To make their selection, all the Patroni and Provveditori went to "particularly examine the masts and rudders of pieces made by the three who had applied, as was ordered by Your Highnesses." The Admiral (himself the ex-foreman mastmaker) and the other major foremen also judged the work: ASV:TA, reg. 138, 27 Nov 1619.

73. Few nobles in Venice were considered ready for major posts until reaching at least the age of sixty: Finlay, "The Venetian Republic as a Gerontocracy." For ceremonial duties of the Admiral, see Chap. 5 below.

74. ASV:CRD suppliche, filza 30, 17 Oct 1639; and filza 35, 12 Mar 1644. The foremen and Admiral considered their manual duties as a matter of pride: "We have always been the chiefs, not only in giving commands and orders, but also in working like everyone else; it can be said in fact that our offices are a particularly mechanical, that is manual, art, because we always work manually." ASV:CRD suppliche, filza 38, 31 July 1647. It should be noted, however, that they were petitioning here for inclusion in a tax exemption which had recently been granted to manual workers of the Arsenal.

75. Birth dates from S. Martino parish: *Libro dei battesimi* and *Libro dei morti*; Grandi's successor, Domenico di Fulgentio was also only around thirty-two years old when elected in 1666: ASV:CRD suppliche, filza 71, 15 Jan 1668 m.v.

76. ASV:TA, reg. 139, 25 Sept 1623; ASV:CRD suppliche, filza 49, 11 Sept 1657. Zorzi's successor Lorenzo di Niccolò would also serve twelve years with the fleet: filza 47, 23 Oct 1656.

77. Both successful and unsuccessful candidates had a nautical background: in 1630, there were four admirals, two ship's captains, and the foreman of the carpenters competing; in 1635, two admirals competed against the same foreman; and in 1680, the choice was between two admirals: MC:Mss Gradenigo, bu. 193 I, f. 106r. The position of fleet admiral in Venice was an executive rather than a commanding one: admirals ran a squadron under the orders of a noble *capitanio*: Lane, *Venetian Ships and Shipbuilders*, 151, n. 21. Only one of seven Admirals selected between 1619 and 1723 had earlier been a foreman shipwright (another had been foreman of the mastmakers): cf. Crovato, "Arsenale e arsenalotti," 57; Perocco and Salvadori, *La civiltà di Venezia*, 2:126.

78. Marco Fasoi was elected in 1660: ASV:TA, reg. 141, 22 Feb 1661 m.v., 2 Mar and 17 Mar 1662. Protests were lodged in the 1720s against the Admiral Pasqual Bisson, rumored to be no more than a foundling ("figliolo de pio ospedale") who had served for a while as an apprentice oarmaker in the Arsenal: MC:Mss Gradenigo, bu. 193 I, ff. 107r and 119r–122r.

79. ASV:CRD suppliche, filza 30, 17 Oct 1639; filza 33, 12 Jan 1642 m.v.; ASV:SM, filza 294, 22 Dec 1634; filza 505, 8 May 1659.

80. Thus, Vicenzo Vice served for over a decade as workforce overseer before his election as foreman shipwright, and Francesco Cavazzina was subforeman of oakum before he was chosen foreman of the caulkers. At the time of their election, foremen were required to surrender all such offices: ASV:TA, reg. 139, 5 Mar 1636; reg. 141, 13 May, 6 Feb 1661.

81. Tucci, "L'Alimentazione a bordo delle navi veneziane," 120.

82. Finlay, *Politics in Renaissance Venice*, 44–108, passim. Trying to keep noblemen from colluding with their favorite gang bosses to produce galleys that were too personalized or showy for proper warships, the Senate tried repeatedly (but evidently unsuccessfully) to ban ship commanders from coming into the Arsenal at all: Lane, *Venice: A Maritime Republic*, 365, 415; *Venetian Ships and Shipbuilders*, 212.

83. Indeed, there survives an earlier letter from Ottavio's father, Antonio, which begged Cristoforo Ciuran's help in getting a piece of Cesani

family business through the legislative channels. ASV:SM, filza 252, 7 May 1626. Also ASV:CRD suppliche, filza 46, 26 Oct 1655.

84. ASV:SM, filza 386, 24 Aug 1646.

85. S. Martino parish: battesimi, 19 Jan 1586 m.v., 11 Aug 1601, 7 Dec 1602, 28 Nov 1624, 11 Aug 1627, and 1 Sept 1627.

86. Ibid.; the children's godfathers were the brothers Piero and Bernardo Memo, Piero Barbarigo (twice), Zuane Pisani, Antonio Molin, Bortolo Grimani, Gerolamo Loredan, Anzolo Labia, Alberto Magno, and Marcantonio Bembo. The latter two noblemen were serving as Patroni of the Arsenal when they stood as godfather, and Antonio Molin had done so three years previously, an indication that Cavazzina also knew how to use the connections of his workplace to advantage. On godparenting for promoting networks across social classes, see Bossy, "Godparenthood"; and Klapsich-Zuber, "Parenti, amici, vicini," 976–81.

87. Lane, *Venice: A Maritime Republic,* 364.

88. ASV:TA, reg. 139, 3 Sept 1630. This in fact later happened with the position of chief stores officer: ASV:CRD suppliche, filza 58, 11 May 1662; filza 62, 19 Aug 1664.

89. ASV:CRD suppliche, filza 18, 27 Dec 1627; filza 35, 26 May 1644; filza 56, 4 Mar 1661.

90. ASV:TA, reg. 137, 22 June 1613 and 19 Feb 1613 m.v., reg. 141, 17 Mar 1659; ASV:CRD suppliche, filza 34, 30 May 1643. On punishments for dishonesty: ASV:TA, reg. 137, 19 Feb 1613 m.v.; reg. 139, 12 Oct 1630; reg. 140, 15 July 1649; reg. 141, 17 Mar 1659; on officers swindling masters: ASV:Collegio V (Segreta), bu. 57, Relazione of Francesco Sanudo (1670), f. 4v.

91. ASV:TA, reg. 139, 18 Mar 1633; reg. 140, 3 Dec 1643; ASV:CRD suppliche, filza 45, 23 Sept 1654; ASV:SM, reg. 85, 22 Sept 1627. For rulings against substitutes: ASV:TA, reg. 137, 24 Jan 1604 m.v.; ASV:SM, reg. 100, 1 Nov 1642; ASV:CRD suppliche, filza 32, 21 Oct 1641.

92. ASV:TA, reg. 139, 14 Jan 1632 m.v.; reg. 140, 17 Sept 1639; also reg. 140, 12 and 26 Jan, and 10 Feb 1637 m.v.

93. The sales were held seven times during the century; by 1650 only 5 percent of all government offices were elected on the basis of merit: Mousnier, "Le trafic des offices à Venise."

94. ASV: Deputati et Aggiunti sopra l'Esazione del Denaro Publico, bu. 70: nos. 87, 134, 143; bu. 71, nos. 164, 241; bu. 72, nos. 302, 325.

95. ASV:CRD suppliche, filza 32, 12 June 1641; filza 53, 29 Jan 1659 m.v. For protests of Marine Secretaries that the sale of key guardian offices brought in far less than would be lost through the resulting corruption and mismanagement: ASV:Collegio V (Segreta), bu. 57, Relazione of Piero Mocenigo (1660), f. 27r; Bertucci Trivisan (1669), f. 10r; Francesco Sanudo (1670), f. 5r.

96. The Patroni wrote, "these posts are the reward and the hope of these poor workers, who look forward to them all the course of their lives." ASV:CRD suppliche, filza 53, 29 Jan 1659 m.v. The co-opting of certain workers into management positions would provide a necessary safety valve in the industrial era as well: Spencer, "Between Capital and Labor," 184.

97. Just as the caulker Alvise Moscatello entered into the office market,

making an unsuccessful bid of 20 ducats for the office of workforce overseer on 30 June 1647, and then undaunted, trying again five months later, with 70 ducats this time, and managing to buy the office of supervisor of large hardware: ASV:Deputati et aggiunti sopra l'esazione del denaro publico, bu. 70, nos. 87, 143; and Mousnier, "Le Trafic des Offices," 563.

98. When Antonio Ferari bought the office of appraiser in 1641, the Patroni told him that since he was not enrolled with the Arsenal he could not personally do the work; furthermore, if he intended instead to engage a substitute, he had to pay the full salary of the position, not hire an inferior worker at a pittance, as he had evidently intended to do: ASV:CRD suppliche, filza 32, 12 June 1641. For a similar complaint, from the owner of the office of workforce overseer, see filza 32, 21 Oct 1641.

99. ASV:Deputati sopra denaro publico, bu. 72, no. 325.

100. The Patroni wrote that if an office "is allowed to be bought by merchants and contractors that deliver goods to the Arsenal, then for appearance's sake substituting in the exercise [of the position] someone who is their confident, they would then have the total dependence of the same . . . in the estimates and consignments for their benefit, to the considerable prejudice of Your Serenity": ASV:CRD suppliche, filza 53, 29 Jan 1659 m.v.

101. Most nontechnical officers were only paid the regular 40-soldi daily wage maximum, although they were sometimes paid it seven days per week. The Patroni once complained that since a substitute workforce overseer was paid only his daily wage, he never bothered to carry out his duties: ASV:CRD suppliche, filza 52, 14 July 1659.

102. The owner himself might realize around 250 ducats a year on his post, perhaps a 15–20 percent return: ASV:SM, filza 392, 23 May 1647.

103. ASV:Deputati sopra denaro publico, bu. 70, no. 27, and bu. 74, no. 37.

104. ASV:TA, reg. 140, 10 Oct 1637; ASV:CRD suppliche, filza 32, 21 Oct 1641; and ASV:SM, filza 416, 24 June 1649; for the list of office holders: ASV:Collegio V (Segreta), bu. 57, Relazione of Francesco Cornero (1696), ff. 7r–15v.

105. Thus, in 1696 the post of workforce overseer belonged to a brother of the foreman shipwright, while the office of timekeeper of the oarmakers was owned by the foreman of the oarmakers: ASV:Collegio V (Segreta), bu. 57, Relazione of Francesco Cornero (1696), ff. 7r–15v; Lane, *Venice, A Maritime Republic,* 333–34.

106. That the Patroni were often unaware of problems and activities occurring within the Arsenal is evident from their own edicts: ASV:TA, reg. 137, 9 June 1608 and 24 Apr 1609; reg. 139, 14 May 1624 and 21 Mar 1630; reg. 140, 26 Mar 1639, 23 Sept 1644, and 15 May 1645. For the suggestion that the very number and specialized duties of managers can make an effective barrier between those appointed to administer an industry and its actual workforce and production processes, see Spencer, "Between Capital and Labor," 180–81.

107. The averages for each position were: Admiral, 18.2 years; foreman shipwright, 15.8; foreman of the caulkers, 14.8; foreman of the oarmakers, 23.5; and foreman of the mastmakers, 32.3.

108. ASV:SM, filza 294, 22 Dec 1634; filza 314, 30 Oct 1637; filza 338,

10 May 1641; filza 377, 17 Aug 1645. Petitions of foreman shipwright Vicenzo Vice followed a similar pattern: ASV:SM, filza 340, 6 July 1641; ASV:CRD suppliche, filza 35, 12 Mar 1644.

109. Davis, *Rise of English Shipping*, 14–21, 61–66; Unger, "Technology and Industrial Organization."

110. On foremen promoting their own candidates for minor offices, see ASV:TA, reg. 137, 2 Aug 1603; 3 Jan and 21 Feb 1613 m.v.; reg. 138, 9 Mar 1616; on their supervision of gang bosses, ASV:TA, reg. 137, 10 Sept 1607; ASV:SM, reg. 71, 18 Apr 1613; reg. 73, 19 Feb 1615 m.v.; on their judging the examinations of apprentices, ASV:SM, filza 298, 13 Oct 1635. The importance of the foremen did not derive from controlling positions within their craft guilds, for they rarely if ever served on the guilds' directing board of *gastaldi:* see Biblioteca Marciana:Codex It VII:560 = 7501, *Scuole dei calafati, mariegole,* ff. 100r and 119v; ASV:TA, reg. 140, 25 Oct 1647; and reg. 141, 9 Mar 1660.

111. The gang boss Zuanfrancesco Lazari complained that he had performed his duties "with all punctuality and diligence, while I do not have either a house nor bonuses *(regaglie),* but only my simple wages" (which were already nearly double those of an ordinary master): ASV:CRD suppliche, filza 35, 13 Oct 1644. Likewise, Zorzi di Christofolo, proto of the oarmakers, complained about the "services given with indefatigable faith for centuries in the Arsenal and with the fleet by me, my father, and my grandfather, without ever having received anything [in return]": filza 33, 28 Jan 1642 m.v.

112. ASV:CRD suppliche, filza 31, 28 Oct 1640; for Moscatello's complaint: ASV:SM, filza 359, 2 Mar 1644. Also ASV:CRD suppliche, filza 34, 16 Feb 1643, for a similar request by foreman of the mastmakers, Zorzi Grandi.

113. ASV:TA, reg 141, 25 Aug 1655.

114. Ibid.; on boss's work books: ASV:CRD suppliche, filza 65, 1 Sept 1665; ASV:TA, reg. 141, 4 Mar 1653.

115. This was of course a wartime measure, but it does not appear to have ever been revoked: ASV:TA, reg 141, 24 May 1662.

116. ASV:TA, reg 141, 18 Jan 1672 m.v.

117. Aymard, "L'Arsenale e le conoscenze tecnico-marinaresche," 296–97.

118. Lane, *Venetian Ships and Shipbuilders,* 17, 70–71; and *Venice, A Maritime Republic,* 363–64. Concina, *L'Arsenale della Repubblica di Venezia,* 187–88; compare with the continuing variations in French designs: Bamford, *Fighting Ships and Prisons,* 68–69, 74–75.

119. This indeed was normal Arsenal policy: Lane, *Venetian Ships and Shipbuilders,* 139–45.

120. Figures for all six dates (1503, 1544, 1560, 1563, 1581, and 1583) from Lane, *Navires et Constructeurs,* 138–39, 230. They were obtained by adding together two categories of "new ships," those with "planking unfinished" and with "frame unfinished." Other categories of new ships, such as "unarmed" or "ready to launch" have been omitted, since their actual date of construction could easily have been much earlier.

121. Romano, "The Construction of Warships in Venice," 77; Tenenti, *Piracy and the Decline of Venice,* 93–99; ASV:Collegio V (Segreta), bu. 57, Relazione of Andrea Marcello, 1645; ASV:CRD suppliche, filza 42, 26 Oct 1651; and MC:Mss Gradenigo, bu. 193 I, ff. 285r–288r.

122. Light galleys were not the only ships produced in the Arsenal, even though the best known. During these same fifty years around thirty great galleys were constructed and at least thirty-five of the extra-large galleys *da generalitie,* destined for the fleet's *capitani generali:* ASV:CRD suppliche, filza 30, 17 Oct 1639; ASV:SM, filza 386, 24 Aug 1646; ASV:Collegio V (Segreta), bu. 57, Relazione of Piero Mocenigo (1660), f. 2r. Perhaps even greater actual productive effort, however, went into the vast numbers of armed cutters, or *barche armate,* and other small coasting vessels manufactured in the state shipyards: ASV:SM, reg. 97, 10 Mar, 19 Apr and 27 May 1639; reg. 99, 23 Mar 1641.

123. Compare with the French arsenal at Marseille: in its most productive period during the 1670s, with as many as 700 to 800 master shipbuilders at their disposal, French administrators nevertheless still protested that to build even seven galleys in a single year would be to "do the impossible": Bamford, *Fighting Ships and Prisons,* 76–79; Zysberg, "L'Arsenal des galères de France," 21, 30.

124. Romano, "The Construction of Warships in Venice," 70.

Chapter 3. The Community of the Arsenalotti

1. On the social importance of the public *campo* in Venetian parish life, see Lane, *Venice, A Maritime Republic,* 11–12.

2. The very large parish of San Pietro di Castello, home to at least 8,000 souls during much of this period, was connected to the rest of the city by only two bridges. Beltrami, *Storia della popolazione di Venezia,* table 1–2.

3. On the convulsive growth the Industrial Revolution brought to villages, see Glen, *Urban Workers,* 24–30; and Crew, *Town in the Ruhr,* 46–58, 119–127. Past work on company town formation has not been vast: see Pollard, "The Factory Village in the Industrial Revolution"; and Porteous, "Goole, A Pre-Victorian Company Town," and "The Nature of the Company Town."

4. Thus, caulkers were living on the opposite side of the city from the Arsenal in the fourteenth and fifteenth centuries: Romano, *Patricians and Popolani,* 80; also Caniato, "Squèri da grosso e squèri da sotil," 49–88.

5. The home was attached to the nearby convent of Sant'Antonio, and was known as l'Hospedale di Gesù Cristo di Sant'Antonio: see Pavanini, "Venezia verso la pianificazione?" 9–10.

6. The land had been intended for the *Hospedale* of Sant'Antonio. ASV:Procuatori di San Marco, bu. 107, no. 2, f. 8: 11 May 1531.

7. ASV:DSD (Dieci Savi sopra le Decime): bu. 94, specific *condizioni* cited in Pavanini, "Venezia verso la pianificazione?" 11–12. Later, the houses would be largely bought up by nobles and others seeking investment opportunities, but well into the seventeenth century the Secco Marina still contained the highest concentration of artisan-owned property in the entire area: in 1582, there were "about fifty" arsenalotti families living in this area

227

in *casa propria,* according to Concina, *L'Arsenale della Repubblica di Venezia,* 184. By 1661, arsenalotti and other artisans still owned 28 percent of the properties in the Secco Marina area (compared to a mere 1.5 percent elsewhere near the Arsenal), although only eleven Arsenal families still lived there in their own houses: ASV:DSD, bu. 520, nos. 1427–1526.

8. Pollard, "The Factory Village," 516–19.

9. ASV:SM, filza 336, 22 Jan 1640; ASV:TA, reg. 141, 30 Apr 1675.

10. Foreman of the caulkers, Giacomo dei Grassi likewise lived with eleven others: ASV:PS, bu. 570, San Biagio and San Martino.

11. ASV:CRD suppliche, filza 18, 27 Dec 1627. Edicts were posted "sopra il pergolo dell'Arsenale": ASV:TA, reg. 137, 19 Feb 1613 m.v., reg. 140, 15 May 1645. Anonymous denunciations were also solicited at the campo, in two slits placed under the words, "Denontie Secrete per l'Inquisitori all'Arsenal": Skippon, *A Journey,* 509.

12. ASV:CRD suppliche, filza 19, 20 Mar 1628. The Campo dell'-Arsenale largely came into being in the 1470s, after the Arsenal had acquired and knocked down some of the charitable houses belonging to the parish of San Martino; it was further enlarged in the 1790s: della Puppa, *Storia della Chiesa di S. Martino "de Geminis" in Venezia,* 12–22.

13. Franzoi and di Stefano, *Le chiese di Venezia,* 499.

14. The parish priest of San Martino described his church as "for the benefit of all the parishioners and the infinite number of foreigners who assemble here (since 'all the foreigners and princes who come to this city make the Arsenal a principal stop [*capo*]'), and for the continuous service of the House of the Arsenal, because of its closeness, and of its numerous workforce": Archives of San Martino parish, file B.1, f. 3 and 5; also Martin, "In God's Image," 163.

15. Accompanied by all the other foremen and bosses of the shipyards on his first morning of work, the new officer proceeded to the church of San Martino. Here he was given a ceremonial admittance *(ingresso)* to his office, an event celebrated with a high mass that was read by the parish priest and enhanced by organ music: Archives of San Martino parish, file J.8, f. C (1703).

16. Another four arsenalotti families of long standing were still living on the island of Poveglia (near the Lido) in 1661, largely because the Arsenal maintained a deep-water repair yard there: ASV:CRD suppliche, filza 55, 11 Apr 1661. More isolated, and therefore even less likely to be absorbed into the Arsenal enclave, was the shipbuilding community of Burano, where twenty-eight private yards operated in 1641: ASV:SM, filza 339, 28 June 1641. For a general discussion of the *anagrafi,* the household census conducted by parish priests: see Rapp, *Industry and Economic Decline,* 57, 78–81, 185; and Burke, *Historical Anthropology,* 27–39; figures from MC:Mss Donà dalle Rose, bu. 352 and 354.

17. "Noi fedelissimi servi della Casa dell'Arsenale . . . si atroviamo a star in solita habitation sin san Jacomo dall'Orio et san Baseglio lontanissimi dalla Casa dell'Arsenale che ben spesso si conviene patir di queli incomodi che la Serenità Vostra poterà comprender, ma quel che più importa è che per tal lontanaza non posiamo conforme li ore debite rivar à ora et questo

assai volte risulta in nostro danno . . . et di più che alli botti di campanela non posiamo servirla così alli fochi chome ochorenze di Vostra Serenità non posiamo eser pronti al comando delli Illustrissimi Patroni; però . . . suplichiamo à concedersi begnigna licenza che possiamo afitar dette nostre case afine del fito che di quele caviamo posiamo pagar il fitto de altre case più vicine che possible alla Casa dell'Arsenale": ASV:CRD suppliche, filza 19, 20 Mar 1628.

18. Gramigna and Perissa, *Scuole di arti, mestieri e devozioni a Venezia,* 35–37, for the caulkers; for the oarmakers' and shipwrights' *scuole,* see Soprintendenza ai beni artistici e storici di Venezia, *Arti e mestieri nella Repubblica di Venezia,* 60–65, which gives the church of Santa Maria della Carità instead of the Carmini as the first home of the *scuola* of the caulkers.

19. MC:Mss Donà delle Rose, bu. 352 (1624); ASV:PS, bu. 568 (1633) and 570 (1642); Beltrami, *Storia della popolazione di Venezia,* table 2.

20. So it would appear from the *anagrafi,* which show a scarcity of all such workers except carpenters *(marangoni)* anywhere else in the city. Unfortunately, only a few of the parish priests conducting the census bothered to specify between shipwrights of the Arsenal *(marangoni all'Arsenale)* and regular house carpenters *(marangoni di case).* Of the latter, around 500 worked in Venice, scattered evenly about the city. Scholars who have estimated the size and location of the Arsenal workforce by counting up all artisans in the shipbuilding trades without taking these house carpenters into account have thus counted too many *marangoni,* tending to conclude that arsenalotti households were both more numerous and more diffuse than they really were: Rapp, *Industry and Economic Decline,* 60, 80.

21. The *anagrafi* used the term *artefici,* or "craftsmen" as a kind of catch-all category to include all Venetians who were neither nobles nor *cittadini.* Since this included all manner of widows, beggars, and foreigners, who were by no means all "artisans," it is probably more accurate to use instead the term *popolani,* a contemporary term meaning roughly the same as the English "plebs": Burke, *The Historical Anthropology of Early Modern Italy,* 32–33; and Pullan, *Poverty and Charity in Renaissance Venice,* 18–22. The 1642 breakdown for the four parishes was as follows: 43 arsenalotti families out of 404 *popolani* households in Santa Ternità; 124 out of 545 households in San Biagio and San Martino; and 509 out of 1297 households in San Pietro di Castello.

22. ASV:PS, bu. 570, Santa Ternità; San Biagio and San Martino; also ASV:SM, filza 336, 19 Feb 1640 m.v.

23. All together, these occupations accounted for 772 of San Pietro's 1297 *popolani* households in 1642: ASV: Provveditori alla Sanità, bu. 570. Between twenty and fifty sailors worked in the Arsenal at launching or repairing ships: ASV:TA, reg. 141, 20 Feb 1669 m.v.; ASV:Collegio V (Segreta), bu. 57, Relazione of Francesco Cornero (1696), f. 15v.

24. MC:Cicogna Codice 3161, 1632, 6; and Tamassia Mazzarotto, *Le feste veneziane,* 224–27.

25. As happened with the men (mostly caulkers) who lived in the Quintevalle, on the backside of the island of San Pietro di Castello, where Venice's cathedral was located: ASV:SUP *(Sant'Uffizio processi),* bu. 89, *contra*

Matteo di Lunardo. The men from Quintevalle also formed smuggling gangs together: ASV:SM, filza 559, 19 Nov 1667.

26. Compare the following with the parish endogamy rates in both the Venetian parishes of San Giacomo dall'Orio and San Barnabà, as well as in Florence during the early Renaissance: Romano, "San Giacomo dall'Orio," 133–36; Martin, "In God's Image," 151 and n. 78; Cohn, *The Laboring Classes in Renaissance Florence*, 117–23.

27. Two decade-long samplings from the San Martino marriage registers tallying weddings where at least one spouse was from an arsenalotti family (that is, master, son, daughter, or widow) of the parish show similar results: in the years 1620–29, out of 121 such marriages, 51 were contracted with both partners living inside the parish, and 34 on the same street or campo; between 1655 and 1664, there were 93 such marriages, 43 of which were intra-parish and 28 from the same street. Endogamy appears to have been much higher in San Pietro parish, where 80 out of 102 weddings involving Arsenal families between 1641 and 1644 were intra-parish. The San Pietro *libri di matrimonio* only recorded marriages which actually took place within the parish itself, however, so that the resulting tally tends to exaggerate endogamy rates by omitting those who moved away to marry. In San Martino, by contrast, there also survive the *libri di stride*, or wedding banns, which list all marriages contracted by anyone living within the parish, regardless of where the ceremony was actually carried out; endogamy rates listed here for San Martino take these banns into account.

28. Such parish clusters have been used elsewhere to describe "the ecology of the Renaissance city": Cohn, *The Laboring Classes in Renaissance Florence*, 26–35, 115–28. For a more qualitative treatment of a similar urban unit, see also Kent and Kent, *Neighbours and Neighbourhood*, esp. 48–66. On the ambiguous nature of the Venetian parish as a social unit, see Martin, "In God's Image," 146–53; and Romano, "San Giacomo dall'Orio," 311–30. Also Muir, *Civic Ritual*, 3–8.

29. Compare the similarity of these six parishes of Castello to San Polo, another "central" parish: Favalier, "Le attività lavoritive," 187–97. The occupational groupings which follow are largely based on those devised by Favalier and by Martin, "In God's Image," 526–30.

30. On the social profile of Venice, especially in its central parishes: Ruggiero, *Violence in Early Renaissance Venice*, 64; Beltrami, *Storia della popolazione di Venezia*, 45–49; Romano, *Patricians and Popolani*, 145–50; Lane, *Venice, A Maritime Republic*, 11–12.

31. Foreign residents had their own separate heading in the *anagrafi*, as did servants and maids *(servitori* and *massere)*: Burke, *Historical Anthropology*, 33.

32. Martin, "In God's Image," 168. For a map of the foreign communities in Castello, see Perocco and Salvadori, *Civiltà di Venezia*, 2:772, and text.

33. ASV:Collegio V (Segreta), Relazione of Domenico Lion (1636), f. 2r; Lane, *Venetian Ships and Shipbuilders*, 56–61.

34. MC:Mss Gradenigo, bu. 193 II, 60r; ASV:SM, filza 511, 4 Sept 1660; on the Council of Ten: Sanudo, *I diarii*, 8:17–18.

35. For the sense of worth and worldly contacts enjoyed by such crafts-men, see Martin, "In God's Image," 122–30.

36. Citywide figures for food dealers ranged from 9.2 percent to 14.1 percent for the three censuses: Beltrami, *Storia della popolazione di Venezia*, 206–9; also Perocco and Salvadori, *Civiltà di Venezia*, 631–41. For an artis-tic glimpse at the variety of Venetian street vendors, see Zompini, *Le arte che vanno per via nella città di Venezia*.

37. ASV:DSD, bu. 520, San Pietro di Castello, nos. 430–34, 463–74, 504–21, 562–73, 631–42, 690–93, 703–16, 737–41, 750–63, 781–83, 798–800, 884–88, 899–904, 918–21.

38. Beltrami, *Storia della popolazione di Venezia*, 50–55.

39. Counted as bakers here are both *forneri* and *pistori*; each of the sample parishes also had one or two *scaleteri*, or biscuit bakers, who may have either sold their product to the public or have only worked as employ-ees at the fleet's biscuit oven in San Biagio parish: ASV:PS, bu. 570, passim.

40. ASV:SM, filza 335, 7 Dec 1640. Not surprisingly, wine dealers were far more common near the port: there were nineteen in the three parishes of the zone, over ten times their frequency per household in the Arsenal district.

41. ASV:Collegio V (Segreta), Relazione of Zuane Bernardo (1676), f. 6r; and of Vettor Grimani (1683), ff. 3r–v.

42. ASV:TA, reg. 137, 26 Jan 1608 m.v.

43. For studies on workers and the poor using these sources, see Rapp, *Industry and Economic Decline*, 117–21, 178–82; Pavanini, "Abitazioni po-polari," 63–126; Palumbo-Fossati, "L'Interno della casa dell'artigiano e dell'artista nella Venezia del Cinquecento," 112–14; Romano, *Patricians and Popolani*, 77–90; also Braudel, *Capitalism and Material Life*, 197–212.

44. ASV:SM, 25 Sept 1530 and 29 Nov 1569; ASV:Procuratia di Citra, bu 381, *Specchio-Bilancio delle case*, 1616–1656; ASV:DSD, bu. 420, S. Pie-tro di Castello, 608–32, 823–83, 1421, 1424.

45. ASV:Procuratia Misti, bu. 191 (Case di Marinarezza), ASV: SM, reg. 62, 9 Nov 1590; ASV:CRD suppliche, filza 51, 13 Jan 1658 m.v.

46. Concina, *L'Arsenale della Repubblica di Venezia*, 183–86; Rapp, *In-dustry and Economic Decline*, 80–81; Perocco and Salvadori, *Civiltà di Ve-nezia*, 115–124; Trincanato, *A Guide to Venetian Domestic Architecture*, 21–39.

47. ASV:Giudizi Petizion, bu. 354, 6 Nov 1635 and 12 Dec 1633.

48. As early as the 1590s, each Venetian sailor was accustomed to serve himself "with his knife and spoone, and his forke": Moryson, *An Itinerary*, 1:448. The fork was not in general use in England until the 1700s; not until 1651 did it come into favor in the Viennese court: Braudel, *Capitalism and Material Life*, 138–39. ASV:Giudizi Petizion, bu. 354, 12 Dec 1633 and 17 Apr 1635; bu. 346, 18 Jan 1615 m.v. ASV: Notarile, Angaran Testamenti, bu. 9/123; Bozini Testamenti, bu. 187/428 and 429.

49. ASV:Notarile, Bozini Testamenti bu. 186/37, 187/331; Angaran Tes-tamenti, bu. 9/29.

50. The 800 ducats which the caulker Piero di Donato Zurlin paid for the post of Arsenal doorkeeper was perhaps the highest amount offered

by any ordinary shipbuilder, but many other masters bid from 50 to 500
ducats for positions; payment was usually expected within one month:
ASV:Deputati sopra Denari Publici, bu. 70/87, 124, 127, 134, 143; bu. 71/
164; bu. 72/305; bu. 73/435; bu. 74/77; bu. 75/157 (Piero di Donato); bu.
103/49.

51. Thus, Catharina Crestin had to raise 500 reales to free her brother,
an Arsenal pulleymaker; only half of this, she wrote, had been promised by
"the usual places": ASV:CRD suppliche, filza 34, 19 Oct 1643; for other
ransoms of 200–500 reales, see filza 18, 13 Feb 1627 m.v.; filza 46, 9 Apr
1655; filza 53, 7 Nov 1659; filza 64, 19 June 1665; filza 68, 16 Mar 1667;
and filza 93, 16 Jan 1680 m.v.

52. Chojnacki, "Dowries and Kinsmen in Early Renaissance Venice,"
571–600; Romano, *Patricians and Popolani*, 34–35; Davis, *The Decline of
the Venetian Nobility as a Ruling Class*, 66–67, and *A Venetian Family and
its Fortune*, 106–9.

53. For selected arsenalotti dowries: ASV:Notarile, Testamenti Bozini,
bu. 186/69 (200 ducats) and 124 (440 ducats); bu. 187/456 (400 ducats),
465 (100 ducats), and 518 (275 ducats); Atti Bozini, bu. 1012, f. 171r (150
ducats); ASV:CRD suppliche, filza, 11 Mar 1628 (400 ducats); filza 20, 2
Mar 1629 (140 ducats).

54. Pullan, *Rich and Poor in Renaissance Venice*, 82, 185; interestingly,
when the noblewoman Diana Vendramin established a bequest specifically
to dower the daughters of poor arsenalotti, she gave 30 ducats to each girl,
perhaps an indication of shipbuilders' status relative to other artisans: Biblioteca Marciana: *Scuole dei calafati, mariegole*, ff. 108r–111r.

55. ASV:Giudizi Petizioni, bu. 354, 17 Apr 1635; ASV:Notarile, Bozini
Testamenti, bu. 186/12. For similar hoards of household goods, see also
Bozini, bu. 187/429 (Marietta, widow of Piero di Michele, caulker); and
Angaran Testamenti, bu. 9/123 (Giacomo di Pierantonio, caulker).

56. ASV:CRD suppliche, filza 38, 23 Feb 1647 m.v.; prices from
ASV:SUP, bu. 82, contra Maddalena, filza 2; bu. 104, contra Laura Malipiero, ff. 55v–56r.

57. A price series assembled for Florence, 1520–1630, indicates that
the price of all essentials, from beans to oil to firewood, registered their
sharpest increases after 1570, tending to crest around 1600–1609, before
declining slightly: Damsholt, "Some Observations on Four Series of Tuscan
Corn Prices, 1520–1630," 160. For workers' declining buying power in
other Italian cities, see Vigo, "Real Wages of the Working Classes in Italy,"
388–89.

58. On grain prices in Venice, see Pullan, "Wage-Earners and the Venetian Economy, 1550–1630," 155–56; for Florence, see Goldthwaite, *The
Building of Renaissance Florence*, 318–19, and "I prezzi del grano a Firenze,"
5–36. Prices of grain and flour were probably not as relevant as the price
of bread itself to the average worker, who generally had no means to do his
own baking: Mattozzi, "Il politico e il pane a Venezia," 208–9.

59. Tucci, "L'Alimentazione," 103–10. Food prices from accounts of
ASV:S. Michele in Isola, bu. 49, 1645–70 and ASV:San Nicolò della Latucha, bu. 15, 1667–73.

60. Beltrami, *Storia della popolazione di Venezia*, 223–27. See for com-

parison the tax census for the worker parish of Santa Eufemia (Giudecca), where a household consisting of only a single room (una stanza sola or camera sola in casa) rented for between 6 and 13 ducats per year: ASV:DSD, bu. 424, S. Eufemia, nos. 169, 183, 240, 373, 566, 706.

61. ASV:Giudizi Petizioni, bu. 346, filza 33.

62. ASV:CRD suppliche, filza 41, 14 Mar 1650; also filza 28, 12 Mar 1637; and filza 56, 5 Apr 1661.

63. San Martino parish, libro dei morti.

64. ASV:CRD suppliche, filza 63, 5 Sept 1664.

65. The anagrafi show little variation in this, although the plague did briefly reduce the female surplus: the ratios were 132 women to 100 men in 1624, 124 to 100 in 1633, and 126 to 100 in 1642; the single parish of Santa Ternità parish in 1624 had 146 women to 100 men. The ratio for the city overall also favored women, at about 116 to every 100 men: Beltrami, Storia della popolazione di Venezia, 80–90; for gender ratios in other Italian cities, see Beloch, Bevölkerungsgeschichte Italiens, vols. 2, 3.

66. ASV:SM, reg. 87, 14 Nov 1629; ASV:Collegio V (Segreta), Relazione of Andrea Marcello (1645); ASV:SM, filza 390, 13 Mar 1647. By the end of the century, the ratio had dropped to around 20 percent: Relazione of Francesco Cornero (1696), f. 15v.

67. ASV:TA, reg. 141, 11, 13, and 18 Sept 1663.

68. Venice's prostitute population has been estimated as high as 12,000; most did not live around the port at all, but in the sestiere of San Polo, by the Rialto: Menetto and Zennaro, La storia del malcostume a Venezia; Davis, A Venetian Family, 105; Burke, Historical Anthropology, 32–38.

69. She was not highly esteemed: "Lucretia Mortesina à Castello, pieza lei medma . . . dar quello si vol": MC:mss Cicogna, misc. 2483. On female household heads in pre-modern Italy: Palazzi, "Abitare da sole," 37–57 and bibliography.

70. Brown, "A Woman's Place Was in the Home"; and Wiesner, "Spinsters and Seamstresses"; also Rapp, Industry and Economic Decline, 27–29; Mackenney, Tradesmen and Traders, 23.

71. ASV:TA, reg. 141, 6 Feb 1663 m.v. Despite occasional hearsay accounts by visitors of "200 Old Women daily mending old Sails, and sometimes . . . 700 daily working," there is no evidence at all in either the censuses or Arsenal records of more than a maximum of 40 or 50 women on the payroll: "A True Description," 2; Forsellini, "L'Organizzazione economica," 84, 87; ASV:SM, filza 338, 4 May 1641; filza 572, 1 Feb 1669 m.v.

72. The woman who did all the laundry for the island monastery of San Michele in Isola during this period earned 2 ducats per month: 25 percent less than a sailmaker's pay: ASV:San Michele in Isola, reg. 3, 1669, salariati.

73. In 1642, the four Arsenal parishes had only about eighty live-in maids, compared with 6,500 in the city as a whole. On maids as an indicator of wealth: Rapp, Industry and Economic Decline, 81; also Beltrami, Storia della popolazione di Venezia, 213.

74. The sawyers were in effect seasonal immigrants, returning to Trento every summer: ASV:CRD suppliche, filza 64, 19 Aug 1665; Gallo, "Maestranze trentine," 95–112.

75. For rates paid to balie during the mid-1600s: Tagliaferri, Consomi e

tenore di vita di una famiglia borghese, 166; Cavallo, "Strategie politiche e familiari intorno al Baliatico," 402; also Klapisch-Zuber, "Genitori naturali e genitori di latte," 547–48; Pullan, *Rich and Poor in Renaissance Venice,* 207, 374; ASV:SUP, bu. 103, *contra* Caterina, 12 June 1647.

76. ASV:SUP, bu. 85, *contra* Maddalena, filza 8. The literature on witchcraft is vast: on the Mediterranean Inquisition and folk magic, see Monter, *Ritual, Myth and Magic in Early Modern Europe,* 61–77; and Tamburini, "Suppliche per casi di stregoneria diabolica nei registri della Penitenzieria e conflitti inquisitoriali," 605–59; on the infrequency of trials against such "white" witchcraft generally, see Monter, *Witchcraft in France and Switzerland,* 67–90; Thomas, *Religion and the Decline of Magic,* 244–52; and Levack, *The Witch-hunt in Early Modern Europe,* 201–5.

77. Favalier, "Le attività lavorative," 195. Ten out of Castello's thirty-three spice dealers in 1642 were located in the Arsenal zone. The connection between a scarcity of rural physicians and the flourishing of cunning women has been noted elsewhere: Lingo, "Empirics and Charlatans," 593.

78. Indeed, many doctors believed in witchcraft themselves, and when an illness presented peculiar or inexplicable symptoms, the wise physician would not attempt to intervene but often referred his patient to the proper religious authorities: Estes, "The Medical Origins of the European Witch Craze," 271–73; also Bergamaschi et al., *L'Erba delle donne,* esp. 11–32, 87–124, 149–78; ASV:CRD suppliche, filza 30, 17 Oct 1639.

79. ASV:SUP, bu. 104, *contra* Laura Malipiero.

80. ASV:SUP, bu. 104, *contra* Laura Malipiero, ff. 53r, 80r, 80v, and 87v; such a combination of invocations and herbalism has been called a "first line of defense" for those afflicted with disease: Park, *Doctors and Medicine in Early Renaissance Florence,* 48–49.

81. ASV:SUP, bu. 104, *contra* Laura Malipiero.

82. La Franza sprinkled holy water about Angela's house and then placed three parsley seeds about the place ("una sotto il sogier, fuori della porta, et la terza adosso"). She also made a mixture of bread, salt, and garlic, which she smeared on Angela, while reciting incantations, and gave her medicines ("robba per bocca"): ASV:SUP, bu 85 *contra* la Franza; compare with Park, *Doctors and Medicine,* 50–51, 93.

83. ASV:SUP, bu 103, *contra* Isabella. Isabella was accused by two other witnesses of performing almost the identical "treatment" on their children the following year: ASV:SUP, bu 104, *contra* Laura Malipiero, ff. 30r–32v and 34r–35r.

84. Isabella herself seems to have kept a fairly clear and interesting distinction as to what made for witchcraft. Witches, she told Catharina, accepted payment for their services, while she did the work for charity; thus she refused a shirt the mother had brought her: ASV:SUP, bu 103, *contra* Isabella.

85. Angelica, the wise woman in question, was herself the widow of a shipwright: ASV:SUP, bu. 89, *contra* Angelica; also Monter, *Witchcraft in France and Switzerland,* 167–73.

86. On the use of such chants to ease childbirth, see Martin, "Out of the Shadow," 27; also ASV:SUP, bu. 104, *contra* Laura Malipiero. Holy water,

sanctified rings, and wax candles were also used: ASV:SUP, bu. 105, *contra* Marula Magnata. For different uses of orations: ASV:SUP, bu. 85, *contra* Zanetta; and bu. 103, *contra* Catharina; also Lingo, "Empirics and Charlatans," 594.

87. ASV:SUP, bu. 104, *contra* Laura Malipiero, ff. 32r, 36r–v.

88. ASV:SUP, bu. 85, *contra* Maddalena, filze 7 and 9; also bu. 104, *contra* Laura Malipiero, f. 33r.

89. ASV:SM, reg. 75, 19 Aug 1617. The caulker Piero di Dimitri wrote in a petition that he had been held as a slave in Tripoli for twenty-six years, and "I was never able to get the news through about my disaster to my only sister (who believed me dead)": ASV:CRD suppliche, filza 93, 17 Sept 1680.

90. For arsenalotti held captive in Constantinople, the Venetian *bailio* in the city might be able to intervene, or at least carry news back home of their fate, but those enslaved in Tunis or Algiers could vanish for decades: ASV:CRD suppliche, filza 27, 23 Jan 1636 m.v.; filza 28, 14 Jan 1637 m.v.; filza 29, 1 Sept 1638; filza 61, 14 Jan 1663 m.v.; and ASV:SM, filza 286, 20 Sept 1633. Coco and Manzonetto, *Baili veneziani,* 63–97; also Lenci, "Riscatti di schiavi cristiani dal Maghreb," 53–80.

91. ASV:SUP, bu. 85, *contra* Maddalena; bu. 105, *contra* Marula Magnata; and bu 89, *contra* Angelica.

92. ASV:SUP, bu. 85 *contra* Zanetta, *meretrice;* and bu. 86, *contra* Camilla Padoana. At least one Arsenal shipwright actually dabbled in black magic himself, however: bu. 95, *contra* Alvise Mazzani.

93. ASV:SUP, bu. 85, *contra* Maddalena; bu. 103, *contra* Catherina; bu. 105, *contra* Marula Magnata.

94. "Pensavo che vi fosse qualche persona che dasse la ventura sopra la mano": ASV:SUP, bu. 85, *contra* Maddalena Schiavona; "Andavo pensando io che mi volesse dare la marenda" bu. 105, *contra* Marula Magnata.

95. ASV:SUP, bu. 105, *contra* Regina d'Elia.

96. Herlihy, "Some Psychological and Social Roots of Violences," 146–47. Compare this hypothesis with the claim that a surplus of women would instead lead to a greater public interest in Christian ceremony and "spiritual restorations": Herlihy, *Medieval and Renaissance Pistoia,* 257; also Martin, "Out of the Shadow," 24–28.

97. ASV:SUP, bu. 86, *contra* Camilla Padoana; for denunciations against such foreign women: bu. 85, *contra* Zanetta *meretrice* and *contra* Maddalena *schiavona;* bu. 105, *contra* Marula Magnata and *contra* Regina d'Elia. On the mixing of witchcraft and prostitution accusations, see Lingo, "Empirics and Charlatans," 596. On the social exclusiveness of the "labor aristocracy" and artisan communities generally, see Hobsbawm, *Labouring Men,* 272–75, 290–300; and Walker, *German Home Towns,* 77–107.

98. ASV:CRD suppliche, filza 47, 15 Sept 1656.

Chapter 4. Arsenalotti as Agents of Disorder in Venice

1. De Roover, "A Florentine Firm of Cloth Manufacturers," 12.

2. ASV:Avogaria di Comun-Penale, *processi,* reg. 4309/159, f. 7r.

3. ASV:Arsenale bu 557, *Inquisitori,* 22 Sept 1640, ff. 1–2r.; ASV:SM, filza 341, 12 Oct 1641; SM, reg. 93, 12 Jan 1635 m.v.

4. ASV:SM filza 338, 4 May 1641; for a shipwright requesting his ration of biscuit: ASV:CRD suppliche, filza 93, 18 Oct 1680. On the infrequency of wages in kind: Pullan, "Wage Earners and the Venetian Economy," 172; and Lane, *Venetian Ships and Shipbuilders,* 193.

5. ASV:TA, reg. 141, 5 May 1665; ASV:SM, reg. 127, 23 Aug 1663; Lane, *Venetian Ships and Shipbuilders,* 194–95.

6. ASV:TA reg. 137, 19 Feb 1613 m.v.; reg. 141, 5 May 1665; Nani Mocenigo, *L'Arsenale di Venezia,* 56–57.

7. cf. Thompson, *The Making of the English Working Class,* 59.

8. Forsellini, "L'Organizzazione economica," 87.

9. Franco, "Questa è la porta del meraviglioso Arsenale." The theft of woodscraps was still a problem as late as 1784: Forsellini, "L'Organizzazione economica," 87.

10. ASV:CRD suppliche, filza 18, 27 Dec 1627.

11. The lead thieves were all banished: ASV:CRD suppliche, filza 46, 8 June 1655; also filza 54, 15 Apr 1660. On the price of saltpeter in Venice: Mallett and Hale, *The Military Organization of a Renaissance State,* 401.

12. "Perché come dona non li veneva guardatto dall' guardiani adosso come si suole fare all'huomeni . . . [et] ogni giorno . . . sua consorte et li suoi garzoni portava sempre via della feramenta da detta Casa alla sua bottega come dall'istessi suoi garzoni, che a quello tempo stava con lui . . . [et] quando loro non rubava . . . feramenta sempre li tratava di dare della bastonatte": ASV:Avogaria di Comun-Penale reg; 4309/159, f. 7r.

13. ASV:CRD suppliche, filza 33, 11 Sept 1642.

14. ASV:CRD suppliche, filza 25, 14 Jan 1634 m.v.

15. Aymard, "L'Arsenale e le conoscenze technico-marinaresche," 315; also Thompson, "Eighteenth-Century English Society," 150–65; Pollard, "Factory Discipline," 258.

16. On Christmas, Easter, and Pentecost: ASV:TA, reg. 137, 19 Feb 1613 m.v.; also Nani Mocenigo, *L'Arsenale di Venezia,* 56–57.

17. ASV:TA reg. 137, 19 Feb 1613 m.v.

18. The gatekeeper Zuandomenico Budelli was fined 10 ducats after twice letting masters leave the shipyards with *stelle*: ASV:TA reg. 137, 19 Oct 1605; when in 1649, the Patroni saw *con occhio proprio* that masters were not only carrying out chips but even shafts *(tappe)* of oak under their cloaks without hindrance, they fined each of the gatekeepers 5 ducats: reg. 140, 15 June 1649.

19. For having let these people in, gatekeeper Gerolomo di Baldiserra was fined 5 ducats: ASV:TA reg. 137, 9 June 1608; also ASV:SM, filza 511, 4 Sept 1660. Another time the Patroni came to the shipyards and found "at the care of the gates of the Arsenal only a single gatekeeper": ASV:TA, reg. 137, 24 Apr 1609.

20. ASV:SM, filza 376, 11 Oct 1645; ASV:Collegio V (Segreta), bu. 57, Relazione of Piero Mocenigo (1660), f. 27r; Relazione of Bertucci Trivisan (1669), f. 10r.

21. ASV:SM, filza 392, 23 may 1647; the Patroni claimed that the *ingordiggia dei principali* even lowered substitute gatekeepers to the point of having to support themselves by showing the Arsenal to private tourists:

ASV:SM, filza 578, 24 Jan 1670 m.v. Also ASV:CRD suppliche, filza 20, 14 Mar 1629.

22. ASV:SM, filza 505, 4 Sept 1659.

23. ASV:SM, reg. 111, 21 Jan 1650 m.v.; filza 511, 28 Aug 1660; ASV:TA, reg. 140, 15 May 1645; on several occasions up to ten *banditi* were said to be living in the shipyards: ASV:Avogaria di Comun-Penale, bu. 234; ASV:SM, filza 422, 25 Jan 1649 m.v.; ASV:CRD suppliche, filza 51, 6 Feb 1658 m.v.

24. Customs authorities regularly raided the private shipyards where many arsenalotti worked and found small boats which had been modified with "devilish devices" for concealing cargoes of contraband: Rapp, *Industry and Economic Decline,* 140, n. 6.

25. ASV:SM, filza 376, 11 Oct 1645; also ASV:CRD suppliche, filza 16, 23 May 1621.

26. Mattozzi, "Crisi, stagnazione e mutamento nello stato veneziano sei-settecentesco," 208–10 and n. 20.

27. ASV:Provveditori al Sal, bu. 378, f. 115v, 20 July 1611.

28. ASV:CRD suppliche, filza 42, 29 Jan 1651 m.v.; filza 38, 1 Aug 1647.

29. ASV:Provveditori al Sal, bu. 378, f. 80r, 13 June 1601.

30. ASV:SM, filza 518, 3 Sept 1661. A stiff duty was collected on all goods trafficked in Venice, whether as import, export, or re-export: Lane, *Venice: A Maritime Republic,* 418.

31. ASV:SM, filza 559, 19 Nov 1667. For the size and social composition of the Quintevalle: ASV:DSD, bu. 420, San Pietro parish, nos. 1–75.

32. ASV:CRD suppliche, filza 27, 10 Dec 1636; filza 30, 23 Mar 1639; filza 46, 16 Nov 1655; filza 63, 5 Feb 1664 m.v. Such smuggling communities elsewhere also enjoyed the support of the poorer members of society whom they served: see Thompson, *The Making of the English Working Class,* 60.

33. ASV:SM, filza 559, 19 Nov 1667. In medieval Venice such rewards would only have been offered for an "especially serious offender": Ruggiero, *Violence in Early Renaissance Venice,* 190, n. 45, and 208, n. 3.

34. ASV:CRD suppliche, filza 56, 21 Apr 1661.

35. "Ho sempre sprezzato qual si voglia offerta d'impiego in altro servitio, tutto che di emolumento considerabile, niente stimando mai": ASV:CRD suppliche, filza 31, 6 July 1640. See also filza 39, 24 July 1648; filza 68, 23 May 1667; and ASV:SM, filza 286, 20 Sept 1633.

36. ASV:CRD suppliche, filza 21, 8 July and 23 Feb 1630 m.v.; filza 26, 4 Dec 1635; filza 56, 11 July 1661; filza 61, 15 Oct 1663; filza 65, 14 Jan 1665 m.v.

37. ASV:SM, filza 559, 19 Nov 1667; the two ringleaders had to work somewhat harder before receiving their pardon, but nevertheless succeeded after three years service with the fleet: ASV:CRD suppliche, filza 68, 23 May 1667.

38. ASV:SM reg. 94, 30 May 1636. A similar offer had been made to fugitive sailors shortly after the Black Death in the 1350s: Lane, *Venice: A Maritime Republic,* 169–70.

39. The Patroni suggested putting to work "alcuna donna con sentenza

criminale" in the shipyards' *sale di velle,* sewing sails at half the normal wage for the duration of their sentences: ASV:SM, filza 559, 19 Nov 1667; ASV:Consiglio dei Dieci, Parti Communi, filza 562, 26 Sept 1653. filza 572, 1 Feb 1669 m.v. Women themselves requested the work: ASV:CRD suppliche, filza 42, 5 May 1651; and filza 68, 16 June 1667.

40. The *Provveditori alle fortezze* had nominal control over the facility; in the end the Senate divided it between the two magistrates: ASV:SM, filza 435, 15 Apr 1651.

41. A few of many examples: ASV:CRD suppliche, filza 21, 8 July 1630; filza 26, 23 May 1635; filza 39, 12 May 1648; filza 45, 7 Jan 1654 m.v.; filza 65, 14 Jan 1665 m.v.; and ASV:SM, filza 444, 22 Mar 1652. Their gang violence had been a feature of the city for centuries: Crouzet-Pavan, "Violence, Société et Pouvoir à Venise," 920.

42. On the role of violence in defining elite status, see Ruggiero, *Violence in Early Renaissance Venice,* 66–70, 142; Herlihy, "Psychological and Social Roots of Violence," 137–38.

43. ASV:SM reg 94, 30 May 1636.

44. Zuane managed to make good both the fine and the compensation in only two and a half months: ASV:SM, filza 444, 22 Mar 1652.

45. ASV. Quarantia Criminal, bu. 69, 13 Nov 1654.

46. Over 90 percent of Venetian workers convicted of murder in the fourteenth century were either executed or mutilated: Ruggiero, *Violence in Early Renaissance Venice,* 102–5. The state was not so generous with shipbuilders who fought with patricians, however: ASV:CRD, filza 26, 23 May 1635.

47. ASV:CRD suppliche, filza 45, 7 Jan 1654 m.v.

48. ASV:Quarantia Criminal, bu. 69, 13 Nov 1654.

49. Thus, a gang of four shipwrights complained of the unfairness of being condemned for their part in a brawl, since evidently they had gotten much the worst of it: ASV:CRD suppliche, filza 65, 14 Jan 1665 m.v.; also filza 34, 9 Oct 1643.

50. MC:Cicogna codice 3161 is titled, *Battagliola o guerra tra Nicolotti e Castellani, 1632–1673,* but also details *battagliole* of 1574 and 1585 as well as a free-wheeling account of the War of Candia, which stopped the fights on the home front during the 1640s. The author possibly was intending to use the manuscript for later publication, for marginal notes and cancellations abound; poems and other addenda were sometimes written on slips of paper and inserted in the binding of the manuscript. Too concerned with specific events and personalities of this largely *popolani* world to allow any easy verification of its many details, the manuscript nevertheless does conform in general terms to Venetian popular culture as it is elaborated in Molmenti and Tamassia Mazzarotto, especially in terms of the crowd dynamics, violence, and popular satire. Compare with such contemporary accounts as Caravia's dialect poem of 1550 (reworked in 1603): *La verra antiga dei Castellani Canaruoli e Gnatti, con la morte de Giurco e Gnagni, in lengua brava,* or Basnatio's *Descrittione piacevole della guerra d' Pugni tra Nicolotti e Castellani.* Besides its use by Tamassia Mazzarotto, the manuscript has also been noted by Quarti, *Quattro secoli di vita veneziana;* and Roffarè, *La Repubblica di Venezia e lo sport.*

51. Tamassia Mazzarotto, *Le feste veneziane,* 41–42.

52. MC:Cicogna codice 3161, 1632, p. 2.

53. Padoan Urban, "Feste ufficiali e trattenimenti privati," 591. Three "official" *battagliole* are described in Cicogna codice 3161: for the visit of the French King Henry III in 1574 (the last with sticks instead of fists), for the ambassador of Japan in 1585, and for the Cardinal of Lyons in 1635.

54. MC:Cicogna codice 3161, 1633, f. 5r. Only by the early eighteenth century, when the Venetian patriciate began to lose interest in such violent entertainments, were the Ten able to abolish the *battagliole* for good: Tamassia Mazzarotto, *Le feste veneziane,* 44 and 50, nn. 12 and 14.

55. Another competition was in the formation of human pyramids, the so-called *forze d'ercole.* During the final days of Carnival, the two camps vied to make the taller and more complex living structures; the popularity of the sport especially grew after the *battagliole* were finally outlawed by the Ten in 1705. Tamassia Mazzarotto, *Le feste veneziane,* 31–35, 44.

56. Tradition held the rivalry to be a continuation of a much earlier antipathy between the inhabitants of Jesolo and Eraclea, who on immigrating to the Rialtine islands in the fifth century supposedly settled on opposite ends of the archipelago. The Nicolotti faction consisted of the *sestieri* of San Polo, Santa Croce, and Cannaregio; while the Castellani came from Castello, and San Marco. The *sestiere* of Dorsoduro, along with the Giudecca, was split between the two sides after a dispute in 1311: Tamassia Mazzarotto, *Le feste veneziane,* 40–41. Also MC:Cicogna codice 3161, 1635, p. 4: the Castellani were also joined by the *popolani* from the islands of Torcello, Burano, and Murano; the Nicolotti by the men from the Lido, Malamocco, and the villages on the Brenta canal.

57. One year the author termed the arsenalotti as "quicker and more courageous than the others" ("quelle dell'Arsenale, come più leste e più coraggiose delle altre"); another time he called them "il capo et il nervo principale di tutta la setta Castellano": MC:Cicogna codice 3161, 1634, p. 1; and 1667, p. 21. On the fishermen of San Nicolò, who after the arsenalotti were traditionally among the most honored guildsmen of the city, see Zago, *I Nicolotti,* 59ff; and Molmenti, *Venice,* 91–92. On the importance of border zones in defining and shaping urban conflict: Le Roy Ladurie, *Carnival in Romans,* 211.

58. A *capo* once even tore the mustache right off the face of a captain of the Ten who tried to break up an impending encounter: MC:Cicogna, codice 3161, 1634, p. 12; also 1644, p. 5.

59. The nobleman Polo Morosini was such a fan of the *battagliole* that once when no battles were being held, he had a bridge built in his palace courtyard and staged the event personally for as many as 2,000 guests: MC:Cicogna, codice 3161, 1633, pp. 5–6.

60. MC:Cicogna, codice 3161, 1632, p. 3.

61. They could expect to be fed at the expense of their noble patrons: "la gioventù delle arti e professioni per otto giorni prima del giorno terminato poco o nulla s'applicavano a loro interessi, essendo sempre con loro compagnie, dalli capi e protetori di dinari e di altre provisioni mantenuti e sostentati": MC:Cicogna codice 3161, 1636, p. 4. Also, 1635, f. 5r: when the Collegio called the *padrini* before it in 1635 to arrange a *battagliola* for the

Cardinal of Lyons, they complained that the three days available were too short notice.

62. MC:Cicogna codice 3161, 1636, p. 4; 1635, p. 4; and 1639, p. 16. Another crowd of "30,000 e più" supposedly attended the *battagliola* at the bridge of San Barnaba in 1632: 1632, p. 11.

63. Unquestionably there was general drunkenness: each faction kept large tubs of wine available "acciò il soldato innanimato dell'allegria del vino più pronto e più ardito si preparasse nell'assalti": MC:Cicogna codice 3161, 1639, p. 20.

64. The author called Toppo, "giovane di gran precentia et aspetto ma non molto conosciuto et esperimentato nelle guerre": MC:Cicogna codice 3161, 1637, p. 7. The episode provides an indication that although they were often set off by local brawls between young journeymen, the *battagliole* were in fact the business of mature and experienced artisans.

65. In 1668, the author reported over 100 *mostre*, "ma il numero di venticinque non trovavano scontro, il che diede tal al Nicolotti di rimproverare l'inimico di viltà e di codardia, con mille improperij della plebe fattionaria": MC:Cicogna codice 3161, 1668, p. 4.

66. Especially when their side was weakening: "con l' hore di conflitto così sanguigno minacciava il fine crudele, perciò Castellani . . . . fecero suonare una piva, al suon delle quale uscirono come leoni strenati dalle case Leorze in circa sessanta soldati freschi dall'Arsenale": MC:Cicogna codice 3161, 1638, p. 5.

67. In a such a competitive context, insults were an important way to gain honor: Trexler, "Correre la Terra," 876–77. On the promotion of honor in Mediterranean societies, see Pitt-Rivers, "Honour and Social Status," 29; also Crouzet-Pavan, "Violence, Société et Pouvoir," 916.

68. MC:Cicogna codice 3161, 1632, p. 13.

69. Ibid., 1634, p. 10.

70. On the use of the medieval Palio to a similar effect: Trexler, "Correre la Terra," 878–78.

71. Mackenney, "Arti e stato a Venezia tra tardo Medio Evo e' 600," 131; and *Tradesmen and Traders*, 135–40; also Rapp, *Industry and Economic Decline*, 15–16 and n. 2. Muir, *Civic Ritual*, 42–44, 157–59, 176–81, and 296; and Lane, *Venice: A Maritime Republic*, 271–73.

72. Romano, *Patricians and Popolani*, 8–9, paraphrases Muir's interpretation of civic ritual: "the patrician government consciously adapted potentially disruptive popular rituals and integrated them into formal civic rituals, thereby rendering them inoffensive to the government." It has been maintained that the *battagliole* were in fact well controlled by the state, such that the combat "concluded when there arrived the gondola of the Council of Ten, with the flag of San Marco at the prow, which enjoined an end to the struggle." Cicogna 3161 records very much the opposite, however, indicating that the Ten's *sbirri* not only completely failed to break up the contests, but were indeed often attacked themselves and thrown into the water: MC:Cicogna codice 3161, 1634, p. 12 and 1640, pp. 1–2; and Padoan Urban, "Feste ufficiali e trattenimenti privati," 591.

73. "Le guerre che di solite a farsi in questi tempi sono come le febri, che

all'improviso assaliscono l'huomo quando sono punte e suscitate da cattivi humori": MC:Cicogna codice 3161, 1638, p. 6; and 1639, p. 1. For similar interpretations of Carnival and saturnalia: see Muir, *Civic Ritual*, 162–4; Thomas, "Work and Leisure," 53; and Natalie Z. Davis, "The Reasons of Misrule" and "The Rites of Violence," in *Society and Culture in Early Modern France* (Stanford, 1975), 97–123 and 152–187.

74. On the relationship between the fragmentation and high specialization of Venetian guilds and their political weakness: Mackenney, *Tradesmen and Traders*, 216–32; and "'In Place of Strife,'" 17–22; Rapp, *Industry and Economic Decline*, 15; and Finlay, *Politics in Renaissance Venice*, 48.

75. Crouzet-Pavan, "Violence, Société et Pouvoir," 918.

76. Some intergroup disputes were inevitably carried over into the *battagliole*, especially during the early days of preparation. Thus, the encounter of 1634 was slow in getting started because the fishermen of San Nicolò were initially angry with the butchers (*becchai*) of Cannaregio for having shortchanged their *compagnia* of San Nicolò for some bulls supplied for an earlier celebration: MC:Cicogna codice 3161, 1634, p. 1; also 1667, pp. 26–27.

77. Turner, *The Ritual Process*, 96–97, 109–30: "There are two major 'models' for human interrelatedness, juxtaposed and alternating. The first is of society as a structured, differentiated and often hierarchial system of politico-legal-economic positions with many types of evaluation, separating men in terms of 'more' or 'less'. The second, which emerges recognizably in the *liminal* period, is of society as an unstructured or rudimentarily structured and relatively undifferentiated *comitatus*, community, or even communion of equal individuals." Weissman, in his *Ritual Brotherhood in Renaissance Florence*, 53, also posits the evolution of *communitas* out of the *liminal* state achieved by Florentine flagellant confraternities during their ceremonies of inversion and penitence: "During liminal states the celebrant is stripped of those objects that are symbolic of his ties to his customary jural, familial, economic, and social status. These symbols are replaced by other symbols, symbols of group allegiance or harmonious behavior. The liminal state allows the attainment of a sense of *communitas*. . . . the sensation of belonging to an undifferentiated humanity, a sensation that may permit spontaneous, unstructured human relations to develop, relations temporarily purged of the complex ties and obligations of the social order."

78. MC:Cicogna codice 3161, 1639, p. 12.

79. MC:Cicogna codice 3161, 1639, p. 22.

80. One of the more notable Arsenal *padrini* was the oarmaker Piero Moro of San Ternità parish, active in the *guerre dei pugni* from 1632 until into the 1660s. The breakdown of participants in 1667 went as follows: "Publicavano i capi da San Nicolò di haver 300 gioveni [pescatori], fattioni in Cannaregio 200, in San Gerolamo 100, Bariotti 150, fra terra et altre contrade, 300; oltre per le compagnie de barcarioli delle barche di Padoa, Mestre e Malamocco. All'incontro i Castellani dassero dalla Casa dell' Arsenale più di 400 combatenti; da' marinari, e Campo delle Gatte, Gnesotti, e Zuechini, 300; fra terra, 300; fra Muran, Torcello e Buranesi, 200": MC:Cicogna codice 3161, 1667, p. 22–23.

81. MC:Cicogna codice 3161, 1635, p, 10; and 1646, p. 1; on the numbers of masters and on those serving at sea: ASV:SM, filza 304, 14 Apr 1636; filza 390, 13 Mar 1647.

82. If a participant held himself to be of higher status in such circumstances, he would after all be dishonored by accepting the challenge: Pitt-Rivers, "Honour and Social Status," 31; Bryson, *The Point of Honor*, 84.

83. On the extremes and social inversions of the Venetian Carnival: Muir, *Civic Ritual*, 156–81; and Burke, *Historical Anthropology*, 186–87.

84. MC:Cicogna codice 3161, 1635, p. 14; also 1637, p. 10. Even before a *battagliola* the arsenalotti contingent might first disembark from their boats and then, led by two of their robed foremen, go to hear mass with all solemnity at a nearby church or *scuola* before going to the battle site: 1634, p. 2.

85. "Ad un tempo . . . quattro o sei capi principali da guerra venero al ponte gridando 'calle! calle' con quattro soldati dell'Arsenale ciaschedun de quali con un sacco di segadure sopra le spalle, sporgendo quelle sopra le prime tre piazze [di] loro confine, gridando, 'adesso siamo per principar la guerra!'" on another occasion: "essi [arsenalotti] gettarono sopra il ponte due sacchi di segadore prese nell'Arsenale per il slicego [slipperiness] grande, che haveva causato la pioggia et il fango il giorno precedente": MC:Cicogna codice 3161, 1634, p. 12: Also 1635, pp. 4, 10; 1639, p. 21.

86. MC:Cicogna codice 3161, 1632, p. 18. Interestingly, parodic content has also been noted in the other great arsenalotti activity of smuggling: Crouzet-Pavan, "Violence, Société et Pouvoir," 910.

87. Cf. Le Roy Ladurie, *Carnival in Romans*, 305–7.

88. "In queste preparatione . . . naquero gravissime difficoltà e sussuramenti tra le militie dell'Arsenale e di Castello con le Gnesotte e Zuecchine, per le parole che queste hebbero à dire nella vittoria havuta da esse nel giorno di San Francesco, cioè che quelli da Castello sono boni di andar à seconda e non à contrario d'acqua. Sì che le maestranze dell'Arsenale pretendevano di voler esse sole far la guerra senza la compagnie de' Gnesotti, il che era da capi malamente inteso, essendo veramente quella militia sì brava e fiera, che si può dire il propugnacolo dell'tutto esercito castellano": MC:Cicogna codice 3161, 1667, pp. 26–27.

89. Authorship of such ephemera is noted but once; interestingly, he was a priest, "Padre Roma dalla Zuecca, notissimo fauttore de' Castellani": Cicogna codice 3161, 1639, p. 12.

90. "Un cartello pendente, sopra il quale vi era dipinto un numero di castellani legati con le mani et cattene à piedi in faccia à Panchia ['Guts,' a *padrino* of the Nicolotti], il quale stava con un bastone in mano vestito et armato come era sopra il ponte nel giorno del combattimento, accompagnatto con le parole seguenti: 'forestieri fermè el pie / questi qua così legai / xe de quei che fa gallie / che pur esser ostinai / à inchinarse ai nicolotti / con zucca e gresotti / à 'sto passo i xe arivai / quando che tornò al paese / fè che à tutti sia palese / che i castellani tutti per so pena / schiavi dei nicolotti, sta in caenna'": MC:Cicogna codice 3161, 1667, p. 41.

91. On the night after a battle, a squad of arsenalotti came to Campo Santa Sofia in Cannaregio armed with long poles topped with grappling

hooks (ancini), hoping to pull down the area's victory crown that hung in the campo and carry it off as a trophy. Caught in the act by a band of armed Nicolotti, many fled, leaving their aste and mazze behind to be later displayed as trophies by the Nicolotti themselves. The complete poem went as follows: "Nu' altri Nicolotti / Spavento de Castello / Femo chiasso e bordello / Poiche i Arsenalotti / Con queste longhe aste / Robade in l'Arsenale / E queste ne' xe zanze / Vengiva per robar / Le nostre corone a Santa Sofia / Ma i grami lassò l'aste e scampè via": MC:Cicogna codice 3161, 1639, p. 21.

92. MC:Cicogna codice 3161, 1639, p. 19.

93. The model was both complex and dynamic, an indication that it may have been built some time in advance: "e di sotto stava pendente un Castello pieno di fuochi artificiosi con gente armata sopra con ponti levadori e guardie come è l'uso, anco quelle incorporate con rochette e scarcavalti [firecrackers], sopra la porta di detto castello veniva fuori uno vestito di habito che usano i protti dell'Arsenale, con una chiave in mano . . . accompagnava la chiave con queste parole: 'Questa è la chiave / che averze e che sera / Il nostro bel Castello / A vù che xe il flagello / Della nostra schiera / D'accordo xe rendemo / E ve la presentemo / Altro no domandemo alla signoria vostra / Se non de far ogn'anno qualche mostra.'" MC:Cicogna codice 3161, 1667, p. 42.

94. "Signori Arsenalotti, per la rotta che havebù / El Castello xe col cul in su!" MC:Cicogna codice 3161, 1632, p. 18.

95. ASV:CRD suppliche, filza 49, 22 Oct 1657; and ASV:SM, filza 500, 11 Oct 1658.

96. ASV:Arti, bu. 61, carbonieri, mariegola, 1476–1781, 1624: cited in Mackenney, "Arti e stato a Venezia," 139–40.

Chapter 5. The Civic Role of the Arsenalotti in Venetian Society

1. A thorough bibliography on the much-discussed "Myth of Venice" is provided by Muir, "Images of Power," 16–18; but see also Grubb, "When Myths Lose Power," 43–94.

2. Tamassia Mazzarotto, Le feste veneziane, 241; Lane, Venice, A Maritime Republic, 114–16, 181–82; Finlay, Politics in Early Renaissance Venice, 119; Ruggiero, Violence in Early Renaissance Venice, 130. According to one chronicle, the arsenalotti promised Falier "di fare tagliare tutti questi becchi Gentilhuomini a pezzi [e] farvi Signore di questa terra": cited in Concina, L'Arsenale della Repubblica di Venezia, 48.

3. Tamassia Mazzarotto, Le feste veneziane, 184–85, 214–18, 224–25; Lane, Venetian Ships and Shipbuilders, 147–48; Finlay, Politics in Renaissance Venice, 121.

4. Lane, Venice, A Maritime Republic, 20, 414–15. For the establishment by the state of the so-called tansa insensibile to hire substitute rowers or pay for slaves, see Rapp, Industry and Economic Decline, 52–53.

5. ASV:CRD, Suppliche, filza 19, 26 Mar 1628, filza 26, 4 Dec 1635; filza 93, 14 Aug and 16 Jan 1680 m.v.; Lane, Venetian Ships and Shipbuilders, 185–86.

6. As when Francesco Cavazzina petitioned on behalf of thirty-four companions who had endured a thirty-five-month odyssey around the

Mediterranean ("nel Regno, nell'armata, e nel arcipelago") only to be paid off in devalued coinage: ASV:SM, filza 498, 2 May 1658.

7. As the shipwright Francesco Casola came to the island of Corfù and stayed several years to complete a whole variety of tasks: "ogni mia opera nelli difficili, et importanti lavori di forni, quartieri, risarcimento del ponte di Santa Giustina, acconcio di galeazzi . . . ecc., da me appaltati": ASV:CRD supplliche, filza 39, 12 May 1648. The so-called *maestranze di rinforzo* was sent out roughly every two years during the war: ASV:SM, reg. 111, 27 Oct 1650 (6 shipwrights and 20 caulkers to Candia and 4 shipwrights and 12 caulkers to Corfù); reg. 115, 30 Aug 1653 (20 shipwrights and 40 caulkers); reg. 119, 8 Nov 1656; reg. 121, 4 July 1657; reg. 128, 13 Nov 1664.

8. One caulker served as *maestro di rinforzo* no fewer than eight times from 1651 to 1669: ASV:CRD supplliche, filza 72, 21 Mar 1669.

9. Thus, the upkeep of Venice's bridges was the special providence of construction guilds; the arsenalotti only worked on a few wooden bridges around the Arsenal or on Murano: ASV:Arti bu. 304, *processi*, f. 13r; ASV:SM, filza 301, 19 Feb 1635 m.v.; reg. 106, 24 June 1648; and ASV:CRD supplliche, filza 66, 25 May 1666.

10. ASV:CRD, Supplliche, filza 18, 28 Nov 1627; filza 25, 24 Nov 1634; filza 30, 17 May 1639; and filza 93, 14 Mar 1680.

11. Lane, *Venetian Ships and Shipbuilders,* 200–205. On ships' contracts, successful bidders were expected to supply the skilled labor force, while the Arsenal provided the sawyers, laborers, lumber, hardware, and wine: ASV:SM, reg. 75, 7 June, 28 Nov, and 9 Jan 1617 m.v.; on using Arsenal materials for the Carnival of 1638: ASV:CRD supplliche, filze 28, 6 Nov 1637.

12. Pontoon bridges were run across the Grand Canal to the Salute and San Vio; from San Maria Zobenigo and (by the 1660s) San Antonio da Padoa; across the Giudecca to the Redentore; and for the doge's embarking on the Bucintoro during the Festival of the Sensa. Such work had been carried out by arsenalotti contractors since at least 1586: ASV:TA, reg. 138, 4 Dec 1619; ASV:SM reg. 126, 27 July 1662. Other bridges were sometimes thrown up for special occasions: ASV:TA, reg. 140, 17 Aug 1637.

13. For new materials, contractors were paid 250 ducats up front the first two years of their contract, to be later deducted at 50 ducats per year: ASV:SM, reg. 113, 26 April 1652; and reg. 126, 27 July 1662. The state could also imprison or send to the galleys masters who failed to keep their side of the agreement: ASV:TA, reg. 137, 12 July 1611. The Senate stipulated that these contracts were only open to shipwrights, not other arsenalotti: ASV:SM, reg. 126, 27 July 1662; ASV:TA, reg. 139, 14 June 1623.

14. To keep the shipwrights from playing favorites too openly, the Patroni directed a clerk (*fante del uffizio*) to inspect the city's boats with them the night before the requisitioning and record which boats were marked with the seal of the Arsenal: ASV:TA, reg. 140, 17 June 1643. For an alternative scheme based on a boat tax: ASV:CRD supplliche, filza 25, 4 Aug 1634.

15. ASV:TA, Reg. 138, 29 Nov 1619; ASV:CRD supplliche, filza 27, 21 Jan 1636 m.v.

16. ASV:SM, filza 274, 14 Dec 1630; ASV:TA, reg 139, 21 Dec 1630.

17. One of the two losers, the son of the foreman caulker, actually offered to pay the State 700 ducats over and above expenses to buy the *apalto*: ASV:CRD Suppliche, filza 40, 23 Nov 1649 and 3 Jan 1649 m.v.; filza 41, 18 Jan 1650 m.v.

18. Here, as in most contracts, the six arsenalotti in the *compagnia* received a flat rate rather than a daily wage, receiving around 74 lire each for two and a half month's part-time work: ASV:Procuratia di Supra, bu. 74/168, filze 32–34.

19. ASV:CRD suppliche, filza 33, 12 Jan 1642 m.v.; ASV:TA, reg. 140, 17 Aug 1637; ASV:Procuratia di Supra, bu. 74/168, filze 32–34; ASV:SM, reg. 113, 22 Mar 1652.

20. For the organization and numbers of the Venetian police forces in the fourteenth century, see Ruggiero, *Violence in Early Renaissance Venice,* 12–15.

21. When three outsiders were appointed as *capi* of the Arsenal guards in 1570, the implacable opposition of the masters soon forced them to resign, and even the nobles on the Zonta of the Council of Ten who had chosen them lost their places: Lane, *Venice, A Maritime Republic,* 364.

22. Traditionally the captain called out, "Dio mantegna 'sta Repubblica!" and the guards were expected to respond, "Dio el fazza e la Madonna!" MC:Mss Gradenigo 193 II, f. 135r (undated but probably 1730s). Any watchmen who failed twice to respond to their captain's call would be fired: ASV:Arsenale bu. 557, Inquisitori, f. 3r; ASV:TA, reg. 140, 26 Mar 1639.

23. Small fires were used in or near galleys as part of the caulking process; evidently many masters were careless about putting them out upon leaving: ASV:SM, filza 323, 2 Apr 1639.

24. ASV:Arsenale, bu. 557, *Inquisitori,* f. 3r.

25. Disbanded after the Cretan War, these guards were told to turn in their *moschetti, alabardi, et feralli,* and their duties were divided between the eighty night guards in their watchtowers and the watchmen of the Dieci, who would continue the boat patrols: ASV:SM, filza 572, 1 Feb 1669 m.v.

26. MC:Mss Gradenigo, bu. 193 II, ff. 136r-137v. For an example of arrests made by Arsenal agents in local neighborhoods: ASV:CRD suppliche, filza 18, 27 Dec 1627.

27. On the harmfullness of the night air: ASV:CRD, suppliche, filza 34, 19 Feb 1643 m.v.; filza 74, 14 Aug 1670. One shipwright who had lost his place with the night guards called the work a "da me stimatissimo bene et benignissima Publica Gratia": ASV:CRD suppliche, filza 73, 15 Oct 1669.

28. ASV:SM, filza 323, 2 Apr 1639; filza 376, 11 Oct 1645; and ASV:TA, reg. 140, 30 July 1650. The men who were chosen as *guardiani festivi* simply were given their day's pay on the holidays when they kept watch: effectively a 30 percent raise for life.

29. Concina, *L'Arsenale di Venezia,* 86; Lane, *Venetian Ships and Shipbuilders,* 163; ASV:Arsenale, bu. 557, Inquisitori, 22 Sept 1640, f. 3r; ASV:CRD suppliche, filza 67, 28 Sept 1666; MC:Ms Gradenigo, bu. 193 II, 135r.

30. ASV:TA, reg. 140, 14 Feb 1645 m.v.; reg. 141, 7 Dec 1658.

31. ASV:SM, filza 376, 11 Oct 1645; filza 422, 22 Jan 1649 m.v. ASV:CRD, suppliche, filza 51, 13 Jan 1658 m.v.; and filza 67, 5 Nov 1666.

32. ASV:SM, reg. 111, 21 Jan 1650 m.v. The amounts involved could be considerable: guards captain Battista di Iacomo Piccolo noted that in just two years he had brought in more than 220 ducats in fines: ASV:CRD suppliche, filza 51, 6 Feb 1658 m.v. On *banditi*: ASV:CRD, suppliche, filza 40, 3 Feb 1649 m.v.

33. The Patroni warned of "various tower windows without the usual bars that open onto the Lagoon [and] that could serve to accommodate the night guards to withdraw from the Arsenal every sort of material": ASV:SM, filza 376, 11 Oct 1645. See also filza 511, 4 Sept 1660, for similar warnings by the Inquisitors; and ASV:CRD suppliche, filza 16, 23 May 1621, for the denunciation of holes in the Arsenal walls.

34. ASV:TA reg 137, 19 Feb 1613 m.v. and 23 Jan 1614 m.v. The time-keeper who inspected the night guards as they left the shipyards in the morning was given two little shacks (*luoghetti*) on the *fondamenta* leading from the Arsenal, "per commodo suo et sigurtà della sua vita per venir in tempo di notte à pontar li guardiani": ASV:TA, reg. 139, 1 June 1620.

35. ASV:CRD suppliche, filza 67, 5 Nov 1666; and filza 74, 14 Apr 1670; on Piccolo: filza 51, 6 Feb 1658 m.v.

36. Grego's supplica makes it clear that officers of the Ten shared responsibility with arsenalotti guards for making boat patrols within the shipyards: ASV:CRD suppliche, filza 69, 16 Dec 1667; also Lane, *Venetian Ships and Shipbuilders,* 153.

37. ASV:CRD suppliche, filza 74, 14 Apr 1670.

38. In 1657, the guards had hoped that their usefulness in the Carnival season (when as many as 30,000 tourists might visit the city) would have resulted in at least a partial payment, but instead they only received another pay chit which they were unable to cash ("[un] mandato, che già mai habbiamo potuto resquotere"): ASV:CRD suppliche, filza 48, 22 Mar 1657; Burke, *Historical Anthropology,* 189. On guarding the Piazza and Rialto: ASV:CRD suppliche, filza 40, 28 July and 17 Aug 1649.

39. Arsenalotti valued the duties enough to be sure to find a substitute to hold their place should they be drafted to serve a turn with the fleet: ASV:CRD suppliche, filza 40, 31 May and 28 July 1649.

40. ASV:Consiglio dei Dieci, 20 Sept 1569. Initially, the eighty masters had served in rotations of only one month, but in 1618 the Senate increased the duty to three months, hoping that "by working longer at the job they might become more adept at fulfilling their service": ASV:SM, reg. 76, 4 Dec 1618.

41. If Council meetings dragged on past lunch, the masters would get a full day's wage: MC:Archivio fotografico, m. 24032; ASV:Arsenale, bu. 11, ff. 63–64; MC:Ms Gradenigo, bu. 193 I, f. 126v; Forsellini, "Organizzazione economica," 85.

42. So, at least, wrote Piero di Marco Osimo, one of the four Arsenal arms stewards: ASV:CRD suppliche, filza 34, 10 June 1643.

43. ASV:CRD suppliche, filza 56, 12 Aug 1661. The Patroni had ordered that the names of masters who had the right (and duty) to serve at the

44. Interestingly, the *pozzetto,* like the *Bucintoro,* was entrusted to the keeping of the arsenalotti themselves, stored in the Arsenal rather than at the Ducal Palace: Skippon, *A Journey through Italy,* 508–9.

45. Tamassia Mazzarotto, *Le feste veneziane,* 216–18.

46. They were very possibly the same masters who, also armed with red staffs, kept order among the mob packing the Church of San Marco earlier in the coronation ceremony, when the new doge was presented to the people and swore his oath of fealty: Tamassia Mazzarotto, *Le feste veneziane,* 212–15 and illustration.

47. Sometimes arsenalotti could carry their enthusiasm at crowd control too far: Sanudo reported that during the *giro* for the 1521 coronation of Antonio Grimani, a master swinging his staff struck a foreigner, who promptly drew his sword and cut off the guard's head, saying, "Now go beat with your cudgel!" Finlay, *Politics in Renaissance Venice,* 20.

48. For a description of the Festival of Sensa: *La Festa della Sensa: notizie storiche a cura del comitato "Viva San Marco!"* Evidently, the banquet especially honored the arsenalotti by giving them a chance to gorge themselves on quantities of meat—beef, pork, and fowl—undreamed of by the ordinary Venetian artisan.

49. Though Venice never had a permanent garrison force, such troops were certainly a hallmark of most Italian city republics; fifteenth-century Florence had only a third of Venice's population in the 1600s but maintained a garrison of 500 soldiers to keep the peace: Brucker, "The Florentine *Popolo Minuto* and its Political Role," 174; Lane, *Venice, A Maritime Republic,* 271–73.

50. Two hundred common soldiers would have cost the state at least 9,300 ducats per year in wages alone in this period, not counting the expense of lodging: Mallett and Hale, *The Military Organization of a Renaissance State,* 494–501.

51. Ruggiero, *Violence in Early Renaissance Venice,* 34, 130; Prof. Ruggiero has kindly informed me about this function of the *duodena.*

52. Firemen in medieval Ferrara were traditionally masons, while in Padova the job fell to masons, carpenters, and wine carriers: Goldthwaite, *The Building of Renaissance Florence,* 266.

53. ASV:CRD suppliche, filza 39, 25 June 1648. The arsenalotti's independence in this matter was seemingly never really overcome. As late as 30 September 1705, the masters became so involved in a *battagliole* on the bridge of San Barnaba that they ignored the alarm for a fire across town in the convent of San Girolamo; the church was ruined and the *battagliole* were banned henceforth: Tamassia Mazzarotto, *Le feste veneziane,* 50, n. 14.

54. In addition to this housing and a master's wage from the shipyards, the two men were also paid fairly substantial salaries of 10 ducats per month for the captain of 30 and 5 ducats for the captain of 15: ASV:TA reg. 141, 11 July 1666; also ASV:Collegio V (Segreta), bu. 57, Relazione of Francesco Cornero (1696), f. 9v. Each parish and the Arsenal itself was also to be equipped with necessary firefighting equipment, such as buckets, ladders,

axes, and eventually pumps: ASV:CRD suppliche, filza 15, 10 May 1620.

55. Between 1600 and 1670, these included the churches and convents of Santa Giustina, the Madonna della Carità, Santa Maria Mater Domini, San Stai, San Biagio, San Francesco della Vigna, and the Frari; palaces at San Barnaba and San Stefano, the Fontegho della Farina à Rialto (twice), and six times at the biscuit ovens; in 1659, fire also devastated the *prigioni oscure* of the Signori di Notte Criminal: ASV:SM, reg. 82, 2 Mar 1624; reg. 88, 26 Nov 1630; reg. 91, 9 Dec 1633; and ASV:CRD suppliche, filza 18, 25 May 1627; filza 22, 10 Sept 1631; filza 36, 15 Jan 1645 m.v.; filza 39, 15 June 1648; filza 45, 3 Mar 1654; filza 67, 5 Nov 1666; filza 93, 28 Jan 1680 m.v.

56. ASV:CRD suppliche, filza 32, 29 Apr 1641. In particular, these porters were required to work at the Arsenal; in 1669, ninety-nine were serving their turn, receiving only around 16 soldi per day: ASV:TA reg. 141, 20 Feb 1669 m.v. The taxes paid by *facchini* who wished to avoid service went to meet the expenses of contractors who supplied the shipyards with an adequate supply of manual laborers. It is reasonable to assume that any porter who could afford to would buy an exemption, since much higher-paying work was available at the city's docks and warehouses; some may have been denied good work because they were unfit or because as recent immigrants they had no influence with the men controlling labor on the Venetian waterfront: Forsellini, "L'Organizzazione economica," 91–95; and Pullan, "Wage-Earners and the Venetian Economy," 166. For accusations of corruption and bribe-taking among local dockyard bosses, see ASV:TA, reg. 138, 3 July 1617.

57. ASV:CRD suppliche, filza 19, 20 Mar 1628; also filza 73, 3 Dec 1669. Arsenalotti asserted that they would "oblige themselves in any occasion of fire (God protect us) to be ready at the sound of the [alarm] bell at the piazza of the Arsenal [awaiting] the orders of the Patron di Guardia": filza 39, 25 June 1648.

58. ASV:CRD suppliche, filza 37, 22 Oct 1646; filza 17, 25 Nov 1624.

59. "Egli dell'anno . . . la note di San Biagio che era entrate il foco nella Casa dell'Arsenale et faceva grandissima ruvina nella munitione delli remi, espose la vita sua insieme con li suoi figlioli à manifestissimo pericolo di morire per estinguere detto fuoco, il quale seguitato dal vento faceva grandissima ruvina, et se non erano loro havria brugiato fino alla Tana": ASV:SM filza 307, 28 Nov 1636. "Son stato al fuoco del Palazzo sotto il Principe Mocenigo, al quale fuoco nel butar zo i piombi restò morto do poveri fachini in corte del Palazzo": ASV:CRD suppliche, filza 17, 25 Nov 1624.

60. Without their timely assistance, the supplica went on, the fire might have reached the storehouses of pitch and charcoal located nearby: ASV:CRD suppliche, filza 39, 25 June 1648.

61. ASV:CRD suppliche, filza 46, 15 Jan 1645 m.v.; ASV:SM reg. 104, 25 May 1646; and ASV:CRD suppliche, filza 51,13 Jan 1658 m.v. For his heroism, the Senate eventually awarded him a pension of 3 ducats a month, also suppliche, filza 67, 3 Feb 1666 m.v., when Zorzi's sons recalled his deed once again.

62. ASV:CRD suppliche, filza 38, 6 June 1647.

63. ASV:CRD suppliche, filza 36, 20 Feb 1645 m.v.; ASV:SM, filza 386, 24 Aug 1646.

64. ASV:CRD suppliche, filza 36, 15 Jan 1645 m.v.; also filza 65, 18 Sept 1665.

65. ASV:CRD suppliche, filza 38, 6 June 1647; and filza 43, 22 Jan 1652 m.v.

66. On the average about 200 ducats were given, probably equal to about a week's wages for each participant: ASV:SM reg. 88, 26 Nov 1630; and ASV:CRD suppliche, filza 26, 31 July 1635. For occasions when raises instead of single *donativi* were granted, see ASV:TA, reg. 138, 2 Dec 1619 and ASV:CRD suppliche, filza 93, 12 Dec 1680; also filza 256, 22 Apr 1627, for a reference to masters still receiving their 4 soldi from the fire at the Ducal Palace more than forty years later.

67. MC:Mss Gradenigo, bu. 193 II, f. 59r; Casoni, "Forze Militari," 149–51; also ASV:CRD suppliche, filza 37, 18 Sept 1646.

68. Even Venice's sailors were increasingly of mixed nationality: Lane, *Venice, A Maritime Republic,* 415–17.

69. On good citizenship and the militia in the Myth of Venice: see Haitsma Mulier, *The Myth of Venice and Dutch Republican Thought,* 19, 49; Finlay, *Politics in Renaissance Venice,* 27–37; Muir, *Civic Ritual in Renaissance Venice,* 13–55; and Dooley, "Crisis and Survival in Eighteenth-Century Italy," 323–34.

70. Aymard, "L'Arsenale e le conoscenze tecnico-marinaresche," 313–15.

71. Ibid., 314.

72. Only one minor strike is recorded in the 1600s, over the size of the advance *(soventione)* given to masters about to leave with the fleet: ASV:SM, filza 421, 17 Dec 1649.

73. Finlay, *Politics in Renaissance Venice,* 48; Lane, *Venice, A Maritime Republic,* 364.

74. Lane, *Venice, A Maritime Republic,* 189; Finlay, *Politics in Renaissance Venice,* 51–53; compare with the description of the shipbuilders in Casoni, "Breve storia," 150:

> So, first with childish imitation, then by habit, and finally for love of the craft, they make good example following the profession of their fathers . . . [among them] absences were not frequent, delinquency very rare, and felony and treason completely unknown words. They were in Venice as the Pretorians had been in Rome, without having their license or boldness.

75. See Pecchioli, *Dal "mito" di Venezia all' "ideologia americana,"* esp. 155–67. Not to mention the by now established fecklessness of many Venetian nobles in civic affairs: Queller, *The Venetian Patriciate.*

76. Romano, *Patricians and Popolani,* 150.

77. On the honors in state or public positions, especially those of a military nature: Bryson, *The Point of Honor in Sixteenth-Century Italy,* 19; Pitt-Rivers, "Honor and Social Status," 22–25.

78. Lane, *Venice, A Maritime Republic,* 319, 362–64.

79. Walker, *German Home Towns,* 73–107; Farr, *Hands of Honor,* esp.

122–95. For the class-related activities of a worker group with certain similarities to the arsenalotti, see Sewell, "Uneven Development, the Autonomy of Politics, and the Dockworkers of Nineteenth-Century Marseilles," 604–37.

80. Zanelli, "L'Arsenale," 68–70.

81. Unger, "Regulations of Dutch Shipcarpenters," 503–20; Riege, "The Development of a Small Village to an Important Naval Town in England." For a forthcoming study focusing on this topic, see Safely and Rosenband, eds., *The Workplace before the Factory.*

Appendix 1. Suppliche in Venice

1. Scarabello, "Paure, superstizioni, infamie," 356–57, n. 23.

2. The Collegio was composed of five *savi agli ordini* (Secretaries of the Marine) to handle naval and imperial matters, five *savi di terraferma* (Secretaries of the Land) to deal with warfare and affairs of the mainland, and six *savi grandi* (Chief Secretaries) to oversee the agenda of the Signoria and prepared legislation for the Senate: Finlay, *Politics in Renaissance Venice,* 40–43; da Mosto, *L'Archivio di Stato di Venezia,* 22–23; and Lane, *Venice, A Maritime Republic,* 254–56.

3. In particular the *Giustizia Vecchia, Giustizia Nuova,* and the *Milizia da Mar:* Mackenney, *Tradesmen and Traders,* 223–29, 239, notes 30–45; Rapp, *Industry and Economic Decline,* 15–21.

4. For examples of this sort of corporate petitioning to the Collegio over tax reductions, see ASV:CRD suppliche, filza 60, 8 May 1663 (*tesseri da fustagni*); filza 69, 3 Nov 1667 (*manganeri*); filza 70, 9 May 1668 (*lanieri*); and filza 71, 15 Nov 1668 (*centurieri*).

5. To some extent, sailors too served as state employees: Lane, *Venice, A Maritime Republic,* 166–70.

6. Lane, *Venetian Ships and Shipbuilders,* 72–87; for the loss of guild control over such vital social functions as pensions and funerals, see ASV:TA, reg. 137, 23 Mar 1601, 17 May 1611, and reg. 139, 21 Mar 1630.

7. ASV:CRD suppliche, filza 23, 23 Apr 1632 (for shipwrights and oarmakers) and 28 Oct 1632 (for caulkers); filza 27, 28 Sept 1636 and filza 33, 19 Nov 1642 (both caulkers).

8. ASV:SM, filza 326, 4 Aug 1639.

9. ASV:Collegio V (Segreta), bu. 57, Relazione of Pietro Mocenigo (1660), f. 24r. After their dismissal many ex-arsenalotti let years go by before they petitioned for readmission to the Arsenal, an indication both of the extent to which they were successful in finding employment at sea or elsewhere and of their likely age at the time they petitioned. ASV:CRD suppliche, filza 53, 15 Dec 1659 (*cassato* in 1645) and filza 58, 21 Mar 1662 (*cassato* in 1638) are not atypical examples.

10. Rapp, *Industry and Economic Decline,* 49–54. See the petition of twenty independent oarmakers of the city: ASV:CRD suppliche, filza 48, 4 July 1657. Also, filza 47, 11 Aug 1656 and filza 49, 22 Oct 1657. The Candia War of 1645–69 also pushed many masters of the two arsenals of Crete to seek enrollment in the Arsenal of Venice: filza 38, 15 July 1647; filza 51, 27 Feb 1658 m.v.; and filza 61, 11 Dec 1663.

11. ASV:CRD suppliche, filza 27, 23 Aug 1636; filza 40, 9 Aug 1649; filza 47, 7 Apr 1656; ASV:SM, filza 398, 12 Nov 1647.

12. ASV:CRD suppliche, filza 42, 9 Aug 1651; and filza 43, 12 Aug 1652: by Camilla, widow of a foreman shipwright; filza 60, 4 May 1663; filza 69, 3 Feb 1667 m.v., for petitions by her grown sons. For suppliche from the widow and sons of Francesco di Nicolò Gramolin: ASV:CRD sup-
‹ pliche, filza 385, 31 July 1646; ASV:CRD suppliche, filza 46, 10 Feb 1655 m.v.; and filza 66, 17 May 1666.

13. ASV:CRD suppliche, filza 38, 23 Feb 1647, m.v.; filza 47, 23 Mar and 1 June 1656.

14. ASV:CRD suppliche, filza 42, 9 Aug 1651; filza 43, 12 Aug 1652.

15. Since an average of about sixty arsenalotti died every year, the entire workforce would have had to replace itself twice over between the years 1621 and 1670: ASV:SM, filza 214, 19 Aug 1617; reg. 87, 14 Nov 1629; *libri dei morti* of San Martino and San Pietro di Castello parishes.

16. Besides their working in private shipyards and as sailors, many of these errant arsenalotti found work as pilots, fishermen, and gondolieri: ASV:Collegio V (Segreta), bu. 57, Relazione of Pietro Mocenigo (1660), f. 24r.

17. The 293 petitions were submitted by about 180 different supplicants; over the period of this study, roughly 220 individuals held the 80 management offices.

18. A few arsenalotti petitions requesting offices or pensions were granted by the Maggior Consiglio instead of the Senate. Not numbering more that 30 or 40 through this entire period, they do not appear to have been handled by the Collegio: see ASV:Gratie del Maggior Consiglio, bu. 9–11, passim.

19. ASV:SM, filza 309, 31 Jan 1636 m.v.

20. ASV:Collegio V (Segreta), bu. 57, Relazione of Alvise di Molin (1633), f. 10v, records that 922 masters and apprentices died in the plague; the number of suppliche which masters presented to the Collegio correspondingly dropped from sixteen in 1629 to only three in 1631. Also ASV:SM, filza 390, 13 Mar 1647, noted that more than half of the arsenalotti were currently serving with the fleet.

21. ASV:Collegio V (Segreta), bu. 57, Relazione of Polo Contarini (1643), f. 11v; ASV:SM, filza 572, 1 Feb 1669 m.v.

22. If only because not many other avenues for personal advancement were open to them: Lane, *Venice, A Maritime Republic*, 400–402, 427. ASV:CRD suppliche, filza 93: there were fourteen requests for admission or readmission to the shipyards in 1680, in fact rather more than the yearly average for the late 1660s.

23. For examples of suppliche apparently prepared by worker managers themselves, with the phonetic and rather labored diction and spellings commonly used, see: ASV:CRD suppliche, filza 18, 27 Dec 1627, of stores supervisor Marco di Gasparo; filza 41, 24 May 1650, of Zorzi di Christofolo, foreman of the oarmakers; and filza 33, 24 Oct 1642, of gang boss Gierolamo di Luca, called "Crosetta." Also see two nearly identical suppliche submitted in short order by the sawyers guild, one evidently written by the

guild leaders (*gastaldi*) and the other by a scribe, showing enormous improvements in spelling, diction, and penmanship: ASV:CRD, suppliche, filza 43, 31 Oct and 22 Nov 1652.

24. As in ASV:CRD suppliche, filza 69, 25 Oct 1667.

25. For the costs of such services, see ASV:S. Nicolò della Latucha, bu. 15 (1667–73); see also the discussion of the price of *fedi* below.

26. See ASV:CRD suppliche, filza 33, 1 Aug 1642, for the unusual example of a arsenalotti petition written in ornate script—perhaps because it represented the collective efforts of six masters, who could thus have split the cost between them (two more names in Venetian spelling were later crudely scribbled in as well).

27. ASV:CRD suppliche, filza 34, 15 and 24 Mar 1643. For how this "notarial culture" both preserves and screens the voices of ordinary artisans, see Burke, *The Historical Anthropology of Early Modern Italy*, 110–31.

28. Unlike most of Marin's other schemes, the wine fountain was quite successful and became a famous tourist attraction in the shipyards: ASV:CRD suppliche, filza 18, 25 May 1627; filza 25, 14 Jan 1634 m.v.; filza 38, 12 June 1647); filza 33, 27 Oct 1642.

29. And apparently often the only task they set for themselves: ASV:SM, filza 332, 20 July 1640. There are about 100 arsenalotti-related fedi preserved in the filze of the Senato Mar for the years 1621–70, although hundreds more are referred to in the suppliche they once accompanied.

30. Such was the situation of the shipwright Francesco di Marco Furlan, who came from his service in Corfù with a fede from Orlando Calichopolo, head bookkeeper of the island's garrison, backed up by another fede of the noble governor-general of Corfù, testifying that Calichopolo himself was indeed a "persona et gentil huomo di buona fama": ASV:SM, filza 313, 2 Sept 1637. Foreign noblemen, however, were apparently acceptable as fedi writers: ASV:CRD suppliche, filza 53, 26 Nov 1659 (fede from the Spanish Viceroy of Majorca).

31. ASV:SM, filza 326, 4 Aug 1639.

32. So Zuane da Candia apologized that because of a shipwreck he was unable to document his period of service with Gerolamo da Pesaro: "per la perdità che segui de libri nel naufraggio della galera . . . privo convienmi resta di questi attestati": ASV:CRD suppliche, filza 65, 25 Sept 1665.

33. At least one shipbuilder, however, a pulleymaker named Domenico Crestan, did in fact leave his fedi at home with his sister, who was then able to show them to the Collegio when he was enslaved: ASV:CRD suppliche, filza 34, 19 Oct 1643.

34. ASV:CRD suppliche, filza 44, 21 Mar 1653.

35. The points stressed in Iseppo's notarized statements are good indicators as to which aspects of a sailor's life were of most concern to the Collegio: his childhood residence in Venice, his exclusive and continuous service for the Republic as a sailor, the ranks he held while at sea, and eyewitness accounts of his slavery, including his activities while enslaved and his means of obtaining his liberty. ASV:SM, filza 323, 24 Mar 1639.

36. ASV:SM, filza 349, 1 Nov 1642; filza 351, 4 Feb 1642 m.v.

37. ASV:TA reg. 137, 6 Nov 1607. On 14 May 1608, however, the Pa-

troni ordered the tariff revoked and a return to "the orders and customs used from 1589 until the present in such matters," presumably meaning a more informal system. The timekeepers were thus probably only trying to rationalize and make explicit a system of "tips" for their services, a custom that very likely was followed by most writers of fedi.

38. Scarabello, "Paure, superstizioni, infamie," 347–48, n. 10: "Tutto un universo di 'fedi,' di attestazioni reciproche (ma più dall'alto verso il basso)."

39. "Facio fede ... io Gerolamo Crozeta, fabricante de galee ... qualmente Francesco di Zuane da Venetia sono uno de' mii arlieve e sempre sia diletato et ora chontinia et aprezo l'arte de' fabrichar qual da ogni tempo sì chusi parese ala benignità pubblica avalirsene dela sua persona per fabrica galee sotil aprezo il modo e regola che richiede adun perfeto maestro di tal arte riusirà a tuta perfetione esperto": ASV:SM, filza 356, 31 Oct 1643.

40. ASV:SM, filza 518, 17 Sept 1661, for the fede of the caulker Iseppo di Zuane, written by the doctor Sebastianos Turresirios in 1658. Also ASV:CRD suppliche, filza 46, 10 Nov 1655; filza 47, 1 Dec 1656; and filza 48, 12 Apr 1657: the shipwright Francesco di Zuane Fantebon had been trained as a shipwright, but "per causa di fierissima et lungissima malatia havuta mortalissima, come da fede del medico si può vedere, mi conviene di tralasciarla." On fedi from state authorities: ASV:SM, reg. 112, 18 Nov 1651.

41. ASV:SM, filza 371, 4 July 1645; TA, reg. 138, 20 July 1615.

42. See esp. ASV:SM, filza 347, 9 July 1642; also filza 198, 2 Mar 1613; and filza 376, 31 Oct 1645.

43. ASV:SM, filza 376, 31 Oct 1645 and filza 419, 29 Sept 1649.

44. ASV:SM, filza 399, 14 Dec 1647.

45. See the ship captain's fede accompanying ASV:SM, filza 377, 15 Nov 1645, which testified that no one besides the petitioner Giacomo dei Grassi had been willing to try to salvage his sunken galleon; also filza 395, 29 Aug 1647; and ASV:CRD suppliche, filza 18, 28 Nov 1627; filza 20, 31 Mar and 7 May 1629.

46. The custom extended to women as well: the personal appearance before the Collegio of Ellena and Virginia, daughters of a shipwright named Olivio, was clearly implied when they begged the doge to excuse "Betta, our third sister [who] being crippled in bed accompanies us with her most humble tears": ASV:CRD suppliche, filza 47, 14 Dec 1656.

47. ASV:CRD suppliche, filza 42: the shipwright Vicenzo di Valerio excused himself by saying, "non ho mai ardito di molestare con suppliche la Serenità Vostra, sebene ho sempre vissuto in miserabile stato." See also filza 58, 17 May 1662, of Battista di Iacomo Piccolo: "non ho mai supplicato alcun accrescimento di pagha, desideroso più di meritar che chiedere gratie"; and filza 93, 12 Dec 1680: the shipwright Mattio di Zuane Spada wrote: "ne mai mi son reso noioso col pressumer accrescimento di paga dalla Vostra Serenità."

48. ASV:SM, filza 419, 28 July 1649; also ASV:CRD suppliche, filza 63, 5 Sept 1664.

49. Claiming this connection seems to have done Olivio di Matteo little good, however: the Collegio actually put off granting his request for six

years, perhaps waiting until Erizzo had died. ASV:SM, filza 349, 3 July 1647.

50. ASV:CRD suppliche, filza 47, 1 Dec 1656.

51. For the sorts of background information the Patroni might supply to clarify a petitioner's request, see ASV:SM, filza 313, 4 Sept 1637; filza 315, 20 Nov 1637; filza 342, 27 Dec 1641, and filza 343, 9 Jan 1641 m.v.

52. A supplica could run into difficulties passing the Senate simply because not enough senators showed up to vote on the days when it was presented: one petitioner twice failed because (as it was noted in the margin of the registry of the Senate) "non si computa per non haver il numero di 70": ASV:SM, reg. 98, 20 Oct 1640.

53. Luca's full account reads: "Supplicai fino l'anno 1625 avanti Vostra Serenità di poter per gratia medianti la mia riverenti servitù, esser admesso per maestro tagier della Casa dell'Arsenal. Fù accetata, et commessa le risposte all' Eccelentissimo Provveditori e Patroni all'Arsenale, risposero et fù il tutto portato nell'Eccelentissimo Collegio. Restò parimenti commessa alli Eccelentissimi Signori Savij, li quali con vigliato notorno[?] partì che io dovessi esser gratiato, et fù anco ballottata nell'Eccelentissimo Pien Collegio, dove che quando io speravo con il procurar di far poner la parte nell'Eccelentissimo Senato, ottener la effettiva gratia dalla benignità Publica": ASV:SM, filza 272, 8 June 1630.

54. It took the Senate seventy-two months to issue the edict granting a request for a raise by the four Arsenal stores supervisors. By that time, as the edict itself noted, three of the four had died: ASV:SM, filza 287, 16 Nov 1633. Also filza 256, 22 Apr 1627: nine years had elapsed before the Senate responded to a 1618 supplica from the foreman shipwright: since by then he was dead, the Senators decided to award its *gratia* to his son instead.

55. See the Patroni's advice on awards in ASV:SM, filza 286, 28 Sept 1633; filza 287, 28 Nov 1633; and filza 305, 8 July 1636.

56. Christofolo wrote that he had been granted an *offitio de ducati diezi* by the Senate, "Et benche nella gratia in pergamina sia detto vi son di quelli che pretendono metermi in difficultà et andar avanti di me ... io habbi spesso centinaria di ducati con esterminio della mia casa et creature et con [at]teso lungamente in Palazzo per adempir la sudetta gratia in offitio nel quale son stato posto al possesso in contraditorio con persone grandi et di autorità": ASV:CRD suppliche, filza 19, 28 Mar 1628.

Bibliography

Archival Sources

Archivio di Stato, Venice:
    Provveditori, Patroni, Inquisitori all'Arsenale, *terminazione*
    Inquisitori alle Arti, *terminazioni, processi*
    Esecutori contro la Bestemmia, *raspe*
    Procuratori di Citra, *case*
    Collegio, *Risposte di dentro, filze*
    Collegio V (Segreta), *relazioni*
    Compilazione leggi
    Avogaria di Comun, *processi*
    Dieci Savi sopra le Decime in Rialto, *catastici*
    Deputati e aggiunti alla provision del Denaro Publico, *incanti*
    S. Francesco di Paola, *spese*
    S. Girolamo, *spese*
    Provveditori alla Giustizia Vecchia, *processi*
    Maggior Consiglio, *grazie*
    S. Michele in Isola, *spese*
    S. Nicolò della Latucha, *spese*
    Necrologio
    Notarile, *atti* and *testamenti*
    Provveditori al Sal, *processi*
    Sant'Uffizio, *processi*
    Senato Mar, *registri* and *filze*

Procuratori di supra
Biblioteca Marciana, Venice:
    Mss Ital VII, codice 560 (= 7501), *mariegole*
Museo Civico Correr, Venice:
    Codice Cicogna 3161
    Mss Donà delle Rose, 351–52
    Mss Gradenigo, 193 I, II
Parish church of S. Martino:
    parish archives, *scritture* B, E, G, and J *libri dei battesimi, matrimoni, morti*
Parish church of S. Pietro di Castello:
    libri dei battesimi, matrimoni, morti

Secondary Sources

"A True Description and Direction of what is most worthy to be seen in all Italy." *Harleian Miscellany,* 5:1–40. New York, 1965.
Abrams, Philip, and Wrigley, E. A., eds. *Towns in Societies.* Cambridge, 1978.
Aymard, Maurice. "L'Arsenale e le conoscenze tecnico-marinaresche. Le arti." Pp. 289–315 in *Storia della cultura veneta,* vol. 3, no. 2. Vicenza, 1980.
Bamford, Paul W. *Fighting Ships and Prisons: The Mediterranean Galleys of France in the Age of Louis XIV.* Minneapolis, 1973.
Basnatio, Sorsi. *Descrittione piacevole della guerra se' Pugni tra Nicolotti e Castellani.* Venice, 1663.
Baulant, Micheline. "Le salaire des ouvriers du bâtiment à Paris de 1400 à 1726." *Annales E.S.C.* 26 (1971): 463–83.
Bellavitis, Giorgio. *L'Arsenale di Venezia, storia di una grande struttura urbana.* Venice, 1983.
Beloch, Karl Julius. *Bevölkerungsgeschichte Italiens,* vols. 2, 3. Berlin, 1961.
Beltrami, Daniele. *Storia della popolazione di Venezia dalla fine del secolo XVI alla caduta della Repubblica.* Padova, 1954.
Bergamaschi, Maria Temide, et al. *L'Erba delle donne.* Rome, 1978.
Bossy, John. "Godparenthood: The Fortunes of a Social Institution in Early Modern Christianity." Pp. 194–201 in Kaspar von Greyerz, ed., *Religion and Society in Early Modern Europe, 1500–1800.* London, 1984.
Braudel, Fernand. *Capitalism and Material Life, 1400–1800.* New York, 1975.
Brown, Judith C. "A Woman's Place Was in the Home: Women's Work in Renaissance Tuscany." Pp. 206–24 in Margaret W. Ferguson et al., eds., *Rewriting the Renaissance: The Discourses of Sexual Difference in Early Modern Europe.* Chicago, 1986.
————. *Immodest Acts: Life of a Lesbian Nun in Renaissance Italy.* New York, 1986.
————. *In the Shadow of Florence: Provincial Society in Renaissance Pescia.* New York, 1982.
Brucker, Gene A. "The Florentine *Popolo Minuto* and its Political Role, 1340–1450." Pp. 155–83 in Lauro Martines, ed., *Violence and Civil Disorder in Italian Cities, 1200–1500.* Berkeley, 1972.

Bryson, Frederick. *The Point of Honor in Sixteenth-Century Italy.* Chicago, 1935.

Burke, Peter. *The Historical Anthropology of Early Modern Italy.* Cambridge, 1987.

———. *Popular Culture in Early Modern Europe.* New York, 1978.

Caniato, Giovanni. "Squèri da grosso e squèri da sotil." In *Arte degli squerarioli.* Venice, 1985.

Caplow, Harriet. *Libri di Ricordi* of the Florentine stonecutter Maso di Bartolommeo (forthcoming)

Caravia, Alessandro. *La verra antiga dei Castellani Canaruoli e Gnatti, con la morte de Giurco e Gnagni, in lengua brava.* Venice, 1603.

Casoni, Giovanni. "Breve storia dell'Arsenale di Venezia." In *Venezia e le sue lagune,* vol. 1. Venice, 1847.

———. "Forze Militari." In *Venezia e sue lagune,* vol. 1. Venice, 1847.

Cavallo, Sandra. "Strategie politiche e familiari intorno al Baliatico." *Quaderni storici* 53 (1983): 391–420.

Chabod, Federico. "Usi e abusi nell'amministrazione dello stato di Milano a mezzo il '500." *Studi storici in onore di Gioacchino Volpe* 1 (Florence, 1958): 93–194.

Chirivi, Romano, et al., eds. *L'Arsenale dei veneziani.* Venice, 1983.

Chojnacki, Stanley. "Dowries and Kinsmen in Early Renaissance Venice." *Journal of Interdisciplinary History* 5 (1975): 571–600.

Cipolla, Carlo. *Before the Industrial Revolution.* New York, 1980.

Clarkson, Leslie A. *Proto-Industrialization: The First Phase of Industrialization?* London, 1985.

Coad, Jonathan G. "L'architettura storica della marina reale inglese dal 1690 al 1850." Pp. 189–97 in Concina, ed., *Arsenali e citta.*

Coco, Carla, and Manzonetto, Flora. *Baili veneziani alla Sublime Porta.* Venice, 1985.

Cohn, Samuel K., Jr. *The Laboring Classes in Renaissance Florence.* New York, 1980.

Coleman, D. C. "Labour in the English Economy of the Seventeenth Century." *Economic History Review* 8 (1956): 280–95.

———. "Naval Dockyards under the Later Stuarts." *Economic History Review,* 2nd ser., 6 (1953), 134–55.

———. "Proto-Industrialization: A Concept Too Many." *Economic History Review,* 2nd ser., 36 (1983): 435–48.

Concina, Ennio. *L'Arsenale della Repubblica di Venezia.* Milan, 1984.

———, ed. *Arsenali e città nell'Occidente europeo.* Rome, 1987.

Coryat, Thomas. *Coryat's Crudities,* vol. 1. Glasgow, 1905.

Crew, David. *Town in the Ruhr: A Social History of Bochum, 1860–1914.* New York, 1979.

Crouzet-Pavan, Elisabeth. "Violence, Société et Pouvoir à Venise (XIV–XV Siècles): Forme et Évolution de Rituels Urbains." *Mélanges de L'École Française de Rome* 96 (1984): 903–36.

Crovato, Maurizio. "L'Arsenale e Arsenalotti." Pp. 50–59 in Chirivi et al., eds., *L'Arsenale dei veneziani.*

da Mosto, Andrea. *L'Arsenale di Stato di Venezia.* Rome, 1937.

Damsholt, Torben. "Some Observations on Four Series of Tuscan Corn Prices, 1520–1630." *Scandinavian Economic History Review* 11 (1963): 145–64.

Darnton, Robert. *The Great Cat Massacre and Other Episodes in French Cultural History.* New York, 1985.

Davis, James C. *The Decline of the Venetian Nobility as a Ruling Class.* Baltimore, 1962.

———. *A Venetian Family and its Fortune, 1500–1900.* Philadelphia, 1975.

Davis, Natalie Z. *Society and Culture in Early Modern France.* Stanford, 1975.

Davis, Ralph. *The Rise of English Shipping in the Seventeenth and Eighteenth Centuries.* London, 1962.

della Puppa, Giuseppe. *Storia della Chiesa di S. Martino "de Geminis" in Venezia,* limited edition. Venice, 1978.

de Roover, Raymond. "A Florentine Firm of Cloth Manufacturers." *Speculum* 16 (1941): 3–33.

Donnachie, Ian. "Drink and Society 1750–1850: Some Aspects of the Scottish Experience." *Journal of the Scottish Labour History Society* 13 (1979): 5–22.

Dooley, Brendan. "Crisis and Survival in Eighteenth-Century Italy: The Venetian Patriciate Strikes Back." *Journal of Social History* 20 (1986): 323–34.

Estes, Leland L. "The Medical Origins of the European Witch Craze: A Hypothesis." *Journal of Social History* 17 (1983): 271–84.

Evelyn, John. *Diary and Correspondence,* vol. 1. London, 1854.

Farr, James R. *Hands of Honor: Artisans and Their World in Dijon, 1550–1650.* Ithaca, 1988.

Favalier, Silvia. "Le attività lavoritive in una parrocchia del centro veneziano (San Polo—secolo XVI)." *Studi Veneziani* 9 (1985): 187–97.

Fernet, Jean. *De abditis rerum causis.* Published in Venice, 1555, as *Medicina.*

Finlay, Robert. *Politics in Renaissance Venice.* New Brunswick, N.J., 1980.

———. "The Venetian Republic as a Gerontocracy: Age and Politics in the Renaissance." *Journal of Medieval and Renaissance Studies* 8 (1978): 157–78.

Formicola, Antonio, and Romano, Claudio. "Vascelli napolentani, breve storia degli esemplari realizzati dall'avvento dei Borbone alla conquista garibaldina (1734–1860)." *Rivista marittima* 120 (1987): 57–74.

Forsellini, Marcello. "L'Organizzazione economica dell'Arsenale di Venezia nella prima metà del seicento." *Achivio veneto,* 5th ser., 7 (1930): 54–117.

Franco, Giacomo. "Questa è la porta del meraviglioso Arsenale." In *La città di Venezia con l'origine e governo di quella.* Venice, 1614.

Franzoi, Umberto, and di Stefano, Dina. *Le chiese di Venezia.* Venice, 1976.

Gallo, Rodolfo. "Segadori trentine nell'Arsenale di Venezia." *Archivio veneto,* 5th ser., 26 (1940): 113–24.

Gay, Franco. "Le costruzioni navali nell'Arsenale di Venezia." Pp. 35–48 in Chirivi et al., eds., *L'Arsenale dei veneziani.*

Geertz, Clifford. "Thick Description: Toward an Interpretive Theory of Culture." Pp. 3–30 in *The Interpretation of Cultures: Selected Essays.* New York, 1973.

Gennaro, Paola, and Testi, Giovanni, eds. *Progetto Arsenale: studi e ricerche per l'Arsenale di Venezia.* Venice, 1985.

Glen, Robert. *Urban Workers in the Early Industrial Revolution.* London, 1984.

Goldthwaite, Richard A. *The Building of Renaissance Florence.* Baltimore, 1980.

———. "I prezzi del grano a Firenze dal XIV al XVI secolo." *Quaderni storici* 28 (1975): 5–36.

Gramigna, Silvia, and Perissa, Annalisa. *Scuole di arti, mestieri e devozioni a Venezia.* Venice, 1981.

Grubb, James S. "When Myths Lose Power: Four Decades of Venetian Historiography." *Journal of Modern History* 58 (1986): 43–94

Herlihy, David. *Medieval and Renaissance Pistoia: The Social History of an Italian Town, 1200–1430.* New Haven, 1967.

———. *Pisa in the Early Renaissance.* New Haven, 1958.

———. "Some Psychological and Social Roots of Violence in Tuscan Cities." Pp. 129–54 in Lauro Martines, ed., *Violence and Civil Disorder in Italian Cities, 1200–1500.* Berkeley, 1972.

Hobsbawm, Eric. *Labouring Men: Studies in the History of Labour.* New York, 1964.

Kent, Dale, and Kent, F. William. *Neighbors and Neighborhood in Renaissance Florence: The District of the Red Lion in the Fifteenth Century.* Locust Valley, N.Y., 1982.

Klapisch-Zuber, Christiane. "Genitori naturali e genitori di latte nella Firenze del Quattrocento." *Quaderni storici* 46 (1980): 543–63.

———. "Parenti, amici, vicini." *Quaderni storici* 33 (1976): 953–82.

Krantz, F., and Hohenberg, H. C., eds. *Failed Transitions to Modern Industrial Society: Renaissance Italy and Seventeenth-Century Holland.* Montreal, 1975.

Kriedte, Peter; Medick, Hans; and Schlumbohm, Jurgen. *Industrialization before Industrialization.* Cambridge, 1981.

La Festa della Sensa: notizie storiche a cura del comitato "Viva San Marco!" Venice, 1913.

Lambert, W. R. "Drink and Work-Discipline in Industrial South Wales, c. 1800–1870." *Welsh History Review* 7 (1975): 289–306.

Landes, David P. *The Unbound Prometheus: Technological Change and Industrial Development in Western Europe from 1750 to the Present.* Cambridge, 1969.

Lane, Frederic. *Navires et Constructeurs à Venise pendant la Renaissance.* Paris, 1965.

———. "The Rope Factory and Hemp Trade in the Fifteenth and Sixteenth Centuries." Pp. 269–84 in *Venice and History: The Collected Papers of Frederic C. Lane.* Baltimore, 1966.

———. "Venetian Shipping during the Commercial Revolution." Pp. 3–24 in *Venice and History: The Collected Papers of Frederic C. Lane.* Baltimore, 1966.

———. *Venetian Ships and Shipbuilders of the Renaissance.* Baltimore, 1934.

———. *Venice, A Maritime Republic.* Baltimore, 1973.

Lassels, Richard. *Description of Italy* (1654). Reproduced as pp. 147–231 in Edward Chaney, *The Grand Tour and the Great Rebellion.* Geneva, 1985.

Lenci, Marco. "Riscatti di schiavi cristiani dal Maghreb. La Compagnia dell SS. Pietà di Lucca (Secoli XVII-XIX)." *Società e storia* 9 (1986): 53–80.

Le Roy Ladurie, Emmanuel. *Carnival in Romans.* New York, 1980.

Levack, Brian P. *The Witch-hunt in Early Modern Europe.* London, 1987.

Lingo, Alison Klairmont. "Empirics and Charlatans in Early Modern France: The Genesis of the Classification of the 'Other' in Medical Practice." *Journal of Social History* 19 (1986): 583–603.

Lis, Catharina, and Soly, Hugo. *Poverty and Capitalism in Pre-Industrial Europe.* Atlantic Highlands, N.J., 1979.

Logan, Oliver. *Culture and Society in Venice, 1470–1790.* New York, 1972.

Luzzatto, Gino. "Per la storia delle costruzioni navali a Venezia nei secoli XV e XVI." In *Scritti storici in onore di Camillo Manfroni.* Padua, 1925.

Mackenney, Richard. "Arti e stato a Venezia tra tardo medio evo e '600." *Studi Veneziani* n.s. 5 (1981): 127–43.

———. "Guilds and Guildsmen in Sixteenth-Century Venice." *Bulletin of the Society for Renaissance Studies* 25 (1984): 23–47.

———. "'In Place of Strife': The Guilds and the Law in Renaissance Venice." *History Today* 34 (1984): 17–22.

———. *Tradesmen and Traders: The World of the Guilds in Venice and Europe, c. 1250-c. 1650.* London, 1987.

Mallett, Michael, and Hale, John. *The Military Organization of a Renaissance State: Venice c. 1400 to 1617.* Cambridge, 1984.

Marchesi, Vittorio. "L'Arsenale di Venezia nei ultimi secoli della Repubblica veneta." *Annali del R. Istituto tecnico di Udine* (1888), vol. 2.

Marchionni, Ennio. "L'Arsenale di Venezia. Gli uomini, il lavoro, le galerie: documenti." In *Venezia e la difesa del Levante: da Lepanto a Candia, 1570–1670.* Venice, 1986.

Martin, John Jeffries. "In God's Image: Artisans and Heretics in Counter-Reformation Venice." Ph.D. diss., Harvard University, 1982.

———. "Out of the Shadow: Heretical and Catholic Women in Renaissance Venice." *Journal of Family History* 10 (1985): 27.

Mattozzi, Ivo. "Crisi, stagnazione e mutamento nello stato veneziano sei-settecentesco: Il caso del commercio e della produzione olearia." *Studi veneziani* n.s. 4 (1980): 199–276.

———. "Il politico e il pane a Venezia (1570–1630)." *Studi veneziani* n.s. 7 (1983): 197–220.

Melling, Joseph. "'Non-Commissioned Officers': British Employers and their Supervisory Workers, 1880–1920." *Social History* 5 (1980): 183–221.

Mendels, Franklin F. "Proto-industrialization: The First Phase of the Industrialization Process." *Journal of Economic History* 32 (1972): 241–61.

Menetto, L., and Zennaro, G. *La storia del malcostume a Venezia.* Abano Terme, Italy, 1987.

Miskimin, Harry A.; Herlihy, David; and Udovitch, A. L., eds. *The Medieval City.* New Haven, 1977.

Molmenti, Pompeo. *Venice: Its Individual Growth from the Earliest Beginnings to the Fall of the Republic,* Horatio Brown, trans., 3 vols. Chicago, 1906.

Monter, William E. *Witchcraft in France and Switzerland.* Ithaca, 1976.

———. *Ritual, Myth and Magic in Early Modern Europe.* Athens, Ohio, 1983.

Moryson, Fynes. *An Itinerary.* Glasgow, 1907.

Mousnier, Roland. "Le trafic des offices à Venise." *Revue Historique de Droit Français et Étranger* 4th ser., 30 (1952): 552–65.

Muir, Edward. *Civic Ritual in Renaissance Venice.* Princeton, 1981.

———. "Images of Power: Art and Pageantry in Renaissance Venice." *American Historical Review* 84 (1979): 16–52.

Mulier, Eco O. G. Haitsma. *The Myth of Venice and Dutch Republican Thought in the Seventeenth Century.* Assen, The Netherlands, 1980.

Mundy, Peter. *The Travels of Peter Mundy in Europe and Asia, 1608–1667,* vol. 1. Cambridge, 1907.

Nani Mocenigo, Filippo Maria. *L'Arsenale di Venezia.* Rome, 1938.

Norwich, John J. *Venice, the Greatness and the Fall.* London, 1981.

Padoan Urban, Lina. "Feste ufficiali e trattenimenti privati." *Storia della cultura veneta* 4/1 (Vicenza, 1983): 575–600.

Palazzi, Maura. "Abitare da sole." *Memoria* 18 (1986): 37–57.

Palumbo-Fossati, Isabella. "L'Interno della casa dell'artigiano e dell'artista nella Venezia del Cinquecento." *Studi veneziani* n.s. 8 (1984): 109–53.

Park, Katherine. *Doctors and Medicine in Early Renaissance Florence.* Princeton, 1985.

Pavanini, Paola. "Abitazioni popolari e borghesi nella Venezia cinquecentesca." *Studi veneziani* n.s. 5 (1981): 63–126.

———. "Venezia verso la pianificazione? Bonifiche urbane nel XVI secolo." In *De la Ville Medievale à la Ville Moderne, atti di convegno* of the Ecole Française de Rome. Rome, 1–4 Dec 1986.

Pecchioli, Renzo. *Dal "mito" di Venezia all' "ideologia americana."* Venice, 1983.

Perocco, Guido, and Salvadori, Antonio. *Civiltà di Venezia.* Venice, 1973.

Phelps Brown, Henry, and Hopkins, Sheila. "Seven Centuries of Building Wages." *Economica* 22 (1955): 195–206.

Pike, Ruth. *Aristocrats and Traders: Sevillian Society in the Sixteenth Century.* Ithaca, 1972.

Pinto, Giuliano. "Personale, balie, e salariati dell'Ospedale di San Gallo." *Ricerche storiche* 4 (1974): 113–68.

Pitt-Rivers, Julian. "Honor and Social Status." In J. G. Peristiany, ed., *Honour and Shame: The Values of Mediterranean Society.* London, 1965.

Pizzarello, Ugo, and Fontana, Vincenzo. *Pietre e legni dell'Arsenale di Venezia.* Venice, 1983.

Pollard, Sidney. "Factory Discipline in the Industrial Revolution." *Economic History Review* 16 (1963): 254–71.

———. "The Factory Village in the Industrial Revolution." *English Historical Review* 79 (1964): 513–31.

———. *The Genesis of Modern Management.* Cambridge, Mass., 1965.

Porteous, J. D. "The Nature of the Company Town." *Transactions of the Institute of British Geographers,* no. 51 (1970): 127–42.

———. "Goole, A Pre-Victorian Company Town." *Industrial Archeology* 6 (1969): 105–13.

Pullan, Brian S. *Poverty and Charity in Renaissance Venice.* Oxford, 1981.

———. *Rich and Poor in Renaissance Venice: The Social Institutions of a Catholic State, to 1620.* Cambridge, Mass., 1971.

———. "Wage-Earners and the Venetian Economy, 1550–1630." Pp. 146–74 in Pullan, ed., *Crisis and Change in the Venetian Economy in the Sixteenth and Seventeenth Centuries.* London, 1968.

Quarti, Guido. *Quattro secoli di vita veneziana.* Milan, 1941.

Queller, Donald. *The Venetian Patriciate: Reality versus Myth.* Champagne-Urbana, 1986.

Rapp, Richard. *Industry and Economic Decline in Seventeenth-Century Venice.* Cambridge, Mass., 1976.

Reid, Douglas A. "The Decline of Saint Monday, 1766–1876." *Past and Present* 71 (1976): 76–101.

Reresby, John. *Memoirs and Travels.* London, 1904.

Rice, Eugene J. *The Foundations of Early Modern Europe, 1460–1559.* New York, 1970.

Riege, Astrid. "The Development of a Small Village to an Important Naval Town in England: Chatham, 1550–1697." Paper given at conference of Istituto Internazionale di Storia Economica "Francesco Datini" XIX settimana di studio, 2–6 May 1987, Prato.

Roffarè, Luigi. *La Repubblica di Venezia e lo sport.* Venice, 1931.

Romano, Dennis. *Patricians and Popolani: The Social Foundations of the Venetian Renaissance State.* Baltimore, 1987.

———. "San Giacomo dall'Orio: Parish Life in Fourteenth-Century Venice." Ph.D. diss., Michigan State University, 1981.

Romano, Ruggiero. "Economic Aspects of the Construction of Warship in Venice in the Sixteenth Century." Pp. 59–87 in Brian Pullan, ed., *Crisis and Change in the Venetian Economy in the Sixteenth and Seventeenth Centuries.* London, 1968.

———. "La storia economica dal secolo XIV al Settecento." In *Storia d'Italia* 2/2 (Torino, 1974): 1813–1931.

Ruggiero, Guido. *Violence in Early Renaissance Venice.* New Brunswick, N.J., 1980.

Safley, Thomas Max, and Rosenband, Leonard, eds. *The Workplace before the Factory: Proletarianization in an Age of Manufactures* (forthcoming).

Sansovino, Francesco. *Venetia, città nobilissima.* Venice, 1663.

Sanudo, Marin. *I diarii.* Venice, 1879–1903.

Scarabello, Giovanni. "Paure, superstizioni, infamie." *Storia della cultura veneta* 4/2 (Vicenza, 1984): 343–76.

Sella, Domenico. *Crisis and Continuity: The Economy of Spanish Lombardy in the Seventeenth Century.* Cambridge, Mass., 1979.

———. "The Rise and Fall of the Venetian Wool Industry." Pp. 106–26 in Pullan, ed., *Crisis and Change.*

————. *Salari e lavoro nell'edilizia lombardia durante il secolo XVII.* Pavia, 1968.

Sewell, William E. "Uneven Development, the Autonomy of Politics, and the Dockworkers of Nineteenth-Century Marseilles." *American Historical Review* 93 (1988): 604–37.

Skippon, Philip. *An Account of a Journey Made thro' Part of the Low-Countries, Germany, Italy and France.* In A. Churchill and J. Churchill, *Voyages,* vol. 6. London, 1746.

Soprintendenza ai beni artistici e storici di Venezia. *Arti e mestieri nella Repubblica di Venezia.* Venice, 1980.

Spencer, Elaine G. "Between Capital and Labor: Supervisory Personnel in Ruhr Heavy Industry before 1914." *Journal of Social History* 9 (1975): 178–92.

Symcox, Geoffrey. *The Crisis of French Sea Power, 1688–1697.* The Hague, 1974.

Tagliaferri, Amelio. *Consumi e tenore di vita di una famiglia borghese del '600.* Milan, 1968.

Tamassia Mazzarotto, Bianca. *Le feste veneziane.* Florence, 1961.

Tamburini, Filippo. "Suppliche per casi di stregoneria diabolica nei registri della Penitenzieria e conflitti inquisitoriali (sec. XV–XVI)." *Critica storica* 23 (1986): 605–59.

Tenenti, Alberto. *Piracy and the Decline of Venice, 1580–1615.* Berkeley, 1967.

Thomas, Keith. "Work and Leisure in Pre-Industrial Society." *Past and Present* 29 (1964): 50–66.

————. *Religion and the Decline of Magic.* New York, 1971.

Thompson, Edward P. "Eighteenth-Century English Society: Class Struggle without Class?" *Social History* 3 (1978): 133–65.

————. *The Making of the English Working Class.* New York, 1964.

————. "The Moral Economy of the English Crowd in the Eighteenth Century." *Past and Present* 50 (1971): 76–136.

————. "Patrician Society, Plebeian Culture." *Journal of Social History* 7 (1974): 382–405.

————. "Time, Work-Discipline, and Industrial Capitalism." *Past and Present* 38 (1967): 56–97.

Trexler, Richard C. "Correre la Terra: Collective Insults in the Late Middle Ages." *Mélanges de L'École Française de Rome* 96 (1984): 845–902.

Trincanato, Egle. *A Guide to Venetian Domestic Architecture: "Venezia minore."* Venice, 1982.

Tucci, Ugo. "L'Alimentazione a bordo delle navi veneziane." *Studi veneziani* 13 (1987): 103–45.

————. "The Psychology of the Venetian Merchant in the Sixteenth Century." Pp. 346–78 in J. R. Hale, ed., *Renaissance Venice.* London, 1973.

Turner, Victor. *The Ritual Process: Structure and Anti-Structure.* Chicago, 1969.

Unger, Richard W. *Dutch Shipbuilding before 1800: Ships and Guilds.* Assen, The Netherlands, 1978.

————. "Regulations of Dutch Shipcarpenters in the Fifteenth and Sixteenth Centuries." *Tijdschrift voor Geschiedenis* 3 (1974): 503–20.

————. "Technology and Industrial Organization: Dutch Shipbuilding to 1800." *Business History* 17 (1975): 56–72.

Van der Wee, Herman, ed. *The Rise and Decline of Urban Industries in Italy and the Low Countries*. Leuven, 1988.

Veludo, C. *Cenni storici sull'Arsenale di Venezia*. Venice, 1869.

Vigo, Giovanni. "Real Wages of the Working Classes in Italy: Building Workers Wages (14th to 18th Century)." *Journal of European Economic History* 3 (1974): 378–99.

Walker, Mack. *German Home Towns: Community, State and General Estate, 1648–1871*. Ithaca, 1971.

Weisner, Merry E. "Spinsters and Seamstresses: Women in Cloth and Clothing Production." Pp. 191–205 in Margaret W. Ferguson et al., eds., *Rewriting the Renaissance: The Discourses of Sexual Difference in Early Modern Europe*. Chicago, 1986.

Weissman, Ronald. *Ritual Brotherhood in Renaissance Florence*. New York, 1982.

Zago, Roberto. *I Nicolotti*. Padua, 1982.

Zanelli. "L'Arsenale—storia di industria e di città." Pp. 68–70 in Chirivi et al., eds., *L'Arsenale dei veneziani*.

Zompini, Gaetano. *Le arte che vanno per via nella città di Venezia*. Venice, 1968.

Zysberg, André. "L'Arsenal des galères de France à Marseille (1660–1715)." *Neptunia* 159 (1983): 147–64.

Index

270

Milton Keynes UK
Ingram Content Group UK Ltd.
UKHW041349301124
451822UK00001B/67